Nation-Building
Five Southeast Asian Histories

The **Institute of Southeast Asian Studies (ISEAS)** was established as an autonomous organization in 1968. It is a regional centre dedicated to the study of socio-political, security and economic trends and developments in Southeast Asia and its wider geostrategic and economic environment.

The Institute's research programmes are the Regional Economic Studies (RES, including ASEAN and APEC), Regional Strategic and Political Studies (RSPS), and Regional Social and Cultural Studies (RSCS).

ISEAS Publications, an established academic press, has issued more than 1,000 books and journals. It is the largest scholarly publisher of research about Southeast Asia from within the region. ISEAS Publications works with many other academic and trade publishers and distributors to disseminate important research and analyses from and about Southeast Asia to the rest of the world.

History of Nation-Building Series

Nation-Building
Five Southeast Asian Histories

edited by
WANG GUNGWU

ISEAS

INSTITUTE OF SOUTHEAST ASIAN STUDIES
Singapore

First published in Singapore in 2005 by
ISEAS Publications
Institute of Southeast Asian Studies
30 Heng Mui Keng Terrace
Pasir Panjang
Singapore 119614
<http://www.iseas.edu.sg/pub.html>

The series of Nation-Building Histories was made possible
with the generous support of the Lee Foundation, Singapore and the
Chiang Ching-kuo Foundation for International Scholarly Exchange, Taipei.

ISEAS Library Cataloguing-in-Publication Data

Nation-Building: five Southeast Asian histories / edited by Wang Gungwu.
   1.   Asia, Southeastern—History—1945–
   2.   Asia, Southeastern—Historiography.
   I.   Wang, Gungwu, 1930–
DS526.7 S725   2005

ISBN 981-230-317-0 (soft cover)
ISBN 981-230-320-0 (hard cover)

Typeset by Superskill Graphics Pte Ltd
Printed in Singapore by Oxford Graphic Printers Pte Ltd

Contents

Preface

The essays in this volume are the product of a conference organized in Singapore by the Institute of Southeast Asian Studies in September 2002: "Nation-building Histories: Thailand, Philippines, Indonesia, Malaysia and Singapore". Altogether sixteen scholars were invited to take part in a two-day meeting that focused on these five countries, the founder members of the Association of Southeast Asian Nations (ASEAN). One volume, that on Malaysia by Cheah Boon Kheng, had already been published. Some of the draft chapters of the other four volumes were circulated for the discussants to read and offer comments. All the participants were invited to write up their thoughts, either on the work they had already done or read, or on the general problems of writing nation-building histories, especially of countries recently committed to the tasks of nation-building and issues of writing contemporary history in Southeast Asia. In the end, Cheah Boon Kheng and seven of the discussants agreed to reflect on the questions that the conference had raised. As editor, I included an essay on "Nation and Heritage" I had published earlier and wrote an introduction to place on record some of the broader issues that the whole exercise had helped to illuminate.

After the conference, I had summarized those questions that attracted most comments as follows: When does nation-building begin and how does it fit into the writing of contemporary history? How should historians treat the earlier pasts of each country and the nationalism that guided the nation-building task? Where did political culture come in, especially when dealing with modern challenges of class, secularism and ethnicity? What part does external or regional pressure play when the nations are still being built? When archival sources are not available, how should narrative, social science analyses and personal experience be handled? Each of the ten essays in this volume includes efforts to pose such questions with reference to one of the five countries. It is hoped that their efforts will stimulate interest in the writing of similar histories for the other five members of ASEAN as well as arouse interest in an emerging regional consciousness that will be more than the sum of the ten national experiences themselves.

15 May 2005   Wang Gungwu
                                                          East Asian Institute
                                            National University of Singapore

The Contributors

Cheah Boon Kheng was Professor of History, Universiti Sains Malaysia.

Carol Hau is Associate Professor, Center for Southeast Asian Studies, Kyoto University, Japan.

Albert Lau is Associate Professor, Department of History, National University of Singapore.

Lee Kam Hing was Professor of History, University of Malaysia and is now Research Editor, Star Publications (M) Bhd, Malaysia.

Anthony Milner is Professor and Dean, Faculty of Asian Studies, Australian National University.

Anthony J.S. Reid is Director, Asia Research Institute, National University of Singapore.

Craig J. Reynolds is Reader, Centre for Asian Societies and Histories, Australian National University.

Anthony Stockwell is Professor of Imperial and Commonwealth History, Royal Holloway, University of London.

Wang Gungwu is Director, East Asian Institute, National University of Singapore.

CHAPTER ONE

Contemporary and National History: A Double Challenge

Wang Gungwu

A T THE International Conference of Historians of Asia (IAHA) in Bangkok (1996), there was a panel on nation-building at which it was debated whether it was time for historians to write nation-building histories for Southeast Asia. This appeared rather unadventurous because in 1996 there was much more debate about globalization and transnational developments, even speculation about the end of nation-states. It was pointed out that the break-up of colonial empires in Asia had happened a long while back. Unlike the new nations after the dissolution of the Austro-Hungarian and Ottoman empires, those that were established after World War II faced a world that was changing much faster than it has ever done. Since the 1950s, new global markets have flourished, new technologies have reached out in all directions and new social forces have been released. It was surely more important to examine the new emerging factors in society that were transforming human lives beyond recognition. In many countries, these had begun to render the idea of nation-states increasingly irrelevant.

On the other hand, only a few years earlier, German reunification and the dissolution of the Soviet Empire had led to a new wave of nation-building in Central and Eastern Europe as well as Central Asia. And what a dramatic challenge that has been to the Western European experiment in crossing national borders to build new kinds of communities. Since then, the tension between a European Union seeking to double its size and the

1

murderous struggles of the new ethnic nationalisms has barely abated. This has certainly led to fresh interest in the idea and practice of nation-building. Of course, how to understand what that process now means may have to change. The Southeast Asian efforts of the past half-century show that the region's new nations are not the same as those carved out of the Ottoman and Austro-Hungarian empires. Turkey and Egypt, Austria and Yugoslavia, to take a few examples, are distinct from each other and even more different from the kinds of states that began to "nation-build" with what was left behind in the British, French, Dutch and American colonies. Historians would be the first to admit that there is much that we do not know about how this "building" has been going on. Particularly for Southeast Asia, the historians have so far been hesitant, if not passive, in tackling this issue.

At the end of our discussions in Bangkok, it was clear that there were also other dimensions in Southeast Asia that called for attention. For one thing, most Southeast Asian nations were still struggling in their attempts to build their nations. Even for the five members who first established their own regional organization, the Association of Southeast Asian Nations (ASEAN), national sovereignty was always uppermost even while they tried to embrace regionalism and sought ultimately to include the remaining five nations. Indeed, most of the ten had been "building" their new nations for nearly half a century and their job was far from done. Following these discussions, I became convinced that it was time the story of these fifty years was told. There have been many books about the nationalism that led to de-colonization and guided the establishment of each of these nations. What was still not well studied was what the various national leaders actually did after independence to ensure that their countries would become the fully-fledged nation-states they wanted. I also thought that a most interesting challenge was to ask historians of each of the states to write that story.

Since the Bangkok conference, five historians have agreed to take up the challenge to write the nation-building histories of the five original members of ASEAN (Indonesia, Thailand, Philippines, Malaysia and Singapore), and they would do this under the auspices of the Institute of Southeast Asian Studies in Singapore.[1] Afterwards, one group of them presented their initial thoughts at the International Association of Historians of Asia (IAHA) conference held in Jakarta in 1999, and then one international workshop was held in Singapore in 2002 to examine more broadly the questions that the project had raised. From the contributions of the historians at the latter meeting have come this group of essays on the problems of writing contemporary and national histories. It has been a most challenging enterprise and I owe my colleagues a great debt for the critical ways they tackled the questions and resolved their doubts. Eight of the following essays were produced at that meeting.

One important point was agreed to by all concerned soon after the project was first launched. While we all knew that Southeast Asia has always been extraordinarily varied, we were struck by the fact that the common experience of anti-colonialism and the nationalist movements of the first half of the twentieth century did not reduce the original variations. On the contrary, the different colonial powers, British, Dutch, French and American, introduced varying policies of state-building and each had particular notions of what a nation meant. In this way, they diversified the conditions for nation-building even further. In addition, the metropolitan powers introduced new demographic and technological ingredients into their colonies, and also their respective national templates that reflected their own historical experiences and stages of development at home in Europe and the new world of North America. Under the circumstances, attempts to find common ground for Southeast Asian new nations were limited to broad generalizations about overcoming colonialism and building nation-states on more or less Western models. Whenever the specifics of each country were examined more closely, what stood out were the sharp differences in the basic elements that each new nation had to work with from the start. This was partly because we are historians who do not see our primary task as finding common patterns but tend to be drawn by the unique and the particular that face us everywhere. But, in the end, the fact that the basic ingredients of history like political culture, population, terrain, and natural resources varied so much was undeniable. We agreed that it would be a mistake to simplify and only highlight the commonalties. It is the very distinctive nature of each of the nation-building stories that was most worth telling. It was with that in mind that the 2002 workshop explored those differences while tackling the more general issues of writing contemporary and national history.

Each of the essays has something different to emphasize and readers will note how the authors underline the issues that strike each of them most about each country. Craig Reynolds, writing on Thailand, has focused on the way the state designed and decorated the kind of nation it wanted. He takes the long view and suggests that "the nation is a building that will never be finished". Caroline Hau, taking the experience of the Philippines, is inclined to agree, and stresses the underlying contradictions that have been inherited and the importance of competitive interpretations in shaping attitudes towards the nation. On Indonesia, Anthony Reid emphasizes the discontinuities that have challenged historians again and again to capture the whole picture whether of state or nation. This was already true for the very beginning of national history, not to say the traumatic events of 1965 and the more recent uncertainties after 1998. Taming these discontinuities is likely to be the key task for the young generation of historians the country is producing.

There is perhaps some significance in having five essays on Malaysia and Singapore in this volume. This may be because the workshop was held in Singapore, but there are other reasons. Both countries have inherited strong administrative structures that have been creatively adapted to serve as the backbone of the new national states. Together with that was a sense of continuity among scholars of what British Malaya had been, and the willingness among the historians of each of its several parts to dig deeper into what evolved from that common past. All five authors have worked closely with systematically archived materials. Cheah Boon Kheng has actually finished his task to write the nation-building history of Malaysia. Here he seeks to encapsulate the issue of ethnicity in his book and explore the political balancing that ethno-nationalism seems to demand. Anthony Milner looks for a deeper continuity behind that apparent balance and probes for the more popular sources of contested "nations" within the equilibrium that has been maintained so far. Lee Kam Hing confronts directly the difficulties in writing contemporary history in Malaysia today, given the sensitivities that surface with every initiative, every attempt to change and reform. Tony Stockwell brings us back to the colonial roots of the modern governance that paradoxically has ensured continuity for both Malaysia and Singapore but also played the *deus ex machina* that had planted the seeds for the political tussles between the two. From Singapore, Albert Lau shows a keen sense of the historiographical dilemma for a country with "short cultures" in a short history. When everything is seen as contemporary, where is the historian to find the objectivity he so wishes to have?

I have only briefly outlined what has led to the genesis of these essays and also what I have found most interesting in them. I shall now also offer a few past-oriented thoughts on Southeast Asia and the art of history writing. Some have been presented before and I have decided to include at the end of the volume an essay I had published in the *Journal of the Malaysian Branch of the Royal Asiatic Society* (2000). They reflect some of the thinking generated by the experiences shared with my colleagues. But I shall add some further notes in the rest of this introduction.

The Historian's Dilemma

It is widely acknowledged that the work of professional historians is not getting any easier. On the one hand, historians have to face the challenge mounted by those social scientists who try to ask different questions of similar data. Trying to turn history into a social science in its own right is not the answer. History has a distinguished lineage and historians have a different job to do. On the other hand, such historians are also challenged by the work of those outside academia who write well. And many of these historians do so with literary flair, verve and imagination. The academic historian today is often discouraged from venturing into such writing by some universities that are narrowly focused on work published in highly specialized journals and read only by other professionals. By the time young scholars have passed through that barrier, many are no longer able to write for a wider audience to read.

For many countries in Asia, historians today are further taxed by at least two other demands: the need to contribute to nation-building efforts by writing national history, and the urge to use their skills to record and explain contemporary events. Altogether thirteen historians have agreed to write for this ISEAS project. There are the five authors who committed themselves to write the nation-building history for the five new nations. They have taken on the double challenge of writing contemporary and national history. The other eight (with a reflective Cheah Boon Kheng adding his own essay) in this volume too are conscious of the twin burdens that the historian of nation-building today must carry on their shoulders. Their essays also throw light on the countries of the region where historians are struggling with the national and the contemporary simultaneously. These eight were all asked to read the writing plans of the five nation-building historians and comment and raise questions about their various approaches. They have put their thoughts down here for the consideration of all those interested in the larger question of writing nation-building history in Southeast Asia.

Let me emphasize again what I mentioned earlier. The historians who agreed to write about the five countries all recognize that the five could hardly be more different from one another in their earlier histories and cultures as well as in their modern transformations. Thailand could be said to have begun its modern phase of nation-building in 1932 following the coup that ended the absolute monarchy, but the post-1945 phase under King Bhumipol Adulyadej has had a distinct trajectory that few could have predicted.[2] The Philippines had its first chance at independence aborted at the turn of the twentieth century and was given a second chance in 1945 for which its leaders were better prepared, partly by American tutelage and partly through the baptism of the Pacific War.[3] The pioneer generation of nationalists in the Netherlands East Indies seized their opportunity to revolt decisively against Dutch colonial rule in 1945–50 and took on the immense and tortuous task of building a new Indonesian nation.[4] As for Malaysia and Singapore, they were the products of a failure to gather together all the untidy remains of British colonies and protectorates in the heart of Southeast Asia. The leaders of the two countries, however, have been surprisingly successful in making their two potential nations credible and hopeful against all expectations.[5]

It is obvious that any attempt by the historians to examine the task of nation-building in their respective countries would be a new experience. For most countries outside of Western Europe and the Americas, "the nation" is a twentieth century enterprise. Whether writing about the work of nation-building is necessarily national history or merely contributing to what might eventually become key parts of a future national history is still a question. The combination of the national and the contemporary, however, is the real challenge. National history rarely begins with the past few decades. On the contrary, there is the well established tradition in the modern West of tracing every national history to its ancient past in an effort to connect everything that happened within the country's boundaries to the "final" outcome, the present nation-state. Indeed, national historians are often expected to concentrate on earlier periods that enhance the sense of nationhood and support the nation's ultimate rise and development. Some might even see that as their primary contribution to enable present and future generations of their fellow citizens to recognize the continuities in the past and identify with them. Only in that way could citizens develop the deep-rooted sense of pride that all nation-states need.

Thus any focus on the beginnings of nation building in post-colonial territories faces two sets of challenges. The first assumes that the nation did not exist before the task of building began. It needs to be constructed or, as Benedict Anderson puts it, "imagined", and the task would begin from a given moment of time. The phenomenon that is most commonly recognized is that, in the post-colonial "potential nations" of different parts of Central and Eastern Europe, as well as those in the Americas, Australasia, Asia and Africa, that moment is usually the day that independence was declared. There are exceptions. In Asia, these would be the examples of Japan, China and Thailand, where the new efforts at nation-building were linked with an enlightened king or emperor who needed to emphasize continuities or a revolutionary leader who needed to highlight his role in replacing the overthrown regime. But, no matter how the date was determined, it is understood that the new nation-state had a beginning. What then normally follows are efforts to show that the nation was in some way predetermined by centuries of common history and shared values. The national historians would trace this development forwards from the earliest times, often on the assumption that the further they could bring their story close to prehistoric man living in their lands, the stronger the bonds that would strengthen the nation.

National history, therefore, tends to look backwards to find the nation's beginnings far back in the past and thus tackle later developments teleologically so that patriotic citizens can connect them with a meaningful present. This makes the writer of national history different from someone engaged in the task of writing the history of actual nation-building. The national historian is not so much concerned with the contemporary tasks that each new government faces after the day of destiny whenever that may be, notably when one flag goes down and a new national flag is raised. Thus the five historians who responded to the ISEAS call have had to face the additional challenge of writing contemporary history. All are nationals of the respective countries they are writing about. But they are first and foremost experienced historians who are also keen observers of what has transpired in their lifetimes. They are conscious of the challenge of writing about recent events, that is, how to deal with the questions that these events posed for the future nation and for history-writing. Indeed, these are the same questions that the contributors to this volume have asked.

In short, the five historians faced a double challenge, both the problems of national history-writing and the daunting task of working with the mass of current documentation. Only one of the five, Cheah Boon Kheng, has contributed to this volume and he reflects on what he has tried to do in his *Malaysia: The Making of a Nation* (2003).[6] The other four authors decided to concentrate on the history they are writing and let their books answer the questions that the contributors to this volume would raise. As for the remaining contributors, they have examined the possible issues that such a task has posed for each of the five countries. Their essays in this volume confront a wide range of philosophical and methodological problems that they each expect historians of nation-building in Southeast Asia to tackle. Several have gone further into possible alternative sources and interpretations than expected. For their stimulating efforts to deepen and broaden the scope of enquiry, the editor is most grateful.

The contributors here acknowledge the complexities of writing the history of recent events and each has chosen to concentrate on one or more of the major issues that historians face. Albert Lau has the most immediate knowledge of the problems because he had just completed *A Moment of Anguish*, a study of the separation of Singapore from the original Federation of Malaysia. This was a controversial event of immense sensitivity to those concerned who are still alive. Not surprisingly, he has given more space to surveying the issue of contemporary history itself and shares his experience of so doing with some poignancy.

Let me now offer some reflections on the idea of the contemporary and the nation-building. There are at least three major recording traditions embedded in Southeast Asian polities that modern states may claim a connection with, and from which some of their historians could draw inspiration if they chose to. These are the Hindu-Buddhist chronicles of kings mostly recorded after their deaths, the Sino-Vietnamese annals and historical records compiled by royal officials, and the Perso-Arab *tarikh* or *tawarikh* and genealogical traditions that have helped to shape the Malayo-Javanese chronicles, and the various *sejarah* and *hikayat*. None of them spoke to "nations" but many of them played a part in the formation of early states. Thus, at least in terms of royal or imperial states, there could be documentary support from early writings about the past. The question is whether those traditions still have a role to play in the shaping of modern nation-building history.

Dealing with the Contemporary

The formal writing of works that we call history today was not found in classical Sanskritic civilization. That civilization dominated not only much of the lands of South Asia but also large parts of Southeast Asia before the fifteenth century. For long periods of early South and Southeast Asian history, historical data consisted of skimpy accounts recorded by the Chinese and the Muslim officials and merchants and, after the sixteenth century, by newly adventurous Europeans. These had little to do with history-writing, but many of the details thus preserved were contemporary observations that included current stories told to the foreign travellers or merchants. Occasionally, these accounts were also accompanied by a brief resume of the polity's history as known to the people at the time. This was a kind of indirect contemporary history, albeit rather shallow and fragmentary.

Nevertheless, civilization in Southeast Asia was extremely rich in epigraphic documents that could be seen to represent efforts to depict contemporary history. The inscriptions that have been collected for the various kingdoms in Java-Sumatra, and the great Khmer and Cham empires of the Indochina region, have few details about their societies as a whole. They concentrated on particular events, like the fruits of battles or the accession or passing of particular rulers, and sought to immortalize the few high points that someone thought were worth recording. They obviously cared enough to want their selected representations to last among their people, so these were inscribed in stone or metal. Let me mention two examples.[7] One declared that Sri Harsavarman, the grandson of Isanavarman, had expanded the sphere of his glory and had obtained the Lion Throne through regular succession. This was recorded in the mid-seventh century on a copper plate found in central Thailand. The text was followed by a list of gifts that indicated that the realm was devoted to Siva. A later inscription in stone found nearby recorded the offerings of slaves to a Buddhist monastery, thus pointing to a shift in attitudes towards the Buddha. Although these accounts were not dateable facts, that they were recorded in this form indicates that the people of the time had specific attitudes concerning the use of power for state-building. Each successful step towards state formation was worthy of a record that would have been an expression of historical consciousness. Such fragments that have been preserved tell us too little. We certainly demand more today to trace the stages of modern nation-building, but the respect paid to decisive changes in history requires no less than the same consciousness found in the inscriptions in stone and metal.

The epigraphic documents were numerous and, taken together, revealing. They are sometimes supplemented by efforts to depict the events and people concerned in statuary friezes, notably in palaces and monasteries. These, too, served to commemorate what was significant and at the same time conveyed a sense of actuality that could be compared with some kinds of contemporary notes that are now recorded on paper. Of course, the inscriptions did not carry a continuous story and the impact on the peoples within range was probably limited. What makes them worth noting is that they reflect the desire of kings and ruling élites, and those who served them, to show what they considered were events of importance for the preservation and stability of the polity.

Contemporary history for a nation that is undergoing a process of building has similar concerns. It could be both the record of a significant job being done or of the failure to overcome the complexities that a new nation faces. What challenges the historian today is, of course, the presence of full political and administrative records on almost every subject imaginable, from the economy, the defence forces and foreign relations, to social and cultural change and the different perceptions among different sectors of a relatively sophisticated population. This immense challenge to the historian, of course, could be considered as largely self-inflicted. Its enormity stems from the fact that professional historians today have been trained in the nineteenth century mould of having to chase up every relevant document to ensure relative objectivity. Although this is a necessary skill and responsibility, something very important for any piece of history to be complete, this method does not necessarily capture the essence of a great event, or of a person or persons in and out of power, or of a moment of profound understanding that some earlier kinds of contemporaneity sought to grasp. Perhaps we should not dismiss the mindset that produced our epigraphic documents but consider if it has anything to tell us about how our ancestors chose to highlight what was truly significant in their lifetimes.

It was also true that the Sino-Vietnamese tradition began with a concern for the contemporaneous. It drew its inspiration from the style of the Spring and Autumn State Records compiled during the time of Confucius in the sixth century B.C. After several centuries of gestation and debate, this method of recording was institutionalized as dynastic history during the Han dynasty (206 B.C.–A.D. 220) and perfected in the History Office of the

Tang dynasty (618–907).[8] The records later kept in independent Vietnam were also meant to be accounts of what the rulers actually did. Getting the words and acts noted down as soon as they happened, as was done in the Imperial and Court Diaries of the Tang dynasty, was deemed to have been more important than waiting for historians to explain what these actions really meant. Understanding their place in history was left for later after the results were clear. This is comparable to the saying that no judgement should be made about anyone until the person was dead, or about any event until it was well and truly over when most of the details would have been forgotten and only the essence remained. But there was a stress here on the instant record that marked the nature of that historical tradition. This clearly did not encourage anyone to trust later memory or future insight. Thus these contemporary accounts bound future historians to hold to the framework of events that the official History Office had produced day by day. If that was not what we mean by contemporary history, it was certainly done to make later historians hew to a particular sequence of events. Perhaps this also enabled later historians to share the sense of immediacy that had determined what was worth recording, and did so in a way that underlined the importance of the contemporaneous.

The Perso-Arab traditions of history came late to Southeast Asia and were adapted to existing oral and visual practices. They also had to vie with earlier Hindu-Buddhist practices of inscribing the significant present. Their contributions did, however, give the whole of the Malay world a sense of time and causality that had not been emphasized before.[9] The resultant mixture of royal and princely acts and morality tales captured the present in the past in enjoyable ways. It so enriched the underlying sequence of happenings that the *sejarah* and *hikayat*, and even the poetic *sha'ir*, genres that were produced are much more endearing and unforgettable than any official work of history could ever hope to be. We are also reminded that there was a greater dependence on oral transmission in the Southeast Asian mind than was found in the Sino-Vietnamese or the Perso-Arab traditions. This oral tradition helped to convey the sense of immediacy, even though it did not lead to the official keeping of contemporary records, and left the preservation of meaningful events very much to chance.

Nation-Building

None of these traditions are actively in play today. The prevalent bureaucratic systems in each of the five countries covered are organized to generate data in totally different ways. And their documents will receive in time the respect due to them by future historians. But there are documents and commentaries that are not hidden but more open to public gaze. Modern pressures towards accountability ensure that more records will surface earlier rather than later. We need different kinds of historians to take advantage of these trends, or at least historians with a different kind of mindset. In considering the efforts of the five historians engaged in writing nation-building history, the authors in this volume have probed far and wide to assess the challenges they face.

Nation-building is an immediate and pressing task in Southeast Asia. It started in earnest from the day after the celebrations were over and the new leaders of new governments got down to work. The nationalist slogans that promised a great new beginning had now to be translated into policies and actions that not only confirmed the power of the state but also launched the project to make nationals of every citizen. Since it is still going on, is it really too early to write its history? Would it not have been wiser to leave it to journalists, economists and political scientists and only bring in the historians a century or two later when all the accessible records are known? These questions were among the first that the ISEAS workshop was asked to think about. At the same time, it was noted that some fifty years have past, a couple of generations of protagonists have come and gone, the bulk of documentation available is already overwhelming and, in the eyes of some, the main outlines of the key stories are clear. So do historians have to wait till everyone concerned is dead, every archive opened and, to put it strongly, only left with the reinterpreting and refuting of what has been written, with the work of dotting the i's and crossing the t's?

Obviously, some historians have accepted these challenges. After all, there is such a thing as contemporary history, something that Geoffrey Barraclough and John Lewis Gaddis have made respectable.[10] So the real doubt was not so much with the contemporary as with the problem of national history. If this were simply another kind of national history, would the historians have to adopt the conscious stance of contributing towards that? Of course, national history too is itself necessary and respectable. It is really a question of writing it well. But would the writing of nation-building history really qualify?

Most of the authors of the essays in this volume have actually confronted the writing of contemporary history some time or other in their careers.[11] Craig Reynolds has written on pressing issues of national identity and the emergence of radical thought in modern Thai politics.[12] Caroline Hau explored the role of literature in a people's sense of nation.[13] Anthony Reid has taken time off from his major historical writings to tackle questions of Aceh, underlying ideas of freedom, the Indonesian revolution and its heroes, and the Chinese minorities in the region.[14] Anthony Milner drew on his studies of earlier periods of Malay history to examine how the Malay majority was constructed. He has also confronted the debates in Malaysia and Singapore about the relevance of "Asian values".[15] Lee Kam Hing has written on several national and local elections, on business groups and their ability and willingness to change, and also some of the immediate problems of education.[16] A.J. Stockwell has on the whole stayed carefully with archival sources but has come close to the contemporary with his examination of neo-colonialism and aspects of colonial policing.[17] As for Albert Lau, he certainly engaged in a key period of nation-building when he wrote on Singapore's separation from Malaysia.[18] Their various brushes with contemporary history and with the edges of national history have led them all to think deeply about the challenges that both the contemporary and the national poses to historians. The essays here reveal their prior exposure to the questions that they have raised.

The main difference between them and the five who have taken on the history of nation-building lies in that most of the authors here have not had to engage the problems of national history directly. Four of them have written as nationals about their own countries, that is, Cheah Boon Kheng, Caroline Hau, Lee Kam Hing and Albert Lau. But, except for Cheah Boon Kheng who set out to write one of the five volumes on nation-building, the others had previously focused their writings on specific events and issues. I believe that they have contributed to future national history. Their own current concerns with the contemporary, however, have been thankfully free from the pressures that national historians often have to face from politicians and governments.

It remains to ask whether historians can do better than other social scientists and contemporary commentators and journalists in writing nation-building history. It is a difficult one for historians to answer because they see themselves as writing works of history. The others have the advantage of not professing to write history. They observe, they comment on the available data, they query the protagonists and they try to gauge public responses to striking events. What they write summarizes the situation as is and each of their books informs, stimulates action or arouses angry rebuttals, or simply amuses and entertains. None would have behind them a phalanx of fellow historians who are sceptical or downright dismissive of their foolishness if not hubris. None have to ask if they risk their professional reputations to describe something as contemporary as nation-building as history. None would have the added doubt whether a national of any country could write anything so close to national history in the making with any objectivity.

This is the context in which this volume of essays seeks to complement the series of nation-building histories. The authors have thought deeply about the issues that the five historians have to deal with and tried to put them not only in the perspective of Southeast Asian developments of the past five decades but also of the larger areas of historiography today. The key rests with the formidable task of combining contemporaneity with mapping nationhood in an era of regionalism and globalization. This is the challenge that our five colleagues have embarked on with courage and conviction. This volume is dedicated to the completion of that enterprise.

NOTES

1   The five historians are Cheah Boon Kheng on Malaysia [*Malaysia: The Making of a Nation* (Singapore: Institute of Southeast Asian Studies, 2002)], Reynaldo C. Ileto on the Philippines, Edwin Lee on Singapore, Taufik Abdullah on Indonesia and Charnvit Kasetsiri on Thailand.

2   Charnvit Kasetsiri is an authority of pre-modern Thai history and the

distinguished historian of the kingdom of Ayudhya. In recent years, he has written on modern Thai politics, notably on democratic student movements, including Thailand under Phibun Songkhram (1897-1964). He has also written the history of Thammasat University. In 1999, he produced a video recording of the 14 October 1973 student uprising that has reached a wide international audience.

3   Reynaldo C. Ileto is best known for his classic study of popular movements, *Pasyon and Revolution: Popular Movements in the Philippines, 1840–1910* (Quezon City: Ateneo de Manila University Press, 1979). His work, taking the story of revolution forward to contemporary attitudes, may be found in *Filipinos and Their Revolution: Event, Discourse, and Historiography* (Quezon City: Ateneo de Manila University Press, 1998).

4   Taufik Abdullah has contributed richly towards the study of the wide range of factors underlying the Indonesian Revolution. His work on Islam is of special importance to our understanding of contemporary Indonesia, "The Formation of a Political Tradition in the Malay World", in *The Making of an Islamic Political Discourse in Southeast Asia*, edited by Anthony Reid (Clayton, Vic: Centre of Southeast Asian Studies, Monash University, 1993), pp. 35–58. Another important work is Taufik Abdullah and Sharon Siddique, eds., *Islam and Society in Southeast Asia* (Singapore: Institute of Southeast Asian Studies, 1986).

5   Although Edwin Lee is now best known through his book on the British as rulers when they governed a multi-racial Singapore from 1867 to 1914, he has also written on more contemporary subjects, notably *The Towkays of Sabah: Chinese Leadership and Indigenous Challenge in the Last Phase of British Rule* (Singapore: Singapore University Press, 1976); and (with Tan Tai Yong), *Beyond Degrees: The Making of the National University of Singapore* (Singapore: Singapore University Press, 1996).

6   Cheah Boon Kheng has produced authoritative studies of the great social and political changes just before and after the Japanese Occupation of Malaya in 1942–45: *The Masked Comrades: A Study of the Communist United Front in Malaya, 1945-48* (Singapore: Times Books International, 1979); and *Red Star over Malaya: Resistance and Social Conflict during and after the Japanese Occupation of Malaya, 1941–46* (Singapore: Singapore University Press, 1983).

7   There are innumerable examples from later inscriptions, including those coming from the ancient Khmer empire, and even the friezes at Angkor Wat and other sites. I have taken these two early examples pertaining to what has been called the Dvaravati *mandala* of the Chao Phraya plains from Charles Higham, *The Archaeology of Mainland Southeast Asia, from 10,000 BC to the Fall of Angkor* (Cambridge: Cambridge University Press, 1989), pp. 270–72. The sense of the

contemporaneous in linking the past with present and future is illustrated in the essay on "Local Writings" by O.W. Wolters, in Postscript V of the revised edition of his *History, Culture, and Region in Southeast Asian Perspectives* (Ithaca and Singapore: Cornell University Southeast Asia Program Publications and Institute of Southeast Asian Studies, 1999), pp. 176–205.

8   The institutionalization of the History Office during the Tang dynasty (618–907) marked the climax of a thousand years of Chinese "historiography". This set out the way that future history-writing could be largely shaped by contemporary perspectives. Denis Twitchett, *The Writing of Official History under the T'ang* (Cambridge: Cambridge University Press, 1992), pp. 33-61. Although this did not impact on the Vietnamese directly, the influence of Chinese approaches towards Vietnamese official history was very strong; Keith Weller Taylor, *The Birth of Vietnam* (Berkeley: University of California Press, 1983); note the discussions in the series of appendices, especially Appendix O, "Sources for Early Vietnamese History", pp. 349–59. The influence is even more pronounced later, when the Vietnamese produced their own official history; O.W. Wolters, "Historians and Emperors in Vietnam and China: Comments Arising out of Le Van Huu's History, Presented to the Tran Court in 1272", in *Perceptions of the Past in Southeast Asia*, edited by Anthony Reid and David Marr (Singapore: Heinemann Educational Books for the Asian Studies Association of Australia, 1979), pp. 69–89.

9   Not all historians today are agreed on this. See the discussions on the various interpretations by modern scholars, Abdul Rahim Haji Ismail and Badriyah Haji Salleh, "History through the Eyes of the Malays: Changing Perspectives of Malaysia's Past", in *New Terrains in Southeast Asian History*, edited by Abdul Talib Ahmad and Tan Liok Ee (Athens, OH and Singapore: Ohio University Press and Singapore University Press, 2003), pp. 168–98. For contrast, J.C. Bottoms, "Malay Historical Works: A Bibliographical Note on Malay Histories as Possible Sources for the History of Malaya", in *Malaysian Historical Sources*, edited by K.G. Tregonning (Singapore: University of Singapore Department of History, 1962); and Muhammad Yusoff Hashim, *Persejarahan Melayu Nusantara* (Kuala Lumpur: Teks Publishing, 1988).

10   Several of the contributors here refer to Barraclough's influential book, *An Introduction to Contemporary History* (New York: Basic Books, 1965). Possibly the most consistent practitioner of this fine art is Gaddis who went on to found the distinguished Institute for Contemporary History at Ohio University. He reflects on his personal experience writing history in *The Landscape of History: How Historians Map the Past* (New York: Oxford University Press, 2000), but more pertinent is his essay on re-writing Cold War History: "The New Cold War

History: First Impressions" in his *We Now Know: Rethinking Cold War History* (Oxford: Oxford University Press, 1997), pp. 281–95. Also of interest here is Eric Hobsbawm's Creighton Lecture, "The Present as History: Writing the History of One's Own Time" published in his collection *On History* (New York: The New Press, 1997), pp. 228–40.

11 Cheah Boon Kheng, before his *Malaysia: The Making of a Nation* (Singapore: Institute of Southeast Asian Studies, 2002), has refrained from writing on post-independence Malaysia, but I believe that his authoritative books on the events just prior to nationhood have prepared him well to take the plunge.

12 At the risk of leaving out writings that my colleagues would themselves have chosen, I draw attention to some that have appealed most to me. With Craig J. Reynolds, he has a revised edition (first published in 1991) of his pioneering study, *National Identity and Its Defenders: Thailand Today* (Bangkok: Silkworm Books, 2003). In addition, there is his *Thai Radical Discourse: The Real Face of Thai Feudalism Today* (Ithaca, New York: Southeast Asia Programme, Cornell University, 1987), and "On the Gendering of Nationalist and Postnationalist Selves in 20th Century Thailand", in *Genders & Sexualities in Modern Thailand*, edited by Peter A. Jackson and Nerida M. Cook (Chiang Mai: Silkworm Books, 1999), pp. 261–74.

13 Caroline Hau, *Necessary Fictions: Philippine Literature and the Nation, 1946–80* (Quezon City: Ateneo de Manila University Press, 2000).

14 Anthony Reid, "Merdeka: The Concept of Freedom in Indonesia", in *Asian Freedoms: The Idea of Freedom in East and Southeast Asia*, edited by David Kelly and Anthony Reid (New York: Cambridge University Press, 1998), pp. 141–60; "Entrepreneurial Minorities, Nationalism, and the State" in *Essential Outsiders? Chinese and Jews in the Modern Transformation of Southeast Asia and Central Europe*, edited by Daniel Chirot and Anthony Reid (Seattle: University of Washington Press, 1997), pp. 33–73; and Henri Chambert-Loir and Anthony Reid, eds., *The Potent Dead: Ancestors, Saints and Heroes in Contemporary Indonesia* (Crows Nest, NSW and Honolulu: Allen & Unwin and University of Hawaii Press, 2002).

15 Anthony Milner, "Ideological Work in Constructing the Malay Majority", in Dru C. Gladney, *Making Majorities: Constituting the Nation in Japan, Korea, China, Malaysia, Fiji, Turkey, and the United States* (Stanford: Stanford University Press, 1998), pp. 151–72; "Mahathir, Australia and the Rescue of the Malays", in *Malaysian Economics and Politics in the New Century*, edited by Colin Barlow and Francis Loh Kok Wah (Northhampton, MA: Edward Elgar, 2003), pp. 132–42; *Region, Security and the Return of History* (Singapore: Institute of Southeast Asian Studies, 2003); "What Happened to 'Asian Values'?" in *Towards Recovery in Pacific Asia*, edited by Gerald Segal and David S.G. Goodman (New York: Routledge, 1999), pp. 56–68.

16   Lee Kam Hing, "Malaysian Chinese: Seeking Identity in Wawasan 2020" in *Ethnic Chinese as Southeast Asians*, edited by Leo Suryadinata (Singapore: Institute of Southeast Asian Studies, 1997), pp. 72–107; "The Political Position of the Chinese in Post-independence Malaysia", in *The Chinese Diaspora: Selected Essays*, edited by Wang Ling-Chi and Wang Gungwu (Singapore: Times Academic Press, 1998), pp. 28–49; "Economic Reconstruction and Political Rebellion: The Insurance Industry in Malaya", in *Europe-Southeast Asia in the Contemporary World: Mutual Images and Reflections, 1940s–1960s*, edited by Piyanart Bunnag, Franz Knipping and Sud Chonchirdsin (Baden-Baden: Nomos Verlagsgesellschaft, 2000), pp. 233–50; "Establishing an Enduring Business: The Great Eastern-OCBC Group", in *Capital and Knowledge in Asia: Changing Power Relations*, edited by Heidi Dahles and Otto van den Muijzenberg (London & New York, NY: Routledge, 2003), pp. 146–70.

17   A.J. Stockwell, "Malaysia: The Making of a Neo-Colony?" in *Managing the Business of Empire: Essays in Honour of David Fieldhouse*, edited by Peter Burroughs and A.J. Stockwell (London: Frank Cass, 1998), pp. 138–56; "Policing during the Malayan Emergency, 1948–60: Communism, Communalism and Decolonisation", in *Policing and Decolonisation: Politics, Nationalism, and the Police, 1917–65*, edited by David M. Anderson and David Killingray (Manchester: Manchester University Press), pp. 105–26.

18   Albert Lau, *A Moment of Anguish: Singapore in Malaysia and the Politics of Disengagement* (Singapore: Times Academic Press, 1998).

CHAPTER TWO

Nation and State in Histories of Nation-Building, with Special Reference to Thailand

Craig J. Reynolds

W HEN FIVE Southeast Asian historians took up the challenge to write five nation-building histories, they embarked on a project that took as its main point of reference the nation-state. While the five histories in their final form will be very different in how they approach their respective countries, each historian accepted the nation-state as worthy of serious attention. It was not an abstraction; it was not an illusion. It was not an unwelcome European by-product of the colonial period but a real and meaningful entity that shaped the post-independence history of each country. These historians are not besotted with the nation-state, nor are they uncritical of its mortal rulers. Rather, they are not, or at least not yet, willing to discard the nation-state as the political entity whose unity, multi-cultural membership, and territorial integrity are best able to give expression to aspirations for political participation, social justice, and economic security. Not one of these historians has given up on the nation-state. They have also not given up on the nation.

This willingness to take the nation as a given and something worth fighting for and writing about is not universal in post-colonial societies around the world. A case in point is South Asia, particularly in the writing of India's history. Generalizations are always a little risky, but I would venture to say that a conversation in India today about the nation would move quickly to a discussion about ethnicity, religion, communalism, or caste. Not much hope is invested in the nation, and nationalism is seen as a derivative discourse, an unwelcome legacy of colonialism. The Subaltern Studies group contributed greatly to this shift, and the words of Partha Chatterjee in *The Nation and Its Fragments*, published about a decade ago, are still worth recalling:

> The continuance of a distinct cultural "problem" of the minorities is an index of the failure of the Indian nation to effectively include within its body the whole of the demographic mass that it claims to represent. The failure becomes evident when we note that the formation of a hegemonic "national culture" was *necessarily* built upon the privileging of an "essential tradition," which in turn was defined by a system of exclusions. (Chatterjee 1993, p. 134)

Initially the Subaltern Studies historians were intent on explaining these exclusions and on reconceptualizing the nation in a more inclusive way, particularly with regard to the peasantry. In his manifesto announcing the aims of the Subaltern Studies project, Ranajit Guha spoke of the need to study the *historic failure of the nation to come to its own*.[1] But many members of the group soon became involved in fashioning a historiography that explored the violent effects of that unitary discourse and that explored the histories of peoples and classes excluded by elite nationalism.

To an outsider such as myself, privileged to be involved in the discussions of September 2002 as the nation-building histories neared completion, it was striking that the five Southeast Asian historians had not abandoned study of the nation. They spoke not once about the *historic failure of the nation*, as Guha had once put it so forcefully, and indeed at times they were intent on showing the nation's triumphs as well as its travails. Whether or not this embrace of the nation as an enduringly meaningful political community is a distinctive feature of nationalism in the region I cannot say, nor do I have the space here to explain why Southeast Asian historians seem more willing to embrace the nation than South Asian historians. My contribution to this discussion is rather more modest, namely, to argue at the outset for the distinction that must be made between nation and state and then to suggest why the nation and nationalism are still vital topics for historians of modern Thailand. I also want to suggest why, in all the prolific writings and seminar discussions about the Thai nation and nationalism over the past three decades or so, historians of Thailand continue to find the two decades or so after the change of government in 1932 the most fertile ground for trying to understand where nation-building went wrong.

The Hinge Between Nation and State

The world is now divided up into nation-states, a crazy quilt of countries that every schoolchild learns from coloured maps on classroom walls and globes of the world. What we sometimes forget is that the nation-state is a hyphenated form, a hybrid creature in which two very different entities reside on either side of the hyphen: the nation and the state.

The state has structure and hierarchy. It commands and controls the defence forces as well as the police who maintain public order and enforce the law. The state is concrete; it is rational. Its bureaucracy administers, makes budgets, collects revenue, and dispenses monies. Yet in many parts of the world the legitimacy of the state may be in doubt and fiercely contested. Regimes that control it may have come to power by force of arms, by Machiavellian manoeuvring, even at the ballot box if the American presidential election in November 2001 may be taken as an example. Parliamentary systems may be dominated by two parties, or a single party, and the controlling party or parities may have the backing of military establishments or self-appointed guardians of the public interest, thereby rendering the state illegitimate in the eyes of some members of the community.

The nation, for its part, is more amorphous. It has little structure or hierarchy. Its appeals are emotional and nostalgic. The nation feels grief and pride for those who fell in battle defending it, and it cherishes its egalitarianism. These shared feelings help the national community to cohere and to give it legitimacy. Indeed, in the eyes of the individual members of the national community, the nation is the only legitimate community. The nation is the soul, while the state is the body, the container of the nation that provides the armour for its protection.[2]

This way of describing the hyphenated form makes too stark a contrast between the two entities and fails to do justice to the complex relationship between them. Also, "nation" and "state" are not singular, monolithic entities. Moreover, the nation and the state need each other desperately. To fulfil its role of defender the state requires loyalty to the point of the sacrifice of life itself that only the nation can truly call upon, while the nation lacks the institutional structure that only the state can provide. Occasionally nation and state enter into an uneasy alliance to help each other out. Their relationship is interdependent, but also inherently unstable and a source of conflict, so they quarrel with each other.

Standing between nation and state is a third element, the hyphen, which is a mere punctuation marker in the English language connecting, but keeping separate, nation and state. One might wonder where to search in social, political, and cultural life for this connecting element, this hinge, where nation and state negotiate their uneasy truce.

One place to see this complementary yet conflictual relationship between nation and state is in the history of national monuments. In many Southeast Asian countries national monuments have been battlegrounds where empires, governments and their oppositions, and the disenfranchised have fought to advance their claims.[3] Nation has been pitted against state in these confrontations. Democracy Monument in Bangkok, built by the militarist state in 1939 to commemorate the fall of the absolute monarchy but claimed and occupied from time to time by demonstrators protesting against the state, most memorably in October 1973 and May 1992, is a striking case in point. At these historic junctures, civic groups challenged the state's interpretation of the democracy memorialized by the monument. Another place to see this complex relationship is in the textbook wars, debates over how episodes in the biography of the nation-state should be written up in school textbooks. The education bureaucracy as the arm of the state has kept alive bellicose images of Thailand's neighbours that appeal to nationalistic sentiments and emotions. Still another example would be the flags or names of countries in the region changed by regimes that come to power and then seek to lay claim to particular meanings of the past. From 1960 until the present, for example, there have been five different flags of Cambodia/ Kampuchea, all of which feature the silhouette of the central quincunx of towers on Angkor Wat, the twelfth-century temple in northwest Cambodia.

Finally, in Thailand's case, the hyphen between nation and state may be found in the monarchy, rebuilt and refurbished by the military regime in the late 1950s and early 1960s at a time when the state needed a softer, more attractive face. The monarch is Thailand's head of state, but the monarchy is also the cherished symbol of the nation, both because of the achievements and political savvy of the incumbent monarch and because the monarchy embodies sentiments of loyalty, affection and shared suffering characteristic of the nation. The beauty and pageantry of the monarchy surround state ceremonies with an irresistibly attractive aura. For many Thai citizens the monarch is a national leader more legitimate than any government, elected or otherwise, and for this reason, battle groups staging a coup in the centre of Bangkok, protestors demonstrating at Government House, and governments of all persuasions proudly display an image of Their Majesties, the King and Queen of Thailand.

My remarks here about the distinction between nation and state and their conflictual and complementary relationship are a necessary preliminary to discussing nation-building in Thai history, because the term "nation-building history" begs to be scrutinized carefully. Who or what was the architect of this building? Who engineered the building? Who were the labourers and of what material was the building made? Who was responsible for decorating the building's façade? More often than not in the biographies of the nation-states throughout the region it is the state that has designed, built, and decorated the nation. Heads of states and their officials have been creative in nurturing the nation, sometimes ingeniously and sometimes oppressively, at the same time that individual members and community associations contribute to its growth and well-being. The state instinctively reaches out and claims to speak on behalf of the nation, for the nation embodies the sentiments of shared suffering, egalitarianism, and hope so lacking in the rational, impersonal state. It is as if the state donned the mask of the nation in order to appear as compassionate, as impressive and as pretty as possible, at least in terms of the state's own aesthetics.

Nation and Nationalism in Thai Historiography

One of the ironies of the nation is that it is simultaneously new and ancient. The nation manages to loom out of an immemorial past, when in fact it is a modern creation. In looking for the origins of nation-building in Thailand the historian naturally turns to 1932, for it is at this moment, when the absolute monarchy was gently pushed to one side by a new civilian and military leadership, that a project of fashioning the nation-state visibly unfolds. The architects of this project are fairly easy to identify, although some of the minor ones deserve more attention than they have received to date, but what tends to be forgotten is that the architects and engineers did not start from nothing. In responding to domestic and international challenges in its last decades the absolute monarchy had already contributed materials crucial to the building of the nation-state, and the new post-1932 leadership was quick to turn those materials to its advantage. It is important to remember that the 1932 event was not a revolution, despite the revolutionary tag that is often affixed to the change of government.[4] The political thinking that ultimately came to dominate the coup group was profoundly conservative and hierarchical, even though the new oligarchy was intent on stripping the king of all political power and denying the princes their privileges.[5] At the same time, the new oligarchy, more specifically its chief ideologues, cleverly exploited and recycled the most progressive political thinking of the last absolute monarchs that suited the new nation-building project.

Two well-known examples of the earlier "design-work" contributed by the absolute monarchy will suffice here. One was the rhetoric of community, expressed as *chat*, loosely translated as nation but expressing the idea of common ethnic origins as well as loyalty to the ruler who acts according to the moral law or Dhamma (Peleggi 2002, p. 138). "Unity", a related term, was espoused in the fifth reign (1868–1910), most famously by King Chulalongkorn in a 1903 speech in which he emphasized that the unity he imagined could take place only under a king (Copeland 1993, p. 29). In using this particular term for unity and solidarity (*sammakhi*), the king was responding to a word and an idea already in public circulation, most notably through the writings of his younger brother, Prince-Patriarch Wachirayan Warorot in 1898, and the commoner thinker and author, Thianwan, whose essay preceded the king's own. Three decades before 1932 there was thus already a split between princes and commoners in how the nation-state should be designed. Thianwan was clearly taking issue with the Prince-Patriarch's presumption that "unity" could only cohere in a community ruled by a monarch, and he has been a hero ever since for political thinkers in Thailand today (Copeland 1993, pp. 26–27).

The other example of royal absolutism's contribution to the project may be attributed to Chulalongkorn's son and successor, King Vajiravudh, who fostered a debate about the membership and meaning of the national community. Vajiravudh has been credited by every historian who has written on the subject with "inventing" Thai nationalism, because he refashioned the model for patriotism, "king, god, and country", which he had learned from his years in England, and Thai-ified it as "nation, religion, and monarch". In fact, through his writings Vajiravudh also enlarged and invigorated the Thai public sphere, beginning in the early 1910s in response to a restive political environment that was far more complex than the one his father had faced (Barmé 1999, p. 146). In an episode that shook the confidence of the new king, the army staged a coup in 1912 just after the reign began. The Chinese republican movement in the early 1910s was another unsettling development. There is plenty of evidence from the reign that the king fostered a love of nation that was deeply homoerotic, an extension of the coterie of male friends and courtiers in which he socialized and in which he felt most comfortable (Fischel 1999, p. 164). When the post-1932 leadership set about its own project of nation-building much of the design work in terms of mutual bonding, defence of the new geo-body, and the rhetorics of community had already been accomplished.

The most important architect in the nation-building undertaken by the post-1932 leadership was Luang Wichit Wathakan, a Sino-Thai whose early education had taken place in a monastery and who had worked his way up the bureaucratic ladder by putting his many talents in the service of several Thai governments, most of them military, from the early 1930s until his death in 1962. With a distinguished diplomatic career already behind him, Luang Wichit made his own contribution to the Thai public sphere through his historical and biographical writings, his plays, and his essays on personal and national self-making. He was put in charge of the Fine Arts Department from 1933 until 1937 when he was made Minister of Education, in which capacity he presided over the refashioning and promotion of Thai culture. Luang Wichit recognized instinctively that Siam's monarchy, which had been gently pushed aside but not sent into exile as had been the fate of the monarchies in Siam's colonized neighbours, was a conduit to Siam's ancient past and needed to be recognized and exploited for its nation-building potential. In his many essays he made it clear that he objected to royalty as a class (*klum jao*) rather than to the monarch as a person, leaving the way open for a strong and astute monarch later in the century to capitalize on the theatrics of royal power that had been modernized in pageantry, architecture, and city planning during Chulalongkorn's reign (1868–1910) (Peleggi 2002).

After late 1938 when Field Marshal Plaek Phibunsongkhram came to power the government needed to develop a new rhetoric of leadership with the abdication of the seventh Bangkok king in 1935. Primary among these was the way the government quickly moved to wear the mask of the nation by writing itself into the biography of the nation-state. In 1936 the Ministry of Interior produced a manual to tutor the people in how to use their rights and meet their obligations as responsible citizens (Connors 2003, p. 45). After the military took power in late 1938 patriotism promoted in daily radio broadcasts soon transformed the national flag into a sacred symbol of Thai sovereignty (Chanida 2003). Security and defence became the hallmarks of the regime. The late absolute monarchy had already contributed to the mythology of the kingdom under siege, a mythology exploited by the military leadership of the late 1930s and afterwards. A chronicle published in 1912 describes in detail found in no other historical source how peasants fortified and defended their villages against Burmese attacks, ultimately overwhelming an enemy with superior force (Sunait 1995, p. 22). Everyman

— and everywoman — was a soldier. This historical "event", the defence of Bang Rachan, supplied writers, playwrights and film-makers in the following decades with material that fed a longing for commoner as well as royal heroes. School textbooks of the 1920s and 1930s continued to develop the theme, as did plays and short stories (Sunait 1995, p. 26).

What purpose was served by circulating this image of the Burmese as an enemy of the Thai nation at a time when Burma had been humbled by British imperialism and was no longer a credible military threat? In a curious displacement of historical fact that continues to have repercussions in relations between Thailand and Myanmar today, the nation-building architects of the 1930s seized on Burma to play the role of the colonial power that Siam had never faced. Even the French, with whom the Siamese court during the absolute monarchy had the most friction, could not be construed as colonial oppressors on Siamese soil. In yet another example of how the architects planning the nation grafted the monarchy's history onto that of the nation-state, praise for hero-kings such as Naresuan (late sixteenth century), Taksin (late eighteenth century), and Rama I (late eighteenth and early nineteenth centuries) as national liberators from the occupying Burmese supplied a motif of independence from colonial domination that was as necessary to the Siamese nationalist self as delimited borders and autonomous sovereignty. The Burmese thus became Siam's colonial Other.

These stories forged an expectation of deliverance from chaos, threat and disorder that could only enhance the reputation of military leadership as the nation's saviour. From the late 1930s until the late 1980s plays and stories about ordinary Thai villagers fighting Burmese colonizers to the death encouraged popular expectations and gratitude for military leadership. *The Blood of Suphan*, a historical play written by Luang Wichit and staged for a visiting Japanese minister in 1937, and *The Blood of Thai Soldiers* are examples of this literature celebrating the sacrifice of life for defence of the homeland (Barmé 1993, pp. 122–23). Nowadays the "wars with the Burmese" genre ranges from academic studies by leading university historians, such as Sunait Chutintharanond, to more populist treatments, such as *Wars in Thai History*, which codify the bellicose relationships between the two kingdoms over two centuries into a well-known series of skirmishes and battles (Sunait 1994; Phiman 1999). Two recent films have augmented the genre of narratives of war between the Thai and Burmese, *Bang Rajan [Rajan Village]* and *Suriyothai*.

Another dimension to the nation-building in these formative decades was a project of self-making that went hand-in-hand with the project of nation-building launched by the country's new elite. Again, Luang Wichit Wattakan was the chief architect. Several of his "how to" books celebrate personal achievement and offer a step-by-step plan to personal growth and success. These include works written before World War II, such as *Brain*, first published in 1928, as well as similar publications that preoccupied him after the war, such as *The Power of Thought* and *The Power of Determination* (Wichit 1998, 1999, 2001). These are manuals for everyman and everywoman on how to cope with the pressures and setbacks as well as the opportunities and potentialities of everyday life. These "how to" books, which he never stopped writing, were cobbled together from Western readings and movements he had encountered during his diplomatic career overseas and from Buddhist precepts and homilies that came naturally to him from his early education. They are manuals in how to be modern in a bourgeois way. Every activity, including recreation, should be purposeful, and the day's routine was set out for readers in a timetable of duties and tasks. *Brain* even contains blank charts and schedules that the willing reader is invited to complete according to his or her own needs. There are regimens for knowledge, observation, good judgement, argument, self-control, clear thinking, right reasoning, and so forth.

Along with this regimen of the inner self, which came naturally to Luang Wichit as a Sino-Thai (*lukjin*), self-made man, the nation-building architects and engineers of the 1930s and 1940s promoted a regimen of the physical body, or "physical culture" as it is more widely known. A recent anthropology thesis at Thammasat University by Kongsakon Kawinrawikun spells out the development of this project in great detail. While historians have known the general outlines of these programs for some time, this new research makes manifest the ambition and vastness of this social engineering. Kongsakon has used the work of Michel Foucault whose notion of capillary networks of power comes to mind when one reads the extent of the Thai leadership's micro-management. Public health, sanitation, and nutrition all came under government scrutiny. In 1939 the Ministry of Education through its Department of Physical Education began to promote regular physical exercise in the school curriculum (Kongsakon 2002, pp. 104–05). The Thai diet was said to be deficient in protein, and the vegetables and fruits consumed by Thai people needed to be grown in soil with improved nitrogen content. A campaign called "proteinism" was launched to increase the protein content in food in order to improve the diet of the Thai population and thus its collective health and economic productivity (Kongsakon 2002, p. 90). Indeed, economic productivity as much as "modernity" was the basis for these programmes. In 1941 royal edicts required that work be provided for the unemployed, and beggars, the disabled, the mentally ill and those without family or support networks were to be dispatched to welfare institutions.

After World War II Luang Wichit published *Success in Life*, which contained brief biographies of international figures who had made an impact on their countries and on world history: Eamon DeValera; Stalin; Mussolini, Hitler; Gandhi; Nehru; Chiang Kai-shek; Mao Zedong; Zhou Enlai; and with passing mention of other American and European leaders. The political proclivities of these men — republican, fascist, communist, pacifist — mattered little to Luang Wichit. For him what was important was that these were all "event-making men", in Sydney Hook's words, who wielded power effortlessly and turned it to their own ends and who could inspire lesser mortals to great feats (Hook 1945). The qualities that distinguished these men — strength of mind, powers of concentration, self-confidence, and will power — were outlined in a 1928 work, *Great Men*, which by 1932 had been reprinted four times (Wichit 1970). One is reminded here of the popularity of biographies in Vietnam in the years leading up to the revolution in August 1945 when Vietnamese writers were likewise captivated by the inspirational lives of powerful Western and Asian political figures (Marr 1981, chap. 6).

Luang Wichit, who was a gifted communicator and a teacher by nature as well as a public servant and official by training and profession, has had a mixed reception by Thai historians. It is impossible to ignore him because of the sheer volume of books and essays he published. His writings on political leadership and personal development have always had avid readers. But because of the service he gave to the two military governments under Field Marshal Phibun (1938–44 and 1947–57) as well as to the dictator Field Marshal Sarit Thanarat in the early 1960s, to say nothing of his celebration of powerful men who rank high on the twentieth-century list of dictators and tyrants, he has long been castigated by the left and by many academics. Typical of the conventional criticism of the first Phibun government, and by implication of Luang Wichit's role in directing the nation-building project, is the following remark of Professor Chai-anan Samudavanija about the creation of "a new state-identity" by the post-1932 elite:

> This new state-identity … negated the principles of constitutionalism. It promoted centralization of state power and authoritarianism, resulting in a modern variant of absolutism…. The identity of the nation and the state became one under the name of Thailand. (Chai-anan 2002, pp. 51–52)

In characterizing the promotion of state power and authoritarianism by the Phibun project as heavy-handed, this criticism overlooks the populism of the nation-building measures. Luang Wichit reveled in the correspondence and criticisms, both positive and negative, that his writing generated. As with many Thai authors, he fed the criticisms back into subsequent editions. The charge of elitism often made of the nation-building project fails to take account of how attractive the new ruling elite made the state to appear as it donned the mask of the nation and peered into every fibre of its being.

The celebration of the centenary of Luang Wichit's birth in 1998 saw the republication of many of his works as well as the usual biographies and reassessments that accompany these occasions, and I detect a current of revisionist history now emerging. An example of this revisionist history is a new book by the Chiangmai-based historian, Saichon Satayanurak, which explains Luang Wichit's political thought with special reference to nationalism (Saichon 2002). It is quite clear from this new research that

Luang Wichit was one of Thailand's most important political theorists for the decades that followed, up to and including the present one. In mulling over the meaning of the change of government in 1932 in relation to the monarchy, the commoner values that he espoused, and the personal discipline he advocated as a key to individual and social well-being, Luang Wichit sketched out a political theory that has been paradigmatic for Thai governments since 1932, be they military or civilian, business or reformist. While he argued for the importance of political parties, a parliament, and for a people's democracy, he also argued for a strong leader to arbitrate conflict. One of his rubrics was "animals follow; people lead" (Saichon 2002, p. 71). And Siam should not be a republic. It is "our custom" to have a king, he said in the year the absolute monarchy ended (Saichon 2002, p. 73).

Surrounded by colonized neighbours that only a half century previously had bowed before Siam's imperial might, the country's new leadership was preoccupied by its status in the world. "If you don't want to be scum you have to be a Great Power," Field Marshal Phibun declared defiantly.[6] Luang Wichit, who had spent the decade before the 1932 change of government in diplomatic posts in Paris and London, was deeply conscious of Thailand's modest place in the world. The new leadership's sense of its status in the international hierarchy of nation-states encouraged it from the late 1930s to edge closer to Japan's East Asian Co-prosperity Sphere and to practise the irredentism that has been the hallmark of the regime's legacy and remembered, somewhat ruefully, to the present day.

Luang Wichit's political theory — the importance of strong leadership, rule by commoners, elected representatives in a parliament — and his books on how to achieve, how to be successful, how to master your fate are connected. Historians usually separate Luang Wichit's political writings from his "how to" manuals as if they came from the pen of two different people. But they came from the pen of the same person. The pop psychological works such as *Brain, The Power of Thought, the Power of Determination,* and *Success in Life* belonged to his nationalist project. These were the qualities on a personal, individual level that he saw necessary for the collective Thai people, the *chat thai,* to pursue.

Conclusion

In summing up, I need to explain why I have chosen to discuss the nation-building project of the post-1932 Thai elite in an essay ostensibly about approaches to writing contemporary history. Thai political and social thought today is still coming to terms with the nation-building project launched by the post-1932 elite. The writings of Luang Wichit Wattakan — his political theory as well as essays on personal and social development — continue to have a place in in contemporary Thai consciousness, even if his reputation has suffered in some quarters because of his service to military governments. The debate about the nation-building project in the 1930s began with momentous events that happen once in a lifetime, the mass uprisings of October 1973 that brought down a military dictatorship. One of the distinctive features of the period between October 1973 and October 1976, when a military coup temporarily suspended Thailand's democratic development, was upheaval in the academic world about the study of economics, the study of contemporary society, and particularly about the writing of history. Dr. Charnvit Kasetsiri, the historian writing on Thailand in this nation-building series, contributed to that upheaval. By encouraging the study of alternative historical interpretations in a fractious academic environment, he played a vital role in breaking the grip of dynastic and conventional historical writing on the Thai academic establishment. He was instrumental in excavating the historical writings of "the political poet", Jit Poumisak, and he enthralled an audience in Canberra in February 1976 with his account of the changing trajectory of Thai historiography long before other historians writing in English grasped what was happening (Charnvit 1974*b*, 1979). In the upheavals of the mid-1970s, the nation-building project of the military regimes in earlier decades was called into question, and here too Dr. Charnvit was an early contributor to an alternative historiography with his assessment of Field Marshal Plaek Phibunsongkhram's nation-building project (Charnvit 1974*a*).

One could point to other developments over the past two decades that have rekindled memories of the first military regime under Phibun. From the mid-1980s until the financial crisis in 1997, the economic boom in Thailand opened up the northern mainland to Thai business, encouraged travel and tourism in the region and reawakened interest in the Tai peoples living in Myanmar, China, and Laos. Academic study of Tai peoples in the region has flourished ever since. For different reasons, Tai irredentism was also distinctive in the regional outlook of the post-1932 elite as it surveyed its colonized neighbours and appealed to Tai brothers and sisters who "shared the same blood lines" to turn to *Thai*-land for leadership (Reynolds 2002, p. 17).

After the 1997 crisis, precipitated in part by massive foreign investment, American dollar loans, and international economic pressures, Thai sovereignty quickly became a political issue. The impact of globalization on the Thai economy had deleterious as well as beneficial effects, and the capacity of the country to withstand the pressures and power of international business was held up to public scrutiny. The issue of sovereignty awakened nationalistic feelings that hark back to the late 1930s when Thailand was surrounded by colonized neighbours, so it is not surprising that the nation-building project of that period should come alive again in contemporary memory. The earlier period of nation-building when *Thai*-land was surrounded by the Western powers is proving to be fertile ground for new historical studies. By declaring itself the guardian of the nation, the state made itself an easy target for historians today to study the co-optation of the nation by the state.

While the contemporary Thai nation-state today owes a great deal to the architects, engineers and workers who laboured to nurture the nation in a way that would serve the state, alternative nationalisms are not so easy to identify. The Assembly of the Poor, for example, a loose coalition of NGO groups, is at heart a classic peasant struggle over rights to land, water and forests (Baker 2000, Missingham 2003). It can trace its struggle back to earlier peasant resistance in the nineteenth century, to the insurgency led by the Communist Party of Thailand, and to the Peasants Federation of Thailand. But in its programmes, advocacy of community consciousness, and its resistance to a state that rides roughshod over the rights of the poor and the disenfranchised, the Assembly of the Poor articulates an alternative vision of the nation contra "the state". But because the Assembly of the Poor speaks on behalf of particular constituencies and thus does not speak with the unitary voice of the centre, its programmes and claims are always seen to be partisan rather than national.

Thailand's nation-builders of today regard the protesters and advocates who march on the parliament or the prime minister's residence as unauthorized renovators of the nation or as squatters claiming a space for themselves in a building that is forever in the act of construction.[7] In the eyes of many, probably most people in the country today, the nation is a building that will never be finished.

NOTES

1   Guha (1982, p. 7), emphasis in the original.

2   The distinction between nation and state elaborated here is based on Anderson (1990, p. 95).

3   See the comparison of the Shwedagon Paya in Yangon with Democracy Monument in Bangkok in Reynolds (2000*b*) and the related essay in Reynolds (2000*a*).

4   Some Thai historians have been willing to tolerate the term "revolution" in view of the debates about the rights of the governed that took place in the decades leading up to 1932; see Nakkarin (1992) and Reynolds (1998).

5   Prajadhipok, the incumbent king who was overthrown in 1932, was quoted as saying that the military "will not tolerate the King taking active command" (Batson 1984, p. 263).

6   Quoted in Kongsakon (2002, p. 24). I am grateful to Villa Vilaithong for bringing Kongsakon's research to my attention.

7   On this point and many others I am grateful to Hong Lysa for comments on an earlier draft.

REFERENCES

Anderson, Benedict R, O'G. *Language and Power: Exploring Political Cultures in Indonesia*. Ithaca: Cornell University Press, 1990.

Baker, Chris. "Thailand's Assembly of the Poor: Background, Drama, Reaction". *South East Asia Research* 8, no. 1 (March 2000): 5–29.

Barmé, Scott. *Luang Wichit Wathakan and the Creation of a Thai Identity*. Singapore: Institute of Southeast Asian Studies, 1993.

———. "Proto-Feminist Discourses in Early Twentieth-Century Siam", in *Genders and Sexualities in Modern Thailand*, edited by Peter A. Jackson and Nerida M. Cook. Chiang Mai: Silkworm Books, 1999, pp. 134–53.

Batson, Benjamin A. *The End of the Absolute Monarchy in Siam*. Singapore, Oxford, and New York: Oxford University Press, 1984.

Chai-anan Samudavanija. "State-Identity Creation, State-Building and Civil Society, 1939–1989". In *National Identity and its Defenders: Thailand Today*, edited by Reynolds, Craig, J. Chiang Mai: Silkworm Books, 2002, pp. 49–70.

Chanida Phromphayak-Phuaksom. "*Thongchat phlengchat sang (rattha) chatthai* [The National Flag and the National Anthem: Building (a Statist) Thai Nation]". *Sinlapa watthanatham* (March 2003): 130–45.

Charnvit Kasetsiri. "The First Phibun Government and Its Involvement in World War II". *Journal of the Siam Society* 62, no. 2 (July 1974*a*): 25–88.

———. "The Meaning of Thai History According to Jit Poumisak". In *Jit phumisak nakrop khong khon runmai [Jit Poumisak: Warrior of the New Generation]*, edited by Suchat Sawatsi. Bangkok: Social Science Association, 1974*b*.

Charnvit Kasetsiri. "Thai Historiography from Ancient Times to the Modern Period". In *Perceptions of the Past in Southeast Asia*, edited by A.J.S. Reid and D.G. Marr. Hong Kong: Heinemann, 1979, pp. 156–70.

Chatterjee, Partha. *The Nation and Its Fragments: Colonial and Postcolonial Histories*. Princeton: Princeton University Press, 1993.

Connors, Michael. *Democracy and National Identity in Thailand*. New York and London: RoutledgeCurzon, 2003.

Copeland, Matthew. "Contested Nationalism and the Overthrow of the Absolute Monarchy in Siam". Ph.D. dissertation, Australian National University, 1993.

Fischel, Thamora. "Romances of the Sixth Reign: Gender, Sexuality, and Siamese Nationalism". In *Genders and Sexualities in Modern Thailand*, edited by Peter A. Jackson and Nerida M. Cook. Chiang Mai: Silkworm Books, 1999, pp. 154–67.

Guha, Ranajit, ed. *Subaltern Studies I: Writings on South Asian History and Society*. Delhi: Oxford University Press, 1982.

Hook, Sidney. *The Hero in History: A Study in Limitation and Possibility*. London: Secker & Warburg, 1945.

Kongsakon Kawinrawikun. "Kansang rangkai phonlamuang thai nai samai jomphon phibunsongkhram pho so 2481–2487" [Constructing the Body of Thai Citizens During the Regime of Field Marshal P. Phibunsongkhram, 1938–1944]. MA thesis, Sociology and Anthropology, Thammasat University, 2002.

Marr, David G. *Vietnamese Tradition on Trial, 1920–1945*. Berkeley, Los Angeles, London: University of California Press, 1981.

Missingham, Bruce D. *The Assembly of the Poor in Thailand: From Local Struggles to National Protest Movement*. Chiang Mai: Silkworm Books, 2003.

Nakkarin Mektrairat. *Kanpatiwat 2475 [The 1932 Revolution]*. Bangkok: Social Sciences and Humanities Textbook Project Foundation, 1992.

Peleggi, Maurizio. *Lords of Things: The Fashioning of the Siamese Monarchy's Modern Image*. Honolulu: University of Hawai'i Press, 2002.

Phiman Jaemjarat [1965]. *Songkhram nai prawattisat thai [Wars in Thai History]*. Bangkok: Sangsan Press, 1999.

Reynolds, Craig J. "Thai Revolution (1932)", in *The Encylopedia of Political Revolutions*, edited by Jack A. Goldstone. Washington, D.C.: Congressional Quarterly, Inc., 1998, pp. 479–80.

———. "The Ethics of Academic Engagement with Burma". In *Burma Myanmar: Strong Regime, Weak State?*, edited by Morten B. Pedersen et al., Adelaide: Crawford House Publishing Pty. Ltd., 2000a, pp. 123–37.

———. *Icons of Identity as Sites of Protest: Burma and Thailand Compared*. PROSEA Research Paper no. 30, Taipei: Academica Sinica, 2000b.

———, ed. *National Identity and Its Defenders: Thailand Today*. Chiang Mai: Silkworm Books, 2002.

Saichon Satayanurak. *Khwamplianplaeng nai kansang chatthai lae khwam pen thai doi luang wijitwatthakan [Changes in the Construction of Luang Wichit Wathakan's "Thai Nation" and "Thai-ness"]*. Bangkok: Matichon, 2002.

Sunait Chutintararanond. *Phama rop thai: wa duay kansongkhram rawang thai kap phama [The Burmese Fight the Thai: On the Thai-Burmese Wars]*. Bangkok: Matichon, 1994.

——— and Than Tun. *On Both Sides of the Tenasserim Range: History of Siamese-Burmese Relations*. Bangkok: Institute of Asian Studies, Chulalongkorn University, 1995.

Wichit Wathakan, Luang [1928]. *Mahaburut [Great Men]*. Bangkok: Soembannakit. Seventh printing, 1970.

——— [1950]. *Kamlang jai [The Power of Determination]*. Bangkok: Sangsanbuk, 1998.

——— [1951]. *Kamlang khwamkhit [The Power of Thought]*. Bangkok: Sangsanbuk, 1999.

——— [1928]. *Mansamong [Brain]*. Bangkok: Sangsanbuk, 2001.

CHAPTER THREE

Rethinking History and "Nation-Building" in the Philippines

Caroline S. Hau

D ISTINGUISHED AMERICAN feminist scholar Joan W. Scott, reflecting on what now counts as "common sense" in her discipline, has argued that "[h]istory is in the paradoxical position of creating the objects it claims only to discover" (2001, p. 85). The fact that historians include and exclude as well as organize and present their "materials" or "data" exposes the interpretive practices that not only underpin their field of study, but constitute the knowledge produced by that field as knowable and intelligible in the first place. Wide-ranging critiques of historical representation (Foucault 1971; White 1973, 1987, and 1999; LaCapra 1983 and 1987) have placed interpretation at the centre of history understood in its double sense as both object of study and verbal account. No longer can interpretation be treated as completely separate and distinct from reality, since interpretations help define and shape that reality. Neither can "materials" or "data" be treated as free-floating and self-contained information awaiting discovery or recovery, since they are embedded within complex, often past systems of thought and action that historians can ill afford to either ignore or discount.

To write a history of contemporary Philippines is not — and, at a time when disciplines and their boundaries are subject to critical interrogation, can no longer be — simply a matter of writing *about* the Philippines with particular reference to its past. The historian must now also attend to the conceptual parameters within which a "history" *of* "the Philippines" is conceivable and practicable as a scholarly undertaking. This entails analysing the ways in which "the Philippines" was imagined and consolidated as a "national" community with "its" own history (Anderson 1991 [1983]; Scott 2001, p. 97). It also demands that historians acknowledge the role that their own project plays in structuring — intellectually and materially — the history of that nation.

Contemporary Philippine history is one of the products, at the same time that it is one of the processes, of producing "the Philippines" as a nation. Indeed, the very concept of *a* Philippine history can only be posited in a circular fashion by recourse to a logical framework that takes for granted, rather than examines closely, a specifically "modern" (re)organization of time, space, matter, and ideas. What we generally call "modernity" is a shorthand for the centuries-long, global transformations of everyday life that created — by elevating to the status of norm — a world system of nation-states. The nation-state became the dominant unit of political, economic, social, and ideological analysis, as well the primary agent of political, economic, social, and ideological action.

The nation-state embodies a particular concentration, distribution, and use of power as well as a particular set of social relationships within a bounded geographical territory (Hobsbawm 1992, p. 80; Elias 1970). Its historical formation is inseparable from the "modernization" of its capabilities for acting within the international arena; for maintaining the territorial integrity of its "geo-body" (Thongchai 1994, pp. 16–17); for extracting and regulating resources and flows (whether of people, goods, capital, ideas); for establishing particular institutions and organizations which allow for certain forms of political, social, cultural, or economic activities; for meeting the needs of and forging links among its inhabitants by fostering their sense of themselves as individuals and as members of a larger collectivity, cementing their attachment and commitment to each other and to the nation-state, and mobilizing them for large-scale endeavours (Smith 1998, p. 20).

Moreover, there is a sense in which these norms, these standards and requirements of nation-statehood, define the horizon of ideals to aspire for and work toward, rather than index fully realized empirical actualities, even in Europe, where they originated (Hroch 1996). Here, the rhetoric and practice of "nation-building" assumed signal importance in the second half of the twentieth century as the key articulator of a theory and programme of attaining nation-statehood. In fact, scholarly literature on modernization equated the reorganization of political life through the establishment of state institutions and the concomitant "training" of individuals in the ideals and values of citizenship with nation-building: "Political development *is* nation-building" (Finkle and Gable 1966, p. 46, underscoring added).

The constructionist overtones of "building" a nation have also meant that the nation came to be thought of in almost mechanical terms as a project that required the "application of design and technical devices to matter" (Smith 1998, p. 3). This application involved a multi-pronged development of politics, economy, and population (Szporluk 1988, p. 164). Scholars differed on which mechanisms — mass education, communications and technology, industrial growth, citizenship training, mass mobilization, and cultural identity-formation — served as functional *sine qua non* of the nation-building agenda of the modernizing nation-state (Deutsch 1966 [1953]; Lerner 1958; Deutsch and Foltz 1963; Bendix 1996 [1964]).

Notwithstanding the differences in emphasis, scholars do agree that the "integration" efforts of the nation-state in establishing authority and administering both territory and people presumed the theoretical primacy and practical challenge of linking the government and the governed (Weiner 1965). The modern state "found itself having to take notice of the opinions of its subjects and citizens, because its political arrangements gave them a voice — generally through various kinds of elected representatives — and/or because the state needed their practical consent or activity in other ways, e.g., as taxpayers or as potential conscript soldiers" (Hobsbawm 1992, p. 80).

While a number of scholars have gone so far as to argue in favour of a strong, if not natural, affinity between nation-states and liberal democracy (Kymlicka 2001, p. 224), few contest the idea that nation-building entails a certain "democratization" of politics, whether the government be self-avowedly democratic or communist. Indeed, the nation-state enabled a new form of social stratification in which people were accorded formal equality (that is, were equal under the law) in the face of existing social and economic inequalities (Elias 1970, pp. 274–79).

The politics of nation-building had a special salience for countries in Asia, Latin America, and Africa that had been subject to colonial rule. During the period of decolonization, especially from the 1940s to the 1970s, the newly independent nation was held up as the agent of sustainable development, social change and redistributive justice, and cultural self-preservation. For countries such as the Philippines, postcolonial national agendas were dominated by modernization and development — a global project that presupposed and required the existence of states, preferably strong ones. It was, in fact, on the principal condition of taking the form of the state that nations could enter the "modern" world system. This condition was so basic to obtaining recognition in the international arena as to become commonsensical, but it also necessitated that political and cultural communities be recognized not just as nation-states in form or on paper, but in substance and in reality. Communities thus needed to be "made" into nation-states, even as these communities themselves took shape within established institutions and territorial boundaries inherited from their former colonizers. The territorial space of such "national" communities had to be filled with political, economic, and cultural "subjects" of the nation whose needs and aspirations could be articulated, and whose activities could be channelled to specific, purposive ends, by the state.

The tendency to think of nation-building in terms of a modular plan that needed to be put into effect or implemented was starkly evident in much of the scholarship on nation-building in the "Third World" (not to mention pronouncements of leaders of those countries), most of which viewed nation-building as a matter of "importing" or "applying" Western norms and models to post-colonial realities (see Chatterjee's critique, 1986). The failure of nation-building projects in many of the former colonies in Asia and Africa has since necessitated a rethinking of basic assumptions about nation-building (Fanon 1963).

This chapter[1] analyses one such effort at nation-building in Southeast Asia — the Philippine case — through a close reading of preeminent Filipino scholar Reynaldo Ileto's account of contemporary Philippine history (2002).

What is striking about the history of nation-building in the Philippines is its exemplariness. As the first country in Southeast Asia to wage an anti-colonial war of national liberation against Spain, it has had a longer experience of nation-building than any of its immediate neighbours. Its peculiar "tutelage" under United States imperialism made it one of the earliest laboratories for nation-building in the region.[2] The American legacy[3] of state-building — particularly the introduction of suffrage, mass primary education, and infrastructure building — in colonial Philippines during the early twentieth century established the conceptual and actual parameters of politics, of what would come to be understood as "the political" in post-independence Philippines (Hayden 1942). Moreover, as Peter W. Stanley has argued, "In a very real sense, Americans in the Philippine government during the first decade of this [i.e., 20th] century conceived of themselves as engaged in building the foundations of a modern nation" (1974, p. 82).

Scholars have stressed the continuity between colonial and post-colonial periods by stressing American ideological and political contributions to both colonial and national state formation (Abinales 2002, p. 605), not least of which was the consolidation, legitimation, and expansion of so-called "elite" power well into the post-colonial period (Stanley 1974, p. 270). The Philippine post-colonial state greatly expanded the programme of nation-building first undertaken by the Americans and continued by Commonwealth president Manuel Quezon in the years leading up to World War II.[4]

Reynaldo Ileto's "History and Nation Building in the Philippines, 1943–1998" (2002) provides one of the fullest discussions of post-independence nation-building in the Philippines. It is also notable for its pioneering attempt at rethinking the concept of nation-building in light of current perspectives on nationalism that, in the wake of the failures of nation-building projects in Asia and Africa during the 1980s and 1990s, sought to "deconstruct" the nation by exposing its constructedness and critiquing the idea of its homogeneity (Smith 1998, p. 3). Ileto's approach stresses the constitutive role of historical discourses in shaping not just nation-building policies in the Philippines, but also ideas about time, power, and change that inform and regulate Filipino nationalist thought and action. The remaining section of this essay engages Ileto's history in an effort to cast into relief some of the characteristic themes and preoccupations of theories of nation-building in the Philippines, and to draw out the "deconstructive" implications of Ileto's reconceptualizing the politics of nation-building.

Ileto's work eschews the standard historiographical perspectives that are brought to bear on nation-building in the Philippines and elsewhere (Kalaw 1926; Hayden 1945; Agoncillo and Guerrero 1984 [1973]; Constantino 1975; Constantino and Constantino 1978; Corpuz 1989). It is not about the state and state-building, even if it rests on the understanding that nation-building took place in interaction with the historical growth and so-called "modernization" of the state. Nor is it about the evolution of "national character" and the construction of cultural, "national" identities. Nor is it about the consolidation of the national economy and the development of political systems and institutions.

Instead, it treats nation-building as a discursive project, one that entails recognition of the Philippine nation-state's "moorings" (to use Ileto's phrase) in specific stories of the country, and one that, moreover, looks into the ways in which understandings of that country's "past" functioned in ways to orient and reorient political action in the present and toward the future. Ileto is concerned to provide a genealogy of repeated and changing ways of imagining a "Filipino" community by tracing the consensus as well as contestation generated around terms and practices that helped to organize Philippine social and political reality. He shows how interpretations of emancipation and transformation inhere in institutions, political systems, social relationships, markets, social movements, and texts. He views the study of history as an analysis of changing and competing interpretations of the Philippine nation.

The term "nation-building" carries with it associations of solidity, concreteness, and structure, summoning up the mental image of an edifice as imposing as it is monumental (cf. Smith 1998, p. 3). Yet, as any scholar or student of nationalism will tell us, the word "nation" in the term "nation-building" is notoriously amorphous, never having been known for its conceptual or theoretical precision (Anderson 1991, p. 5). But if there is one insight that stands out among the many that underpin Ileto's work, it is the idea that the lack of precision of the term "nation" has never gotten in the way of political practice. In fact, the very vagueness of that term may have actually enhanced political practice (see also Vincent 2002, p. 39). It is precisely because the "nation" lends itself to different interpretations that it can be used by different groups for people for different purposes. It may not be far-fetched to claim that the intellectual opaqueness of the nation is one of the conditions for the exercise of politics in the Philippines.

A key argument in Ileto's work concerns the role of writings on the nation, especially writings on the history of the nation, in the "building" of the nation-state. Ileto holds that history functioned as an implement for establishing and regulating "modernity". It served as the scaffolding on which the state constructed its rationale for existence, as well as its policies and practices. In this sense, writings of and on history — even scholarly ones — cannot be treated as abstract commentaries on something called Filipino nationalism. These writings are part and parcel of nationalism, not least in the ways in which both state and society have marshalled these writings about the past to claim legitimacy and validate practice, and in doing so, contributed to fashioning the myths, articulating the aspirations, and formulating the policies of the nation.

And since political meanings and symbols also encode power relations, the often vociferous if not violent contention over "correct" or "valid" interpretations in the Philippines points to real and existing political investments on the part of those who participate in the debate, even as silence also points to the effective marginalization of certain groups and classes of people from that debate. Ileto's own project, the project of academic writing on the history of Philippine nation-building, can arguably be considered *a* history of the nation (cf. Vincent 2002, p. 45).

Ileto's discussion unfurls around a number of important political figures, notably presidents and officially recognized "national heroes", as well as intellectuals "behind the scenes whose ideas gave substance to the rhetoric of presidents". He shows the remarkable continuity in the style and substance of the discourse on nation-building, which can be partly attributable to the staying power of visibly public figures such as Jose Laurel, whose career is exemplary in that it distils many of Ileto's major concerns and arguments in this book. He also brings in lesser-known intellectuals involved either in the nation-building project of the state or in alternative visions of nation-building advanced by progressive movements, or, more often than not, in both. He treats these people as "bearers of discourses" which can be read closely and examined for the style and content of their language and for their "effects on national life". As he has argued elsewhere, proper names do not simply encapsulate individual life-histories; they also designate "a certain preoccupation with, or thinking about power and change" (Ileto 1998, p. 41). Political oratory — the thematic and rhetorical motifs that run through politicians' speeches and papers — can be analysed as a form of theorizing about the source and logic of authority and response.

Ileto argues that politicians, "in order to remain in control and popularly-backed, spoke to crowds of people and elicited responses that might well be described as nation-building responses because they served to establish communication among various forces and social groups". Much as "the national revolution" became the dominant myth of the Indonesian post-colonial state (Taufik 2002, p. 1), rhetoric and response in the Philippines have tended to cluster around interpretations of "key" events in Philippine history, one of which, the anti-colonial revolution against Spain of 1896–98, looms large in the political imagination as a "common point of reference" capable of eliciting strong emotions and mobilizing mass support. Ileto argues that "[w]hen the Revolution of 1896–98 was written into national history as a foundational event — the birth of the nation — it also engendered a set of 'heroes' or 'founding fathers' with whom political leaders and citizens alike could identify." The American legacy of universal education was the crucial apparatus for disseminating a brand of national history — what Ileto calls "national textbook history" because of its deployment within the sphere of mass education — which recapitulated the founding event of the revolution in terms of a historical emplotment of Philippine history that viewed the event as a major step forward in the gradual evolution and progressive realization of ideals of independence and salvation.

This well-worn "plot" of the Philippine story can be used to justify the status quo or to challenge it. Thus, on the one hand, post-war Philippine presidents Manuel Roxas and Elpidio Quirino used the revolution to highlight the virtues of American tutelage of the Philippines, emphasizing that the "United States had fulfilled its promise to nurture the Filipinos politically until the latter were ready to go off on their own as an independent nation-state." But on the other hand, this benign view of American colonialism in the Philippines was subject to criticism by radical intellectuals and peasant groups. The politician Jose Laurel, who headed the Japan-sponsored government during the war, argued that the United States "had never really let daughter Filipinas become fully independent and so the Revolution remained unfinished". In the late 1940s and early 1950s, Huk leader Luis Taruc, to cite another example, drew a parallel between the American occupation of the Philippines, with its brutal suppression of the Filipino populace in the midst of the Filipino struggle against Spain, and the American return to the Philippines in the midst of Filipino struggle against Japan, with its arbitrary intervention in Philippine politics in support of the Filipino elite "collaborators" against the interests of the Filipino people.

A single event such as the Philippine revolution is therefore capable of generating multiple meanings, and becomes itself an object and subject of political debate and contestation over "correct" or "valid" interpretations of Philippine history in light of the exigencies of present concerns. Narratives of the past — particularly the colonial times, of which the American regime was the fraught typecase — are double-edged weapons which may be used to legitimize or challenge the status quo, to generate consensus and conflict among politically diverse individuals and groups.

Given that the force of signification helps to shape the past and condition the present, we readers are forced to critically examine the knowledge that is handed down to us and the knowledge that we ourselves produce. Ideas about the Philippine nation and its history not only inform the way people think and behave and act in society. More important, they set limits on what people can imagine and do at specific moments and in specific locations.

One implication of Ileto's work is that while nation-building took place in conjunction with the Philippine state, and may have well been one of the key practices of the state, the state cannot simply be treated as a prime mobilizer of "nationness", even when it arrogated to itself the task of promoting and realizing certain ideas of the nation. The Philippine case is particularly instructive because of the high visibility of efforts on the part of various social groups to contest or resist the state's upholding of a single narrative of the Philippine nation. Philippine nationalism took shape often as a critique of the state, and often at an assumed distance — both literal and conceptual — from the state.

But what becomes clear from our reading of Ileto's work is the mutual inter-penetration between state and society far beyond that suggested by even scholars and activists working before and since Ileto. This is because both leaders and rebels across social classes shared and drew from a common fund of insights and stories — what Ileto calls a partisan but nevertheless "shared, public discourse" centred on heroes — pertaining to the desirability and necessity of freedom and change. This nationalist imperative toward emancipation and transformation was often couched or framed in the religious and especially Catholic idiom of brotherhood, suffering, martyrdom, and sacrifice, carrying with it the emotive charge of pity and empathy, and provoking readjustment of bodily dispositions and orienting these dispositions toward action (see also Ileto 1979). The impulse animating this understanding of nationalist solidarity and concerted action in the name of the nation does not just inform state efforts to push its "development" agenda. It has empowered those in the fringes of power to challenge the official nationalist agenda.

Crucial to Ileto's argument is the question of "excess", the need to factor in the "remainder" that exceeds the nation-building project's attempt to grasp and organize the Philippine socio-political reality. Ileto assigns to identifiably marginalized groups the epistemic radicalism that is tapped by the ruling classes yet is nevertheless always in excess of the ruling classes' attempts to appropriate it. Thus, while Ileto cogently argues that neither the colonizers nor the elite ruling class that dominated Philippine politics ever really exercised full and absolute control over politics, confronted as they always were by the disruptive presence of the dominated whom they sought to marginalize by criminalizing them or else dismissing them as "ignorant" and "irrational", he also shows how the domination of

Philippine politics and society by one order actually rests not on the ruling order's ability to generalize its principles and ideas and remold society in its own image, but rather on its ability to effectively use the very principles and ideals of the dominated. Allusions to historical events of the past, and to the heroes whose lives consecrate that past "function to disseminate signs that can be apprehended in different ways. Martyrdom, struggle, revolution, independence and national unity are, after all, potent images in their own right".

On the one hand, this would explain the explosive social divisions and political contentions (Hau 2000*b*)⁵ that regularly destabilized Philippine society, ranging from the collaborationism issue that split Philippine society in the brutal aftermath of World War II to the Huk rebellion of the late forties and early fifties to the controversy over the teaching of "national hero" Jose Rizal's life and works and the tug-of-war between the Catholic church and the state over the "proper" content of Filipino nationalist historiography of the mid-fifties to the student activism of the sixties and the communist "insurgency" and Muslim separatist movement of the seventies and beyond. On the other hand, Ileto's work also points to the ineluctable intertwining, or better yet the mutual contamination, of these social groups locked in a tight, ultimately "national" embrace based on the fundamental sharing of ideas about Philippine history and national identity.

Ileto maintains that "politicians of all colors have always felt a need to speak in the idiom of radical nationalism, which originates from the experience and memories of the revolution against Spain (inspired by both 'millenarian' traditions and the enlightened ideals of the French revolution) and the Philippine-American war." He identifies the wellspring of nationalism that has been tapped at various times by various kinds of people to advance their political and social goals or agenda. Notable is his contention that the Communist Party was able to "ride on the backs of peasant nationalist and anti-Japanese sentiments" in establishing the revolutionary Huk guerrilla army and movement.

Paradigms for thinking about Philippine nationalism and history have characteristically taken the form of conceptual oppositions or dichotomies between elite/masses, enlightenment/millenarian, collaborator/

nationalist. By deconstructing these oppositions and showing their co-implication in and reliance on each other, Ileto's work leads to a re-evaluation of historical periods such as the "dark age" of the Japanese occupation, which is now shown as a forcing ground for the articulation of an Asian- and Filipino-centric, critical rereading of the American colonial regime and the post-colonial nation-state in the making: "[T]he Japanese occupation period had cultivated among a segment of the political elite and educated class, if not a proportion of the populace, the idea long entertained by fringe nationalist groups that the destiny of the Philippines need not be entwined with America's."

Ileto's nuanced account of Philippine nation-building traces both the holes and the seams in the fabric of nationalist intentions and practices. His arguments become especially salient when they are posed alongside the question of the impact of nation-building on ethnocultural minorities. One of the main critiques of nation-building programmes, in fact, centres on the homogenizing tendency of the state's integration policies and their implications for these minorities (Kymlicka 2001). If nationalism is concerned with the formation of a political, moral, and symbolic community, what is left out, or marginalized, in this process? Does the nation-building project selectively include and exclude specific groups and individuals?

Factoring in the experiences of ethnic minority groups such as Muslims, Chinese, and indigenous peoples, and of the increasing numbers of Filipinos working and living overseas can contribute to deepening our understanding of the fraught politics of nation-building policies and practices, especially those aimed at ethnic minorities.

Patricio Abinales (2000), for example, has argued that Muslim communal identity was often used during the first half of the twentieth century not to separate Muslims or assimilate them into the "mainstream", but to integrate them into the larger Philippine body politic through the co-optation of "brokering" Muslim elites. The Philippine state had an interest in preserving cultural differences rather than erasing them as part of the process of nation-building and state construction through electoral democracy. Integration was in many ways a brand of "ethnic juggling" — rather than ethnic cleansing — which functioned to frustrate separatist appeals while providing access to the state for "loyal" Muslim allies. Ethnic identity politics can thus be used both ways by separatists and elites who prized historical participation in or separation from the Philippine state.

Mass education was an important element in the development of Moro identity. Through contact with each other and with "other" Filipinos, Muslims educated in Philippine public schools and colleges during the American and post-independence periods grew to be self-conscious of an ethno-religious identity that transcended ethnolinguistic and geographical boundaries. This "insider" identity was further strengthened when, during the years in which Mindanao was viewed and treated as a "frontier" by the government, a big influx of post-war internal migrants and government policies which favoured Christian settlers (in logging and development, for example) created profound economic and social gaps between Muslim and Christian communities throughout Mindanao. This, along with the negative stereotyping of the Muslims by non-Muslim Filipinos, sowed the seeds of the secessionist movement that culminated in the violent clash between the Moro National Liberation Front (MNLF), with its military arm Bangsa Moro Army, and the Marcos state during the Bangsa Moro Rebellion from 1972–77.

That the Muslim struggle took on a pronounced, politico-religious colouring was manifested when the splinter group Moro Islamic Liberation Front broke away from the MNLF. The rise of the MILF marked the entrance of a pronounced Islamic phraseology into everyday political discourse in Muslim Cotabato, but it is also striking that most Muslims resisted their leaders' attempt to "purify" their rituals (McKenna 1989, p. 228).[6] The creation of the Autonomous Region of Muslim Mindanao under the Aquino administration in 1989, and the subsequent peace accord between the Ramos government and the MNLF signed in 1996 have not prevented hostilities from breaking out, with the MILF taking the lead. Shadowed by charges of corruption and mismanagement of funds and development programmes, the Autonomous Region government has had limited success in ensuring that the goodwill and resources of the Philippine state filter down to the ordinary people.

The case of the ethnic Chinese is also revealing. The American occupation basically encouraged the expansion of Chinese economic activities while barring the Chinese from political participation (Blaker 1970, p. 82). The resulting dichotomy between economic integration and political participation (the latter enforced through immigration and citizenship restrictions patterned after the Chinese Exclusion Act of 1882 applied to the Chinese in America) strengthened the ethnic consciousness of the Chinese while cementing the image of the Chinese community as "alien" to the Philippines in both its political loyalty and cultural orientation. The influx of women immigrants and the growth of Chinese nationalism in the waning years of the Qing dynasty during the first decade of the twentieth century created stable family structures within the Chinese community and encouraged the movement toward re-sinification with the establishment of Chinese schools, newspapers, and chambers of commerce, the latter assuming functions that exceeded their economic utility and made them the spokesperson organizations of the local Chinese community (Tan 1972).

The problematic legal status of the Chinese meant that the Chinese would remain confined to mercantile operations, since professions such as law, medicine, and architecture could only by practised by Filipino citizens. As economic anthropologist John Omohundro noted: "By different methods, and for different motives, the Spanish, the Filipinos, and the Americans each contributed to the specialization of the Chinese in a merchant niche" (1981, pp. 43–44). Moreover, the economic specialization of the Chinese, most notably in retail trade and wholesale distribution, was a source of Filipino resentment. Part of the nationalist critique of the Filipino's economic "alienation" from retail trade, one of the most visible and ubiquitous economic niches in the Philippines, expressed itself in a tide of nationalist legislation aimed at breaking the Chinese "stranglehold" over the retail trade in the 1950s and 1960s (Agpalo 1958). In the cultural sphere, the Filipinization of Chinese schools, which had flourished under American rule, cut down hours of Chinese-language study, put schools in majority Filipino ownership, and put the state in charge of supervising Chinese-language textbook production (through the Taiwanese Consulate).

The normalization of Philippine diplomatic relations with China in 1975 saw the passing of the Naturalization Law, which relaxed the constraints against citizenship and enabled the participation of Chinese Filipinos in the political process. The late eighties and early nineties, however, have borne out the truism which identifies Chinese ethnicity with money through the instrumentalization of citizenship (in which the government offers permanent residency status to aliens in exchange for a fee) and the outright commodification of Chinese bodies through kidnap-for-ransom (Hau 1999). Since the late 1980s, the Chinese have become as visible a presence in the political arena as in the business arena, proof enough of the selective "integration" of the Chinese into Philippine mainstream society.

In the case of the indigenous peoples (see Finin 1991), the post-independence years were witness to intensified conflicts between indigenous peoples and "outsiders" and led to political mobilization and activism on the part of the indigenous peoples. Under the Marcos administration, the Presidential Assistant on National Minorities, formed in 1975, promoted Igorotlandia as a tourist attraction and as a the site of "authentic natives". In the late 1970s, the Ministry of Tourism embarked on a cultural enhancement programme that was meant to highlight the distinctiveness and the cultural attractions of the ethnic minorities.

Although the government took pains to showcase the culture of the indigenous peoples, it was unable to redress the grievances of these communities. Cordillera activists resisted the Chico River Basin Development Project in the mid-seventies and criticized Cellophil Corporation pulp mill operations in Abra in 1977 for encroaching on communal lands and damaging the communal irrigation systems. Indigenous peoples also clashed with loggers who conducted their operations in the ancestral lands.

The late 1960s saw the growth of militant student nationalism, which came to be linked to the anti-Marcos struggle in the 1970s, and resulted in political mobilization under the auspices of the Communist Party of the Philippines-New People's Army in the Cordilleras. In 1979, the communist arm, National Democratic Front, gave special prominence to the plight of "minority people". Anti-Marcos groups flourished and formed coalitions with cause-oriented groups. The formation of the Cordillera People's Alliance and Regional Autonomy closed the gap between anti-Marcos, educated urban highlanders and rural highlanders who resisted the government on grounds of local grievances.

The 1980s witnessed the emergence of a proposal by the Cordillera People's Liberation Army for the creation of a Cordillera Autonomous Region to be governed in keeping with the principles of local highland traditions. In 1984, this proposal was brought up as part of the Marcos administration's peace initiatives and was later included in the peace agenda of the Aquino government. Internecine conflict within the Left resulted in a split, two years later, between the Cordillera People's Liberation Army and the Communist Party-New People's Army. Nevertheless, in 1997, Fidel Ramos signed Executive Order 220 creating the Cordillera Administrative Region, based on the administrative grid bequeathed by the Americans.

Both the American colonial state and the Philippine post-colonial state adopted a philosophy of selective "national" integration in their approaches to Muslim, Chinese, and indigenous Filipinos. Instead of assimilating minorities into the dominant Filipino culture, the participation of these groups in the political system and in civil society was premised precisely on their communal differences.[7] In fact, ethnicity may have been cemented or consolidated — rather than simply co-opted or marginalized — by nation-building practices.[8] Moreover, Ronald May observes that the Philippine electoral system and the parochial politics that anchored such a system often worked to impede the effective implementation of the same state-sponsored assimilationist policies that were adopted by other Southeast Asian governments (1997, p. 350).

The experiences of ethnic minorities suggest that the idea of "participation" in the national body politic has long been premised, not on the outright assimilation of ethnic groups to the dominant culture, but on the selective inclusion and exclusion of these groups precisely through the stressing of their communal differences. The Philippine case resonates with Cheah Boon Kheng's (2002) account of nation-building in Malaysia, which stresses the legacy of the "historic bargain" forged among the country's major ethnic blocs and reveals the complex, mutually determining relations between the Malaysian government's integrative strategies and the articulated demands of the various ethnic groups. The Philippine state has, at least on paper, formulated policies that are accommodating of the demands of various ethnolinguistic groups. These progressive policies are, however, largely vitiated by scarce resources and by the state's own failure to effectively implement these policies due to mismanagement, corruption, and lack of political will.[9]

Furthermore, nation-building in the Philippines has had to account for one of the most significant developments in the Philippines over the past thirty years: the large-scale export of Filipino labour. While the "exodus" of so-called overseas contract workers (OCWs, later renamed Overseas Filipino Workers or OFWs to carry a "national" inflection) from the Philippines since the mid-1970s reflects the general trend in Asia (*The Labour Trade* 1987, p. 1), in no other country in that region has the impact of the phenomenon on people's everyday lives been more visible or dramatic. The Philippines ranks second only to Mexico as the leading country of labour emigration in the world (Martin 1996, p. 11). In 1999, the twenty-fifth year of the Philippine Government's labour export programme, an estimated seven million Filipinos — constituting about ten per cent of the population and twenty per cent of the total labour force — in 182 countries remitted US$3.272 billion or the equivalent of 21 per cent of the country's Gross National Product (GNP) in the first quarter of the year alone.[10] Roughly 22.5 million to 35 million Filipinos, or half of the country's population, are said to be directly or indirectly dependent on these remittances (*Fast Facts on Filipino Labor Migration* 1999, p. 19).

Until the Marcos government began playing a crucial role in promoting and regulating the export of labour in the 1970s, these flows of people from the Philippines were largely self-initiated or family-sponsored (Mangahas 1989, p. 9). With the enactment of the New Labour Code in 1974 and the signing of a bilateral labour agreement between Iran and the Philippines in 1975 began a new era in which the Philippine state reinvented itself as the preeminent apparatus of labour capture (to use a term from Deleuze and Guattari 1987) which sought to actively insert itself into, if not actually create, channel, and manage, labour flows from within its territory to other nation-states.

To a certain extent, this is merely an extension of the state's extractive capacities. In fact, the very concept of the state is inseparable from the "process of capture of flows of all kinds, populations, commodities or commerce, money or capital" (ibid., p. 386). Brokering labour is but one of the many forms — apart from "traditional" ones such as land rents, profits, and taxes — taken by the state's capture of economic flows. Historically, the modern nation-state was a machine of capture that conjoined, on a scale far surpassing that of previous machines of capture, flows of social activity and product through a complex process of coordination, control, and extraction of value and "surplus". The nation-state came to define the horizon of social life to an unprecedented degree, employing multifarious legal, coercive, and political techniques to integrate the bodily care and disposition of its "people" while supporting technologies of subjectification which endowed individuals with identities and cemented their attachments to the nation-state. The state was at once totalizing and individualizing in its reach and function (Foucault 1994, pp. 229–32). The state's reach and function, in turn, rested on the idea of "sovereign power", that is, on the foundational and legitimating principle of the state's supreme command over life within its borders and its authority to act on behalf of its "community" *vis-à-vis* other states.

The Marcos state had initially viewed the labour export programme as a "temporary measure" aimed at "eas[ing] under-employment" that would be "increasingly restrained as productive domestic employment of opportunities are created. This will ensure the availability of talents and skills needed to raise production efficiency in all sectors of the economy". When the financial crisis worsened in 1983, the Central Bank again turned to labour export as a stop-gap measure: "Tapping the remittance of Filipino workers would be the most immediate and obvious means by which the country could improve her BOP (balance of payments) position which was estimated to be US$1 billion in the red last year" (*The Labour Trade* 1987, p. 18).

Developments outside the Philippines were equally crucial in institutionalizing the export of Filipino labour. The oil boom in the Middle East during the 1970s, and the rapid growth experienced by East Asian and

Southeast Asian economies in the 1980s and 1990s made countries like Saudi Arabia, Japan, Malaysia, Hong Kong, Taiwan, and Singapore major sources of employment for Overseas Filipino Workers. Filipino labour tended to fill gender and occupational niches vacated by the "reserve army" of each labour-receiving country. Scholars have pointed to the feminized and "domesticated" nature of Filipino overseas work: From 12 per cent of deployed workers in 1975, the percentage of female OFW's increased to 47 per cent in 1987, 58 per cent in 1995, and 61 per cent in 1998, and 72 per cent in 2001 (*Fast Facts on Filipino Labor Migration* 1999, p. 13). Women are employed mainly in the service industries as domestic helpers, nurses, and performing artists. In 1998, nearly 95 per cent of the 47,017 Filipino entertainers abroad were working in Japan. The majority of the men are employed in production or related work as transport equipment operators, construction workers, electrical and electronics workers, plumbers and welders, and machinery workers. They made up 80 per cent of the managerial sector deployed overseas in 1998 (15).

What was initially viewed as a "temporary" solution to the Marcos government's inability to work out economic, political and social solutions to the crisis it encountered in the late seventies and early eighties would become the cornerstone policy, by the Estrada and Arroyo years, of the Philippine state. Less than two years after the onset of the Asian crisis, an embattled Joseph Estrada was calling on the OFWs to "help prop up the heavily battered economy and to help in praying for his critics and political opponents" while Gloria Macapagal Arroyo not only stated in 2001 that the Philippine economy would be "heavily dependent" on OFW remittances "for the foreseeable future", but went so far, in her keynote speech in Kuala Lumpur, as to suggest a new moniker for the OFWs: OFI, or Overseas Filipino Investors (De Guzman 2003, p. 4).

The Aquino administration had been the first to capitalize on — and officially recognize — the OFWs remittances by calling the OFWs the "new heroes" (*bagong bayani*). In large part, this was aimed at containing public criticism of the government's inability to protect its workers abroad from physical and sexual abuse in the hands of their foreign employers. The outcry provoked by Filipino maid Flor Contemplacion's hanging in

Singapore in 1995 prompted Fidel Ramos to push for the passing of Republic Act 8042 (The Migrant Workers and Overseas Filipinos Act of 1995).

The overseas Filipino worker is defined in terms not so much by her desire to return to the Philippines, but by the certainty of her return (Austria 2002, p. 7). The guarantee of eventual return to the Philippines, therefore, locates the OFW firmly within the Philippine national imagination. At the same time, the revolving-door policies adopted by some states ensure that OFW's can only ever remain "aliens within the country of employment" who reside "outside of its national class structure" (Aguilar 1996, p. 115). Although the labour of the OFW contributes, often literally, to the "building" of the nation in which he or she works, and the importation of foreign workers to meet the labour shortages in particular sectors after the domestic reservoir of labour has dried up has long been an integral part of "economic development" (Martin 1996, p. 5), the OFW is unable to acquire citizenship in these labour-receiving countries. For this reason, OFWs are particularly vulnerable to exploitation and abuse as they slip through the cracks of the legal system. In Japan, for example, illegal workers cannot enrol in the national health insurance programme, and consequently have difficulty obtaining adequate health care due to the high cost of medication and hospitalization.

Moreover, in countries like Japan or Saudi Arabia, linguistic and cultural barriers may also strengthen OFW perception of their alienation from the societies in which they live, thereby inflecting the word "Filipino" in the term "Overseas Filipino Worker". Filipinoness coalesces — as language, lifestyle, "mentality" and group belonging — in contrast and even opposition to "Singaporeans", "Japanese", "Taiwanese", "Arabs", and so on.

State policies also play an important role in "racializing" differences between workers and employers. In Japan, foreign workers are categorized and organized in terms of a racial hierarchy rather than by skills and qualifications: "Japanese view certain races and nationalities as being uniquely qualified for certain kinds of labour and they grant privileges and legal rights to workers on this basis" (Shipper 2002, p. 41). Japanese-born Koreans and Chinese are seen as "special foreigners", while foreign-born Japanese (*nikkeijin*) are "almost Japanese"; both groups are entitled to work legally, and have workers' rights to medical insurance and legal mediation on labour-related problems. Filipinos and Thais occupy the middle of the spectrum: their looks, cultures, and "racial descent" are similar enough to the Chinese and Koreans to make them appear "less foreign" to Japanese compared, say, to the "darker-skin" Indians, Pakistanis, Bangladeshis, and Iranians. This racializing discourse partly shapes government policies which not only greatly affect the lives and working conditions of the foreign workers, but heighten these workers' sense of alienation from the larger society.

Thus fuelled by the experience of alienation abroad, absence from the homeland carries with it strong associations of enforced uprootedness and "reluctant" migration (Laguidao 1988), of exile and nostalgia, and most of all, duty and sacrifice. But the rhetoric of sacrifice is a two-edged sword. If the Philippine state has routinely invoked the principles of sacrifice, responsibility, and discipline to induce OFWs to continue remitting their earnings back to the Philippines, the OFWs have in turn seized on the state's definition of *"bagong bayani"* to call attention to the state's dependence on their remittances, and to pressure the state to grant them the right to vote, and to abolish the taxation of their income. The "nation" becomes a reference point for articulating new relations between citizens and state, even as the parameters of the nation are expanding beyond the borders of the territorial state.

Although it does not directly address nation-building policies on ethnolinguistic minorities and the impact of the so-called Filipino labour diaspora on nation-building policies and the national imaginary, Ileto's study of nation-building in the Philippines remains invaluable for its highlighting of the rich lode of radical populist aspirations and ideals which can yield important insights into the limits of protest and other forms of "alternative" political action conceived within the most radical movements and contexts. "Limits" as used in this argument does not mean the negative sense of limitations, but the positive sense of mapping the farthest reach and testing the efficacy of conceptual parameters. The importance of Ileto's work resides not just in its illumination of the discursive contours of nation-building, but in its mapping of the bounded intellectual terrain within which nation-building takes shape as a self-conscious project of the state. While groups may and often do protest against the injustice of the established order, their reliance on the same, identical principles and visions of change raises the question of whether Filipino politics can be viewed as a way of dealing with or coming to terms with the ambivalence of shared principles.

There exists a consensus on the essential "goodness" of nations, and on the essential desirability of nation-building. Yet what is striking about the Philippine discourse of nation-building is that its idealistic belief in the goodness of the nation and the necessity of nation-building appears in the face of the everyday living reality of constant, seemingly insurmountable crises which constantly threaten if not actually undermine the project. Those who are familiar with the Philippines always note the peculiar despair, compounded by equal measures of extreme optimism and pessimism, that attends any discussion of the Philippine nation — the endless catalogue of failures, near-misses, could-have-beens or should-have-beens, the lamentations regarding the absence of Filipino identity, and the lack at the heart of Filipinoness that shadow even the most optimistic assessment of nation-building (Cannell 1999, pp. 6–9). The nation-building project is perennially shown to rest on fragile, if not dubious, foundations. Even the most intoxicated enthusiast of nation-building is always sobered by the very real possibility of failure.

But far from suggesting that the unbearable fragility of the nation-building project refutes or negates the project itself, I argue instead that the fragility of the nation-building project is the condition of possibility of nationalist thought and action, of politics and history in fact. The ambivalence about nation-building is ineradicably linked to the very conception of the politics of nation-making because the project itself is not just "unfinished" but, rather, "unfinishable" (Ileto 1998, pp. 177–201; Hau 2000a, pp. 214–42). And it is this unfinishability of the project of nation-building — the fact that the "nation" is always made and unmade and remade — that makes it impossible to ever speak of the end of "history", the end of politics. It is this unfinishableness of the so-called "Philippine revolution" that gives this country its chances, turning every crisis into opportunity, conferring on that country the possibility of a future, or, to use religious parlance, the promise of paradise and salvation in the face of the present nightmarish repetition of everyday violence.

NOTES

1   The author thanks Takashi Shiraishi and Patricio Abinales for commenting on drafts of this chapter.

2   What is peculiar about this experiment in nation-building is that until the Commonwealth was established in 1935, it proceeded without any reference to nationality or political independence. "Few [Americans in the colonial government] had any sympathy for the notion that the result [of nation building] would be an independent Philippine nation" (Stanley 1974, p. 82). Glenn Anthony May (1980) has argued that American efforts at "social engineering" (what he calls "an experiment in self-duplication") in the Philippines — efforts centred on the three-fold policy of "preparing Filipinos to exercise governmental responsibilities", "providing primary education for the masses", and "developing the economy" — were largely failures, serving principally to consolidate the power of the indigenous elite and being unable to alleviate poverty and solve the land tenancy problems in the countryside.

3   I should qualify my generalization by stating that there had never been a monolithic and consistent American colonial policy on the Philippines. Various colonial actors from America with different, sometimes contradictory agenda sought to implement their vision in the Philippines. One example of this would be the debate on whether to make English the basis of public school instruction, with the third director of education, David Barrows, and Vice Governor-General George Butte advocating instruction in the vernacular at various times during the American period.

4   Apolinario Mabini, who was in charge of re-organizing the Philippine revolutionary government under its first president, Emilio Aguinaldo, in the closing years of the nineteenth century, arguably provided one of the first important theorizing of the "Philippine Revolution" (*la revolución filipina*), even as he was one of the key figures involved in the conceptualization of the first republic (Majul 1960 and 1967). His idea of strengthening the executive power of the republic was defeated, and in its place, a state with a strong legislative branch was put in place. The Commonwealth government under Manuel Quezon, however, oversaw the strengthening of executive power *vis-à-vis* the legislative and judicial branches through the creation of a single, "monolithic" political party claiming to speak on behalf of the Filipino majority, and headed by a preeminent national leader (Golay 1998, p. 354). Seen against this backdrop,

Ferdinand Marcos' authoritarianism appears less as a political aberration than a recurrent tendency in Philippine history.

5   Cf. Taufik's (2002) account of Sukarno's appeal to national unity and integration while dexterously managing — by pitting against each other — the contending political parties under Guided Democracy, and the Suharto government's subsequent and largely successful attempts at containing the "anarchy" in politics and economy.

6   Recent studies show that Muslims joined the Moro rebellion for reasons other than simple devotion to Islam or their "Moro" identity. Self-defence, rather than nation-building or Islamic reform, was a key motivation for ordinary people who joined the MILF or MNLF (McKenna 1989). Careful not to downplay the religious element in the Muslim struggle, these studies posit a tiered identification structure, with clan affiliation, followed by ethnic membership, religion, participation in the "Moro" struggle and finally the nation as the most enduring sources of Muslim identity (Guialal 1997).

7   A look at the "Rules and Regulations Implementing Republic Act No. 8371" (Indigenous Peoples' Rights Act of 1997), for example, reveals that the government, in theory, "recognize[s] and respect[s] the rights of the ICCs/IPs [indigenous cultural communities/indigenous peoples] to preserve and develop their cultures, traditions, and institutions." Respect for "cultural integrity" here extends to allowing ICCs/IPs "to exercise their rights to establish and control their educational systems and institutions", and pledging to establish, maintain, and support a complete, adequate and integrated system of education "relevant to the needs of the ICCs/IPs, particularly their children and young people", and to develop school curricula "using their language, learning systems, histories, and culture".

8   Scholars such as Benedict Anderson have even argued that although the Philippines contains far more ethnolinguistic groups than, say, Myanmar, "ethnicity" as such has played a relatively minor role in Philippine politics (1987, p. 9).

9   The vicissitudes of language-policy planning and implementation in the Philippines — another crucial prop of nation-building programmes — underscore as well the dilemmas and possibilities engendered by the co-existence of nationalist aspirations, pragmatic concerns, and sub-national group loyalties within a multi-lingual setting (Hau and Tinio 2003). Since 1935, the Philippine state has embarked on the difficult project of developing a *Wikang Pambansa* or national language. Initially called "Pilipino" and based on one major language (Tagalog), the national language was renamed "Filipino" in 1973 and made inclusive of all existing Philippine languages and dialects. This shift in policy conceptualization occurred largely as a consequence of the objections raised by

non-Tagalog speakers to the "ethnic bias" of a Tagalog-based national language. Far more seriously, state efforts to promote the national language are complicated by the existence of a hierarchy of languages that privileges English over and above F/Pilipino and other indigenous languages, and secures the former's place as the language of command in the country. Much of the critical impetus behind the national-language project has its origins in the colonial history and the legacies of that past. This impetus takes the form of a specific understanding of the symbolic and unifying power of a common language to facilitate social exchanges across class, ethnic, religious, and other divides within a markedly heterogeneous population. In a formal-legal sense, the state has been generally accommodating of the demands of various ethnic groups. Unfortunately, poor implementation and scarce resources undermine whatever goodwill is generated by the policies of the government. Ironically, the partial failure on the part of the state to implement its language policies has helped ease rather than exacerbate inter-ethnic tension by preventing language from becoming one more mobilizing issue in instances of ethnic conflict in the Philippines. The mitigating effects of this failure in implementation are, however, cancelled out by the wasted opportunities afforded by a common language which can be used by the state to effectively address the social, economic and political problems in the Philippines. While the use of English, for example, has downplayed ethnic differences, it has reinforced class divisions across ethnic groups. Moreover, its relative preeminence, entrenched through a policy of bilingual education, poses constraints on the capacity of the state to fully maximize the development of an existing national *lingua franca*, Filipino, and, in elevating this *lingua franca* into a national language, tap its potential for promoting social justice and facilitating communication among social blocs.

10   Since 1999, more than ten million Filipinos have gone abroad to work, generating at least US$37 billion in official remittances, which have registered an average annual increase of twenty per cent since 1989 (*Fast Facts on Filipino Labor Migration* 1999, pp. 7, 18–19). In 1998, a year into the Asian financial crisis, official remittances fell to US$4.925 billion, although the Bangko Sentral ng Pilipinas reported the total value as US$7.4 billion (cited in De Guzman 2003, p. 1).

REFERENCES

Abinales, Patricio. *Making Mindanao: Cotabato and Davao in the Formation of the Philippine Nation-State*. Quezon City: Ateneo de Manila University, 2000.
———. "American Rule and the Formation of Filipino 'Colonial Nationalism'". *Southeast Asian Studies* 39, no. 4 (March 2002): 604–21.

Agoncillo, Teodoro A. and Milagros Guerrero. *History of the Filipino People*. Sixth edition. Quezon City: R.P. Garcia Publishing Co., 1984.

Agpalo, Remigio. "The Political Process and the Nationalization of the Retail Trade in the Philippines". Ph.D. dissertation. Indiana University, 1958.

Aguilar, Filomeno V. "The Dialectics of Transnational Shame and Identity", *Philippine Sociological Review* 44, nos. 1–4 (January–December 1996): 101–36.

Anderson, Benedict. "Introduction". *Southeast Asian Tribal Groups and Ethnic Minorities: Prospects for the Eighties and Beyond*. Cultural Survival Report No. 22. Cambridge, Massachusetts: Cultural Survival Inc., 1987.

———. [1983]. *Imagined Communities: Reflections on the Origin and Spread of Nationalism*. Revised edition. London: Verso, 1991.

Austria, Ruben Salvador. "From Temporary Laborers to Long-Term Settlers: The Case of Filipino Workers in Madrid". M.A. thesis. Cornell University, 2002.

Bendix, Reinhard. [1964]. *Nation-Building and Citizenship*. New Brunswick, New Jersey: Transaction Publishers, 1996.

Blaker, James. "The Chinese in the Philippines: A Study of Power and Change". Ph.D. dissertation. Ohio State University, 1970.

Cannell, Fenella. *Power and Intimacy in the Christian Philippines*. Cambridge: Cambridge University Press, 1999.

Chatterjee, Partha. *Nationalist Thought and the Colonial World: A Derivative Discourse*. Minneapolis: University of Minnesota Press, 1986.

Cheah, Boon Kheng. *Malaysia: The Making of a Nation*. Singapore: Institute of Southeast Asian Studies, 2002.

Constantino, Renato. *The Philippines: A Past Revisited*. Quezon City: Tala Publishing House, 1975.

Constantino, Renato and Letizia R. Constantino. *The Philippines: The Continuing Past*. Quezon City: The Foundation for Nationalist Studies, 1978.

Corpuz, Onofre D. *The Roots of the Filipino Nation*. vols. 1 and 2. Quezon City: Aklahi Foundation, 1989.

De Guzman, Odine. "A Cultural Biography of Overseas Domestic Work, 1990–2002: Letters and Autobiographical Narratives of Women OFWs". Unpublished manuscript, University of the Philippines, Diliman, Quezon City, 2003.

Deleuze, Gilles and Félix Guattari. *A Thousand Plateaus: Capitalism and Schizophrenia*, translation and foreword by Brian Massumi. Minneapolis: University of Minnesota Press, 1987.

Deutsch, Karl. [1953]. *Nationalism and Social Communication*. Second edition. New York: Massachusetts Institute of Technology Press, 1966.

Deutsch, Karl and William Foltz, eds. *Nation-Building*. New York: Atherton Press, 1963.

Elias, Norbert. "Processes of State Formation and Nation Building". *Transactions of the 7ᵗʰ World Congress of Sociology 1970*. Volume 3. Sofia: International Sociological Association, 1970, pp. 274–84.

Fanon, Frantz. *The Wretched of the Earth*. Translated by Constance Farrington. New York: Grove Press, Inc., 1963.

Fast Facts on Filipino Labor Migration. Quezon City: Kanlungan Center Foundation, Inc., with support of Evangelische Zentralstelle Für Entwicklungshilfe e.V., 1999.

Finin, Gerard A. "Regional Consciousness and Administrative Grids: Understanding the Role of Planning in the Philippines' Gran Cordillera Central". Ph.D. dissertation, Cornell University, 1991.

Finkle, Jason L. and Richard W. Gable, eds. *Political Development and Social Change*. New York: John Wiley and Sons, Inc., 1996.

Foucalt, Michel. [1971]. "Nietzsche, Genealogy, History." *Essential Works of Michel Foucault, 1954–1984. Volume 2: Aesthetics, Method, and Epistemology*, edited by James D. Faubion. Translated by Robert Hurley and Others. New York: The New Press, 1998, pp. 369–91.

———. *Dits at écrits*, vol. 4. Paris : Gallimard, 1994.

Golay, Frank Hindman. *Face of Empire: United States-Philippine Relations, 1898– 1946*. Wisconsin: University of Wisconsin Centre for Southeast Asian Studies, 1998.

Guialal, Wahab Ibrahim. "Perceptions of Democracy and Citizenship in Muslim Mindanao". In *Philippine Democracy Agenda 1: Democracy and Citizenship in Filipino Political Culture*, edited by Maria Serna I. Diokno. Quezon City: Third World Studies Centre, University of the Philippines, 1997, pp. 159–73.

Hau, Caroline S. "Who Will Save Us from the 'Law'?: The Criminal State and the Illegal Alien in Post-1986 Philippines". In *Figures of Criminality in Indonesia, the Philippines, and Colonial Vietnam*, edited by Vicente L. Rafael. Ithaca, New York: Southeast Asian Studies Programme Publications, Cornell University, 1999, pp. 128–51.

———. *Necessary Fictions: Philippine Literature and the Nation, 1946–1980*. Quezon City: Ateneo de Manila University Press, 2000*a*.

———. "The 'Cultural' and 'Linguistic' Turns in the Writing of Philippine History". *Journal of Commonwealth and Postcolonial Studies* 7, no. 2 (Fall 2000*b*): 89–122.

Hau, Caroline S. and Victoria L. Tinio. "Language Policy and Ethnic Relations in the Philippines". *Fighting Words: Language Policy and Ethnic Relations in Asia*, edited by Michael Brown and Sumit Ganguly. Cambridge, Massachusetts: The Massachusetts Institute of Technology Press, 2003.

Hayden, Joseph Ralston. *The Philippines: A Study in National Development*. New York: Macmillan, 1942.

Hobsbawm, E.J. *Nations and Nationalism since 1780: Programme, Myth, Reality*. Cambridge: Cambridge University Press, 1992.

Hroch, Miroslav. "From National Movement to Fully-formed Nation: The Nation-building Process in Europe". *Mapping the Nation*, edited by Gopal Balakrishnan. London: Verso and New Left Review, 1996.

Ileto, Reynaldo C. *Pasyon and Revolution: Popular Movements in the Philippines, 1840–1910*. Quezon City: Ateneo de Manila University Press, 1979.

——. "The 'Unfinished Revolution' in Political Discourse". *Filipinos and their Revolution: Events, Discourse, and Historiography*. Quezon City: Ateneo de Manila University Press, 1998, pp. 177–201.

——. "History and Nation Building in the Philippines, 1943–1998". Workshop on Nation-Building Histories. Institute of Southeast Asian Studies, Singapore, 23–24 September 2002.

Kalaw, Maximo M. *The Development of Philippine Politics*. Manila: Oriental Commercial Co., Inc., 1926.

Kymlicka, Will. *Politics in the Vernacular: Nationalism, Multiculturalism, and Citizenship*. Oxford: Oxford University Press, 2001.

LaCapra, Dominick. *Rethinking Intellectual History: Texts, Contexts, Language*. Ithaca, New York: Cornell University Press, 1983.

——. *History and Criticism*. Ithaca, New York: Cornell University Press, 1987.

Laguidao, Wendy. "The Filipino as Reluctant Migrant". *Asian Migrant* 1, no. 5 (September–October 1988): 151–53.

Lerner, Daniel. *The Passing of Traditional Society*. New York: Free Press, 1958.

Majul, Cesar Adib. *Mabini and the Philippine Revolution*. Quezon City: University of the Philippines Press, 1960.

——. *The Political and Constitutional Ideas of the Philippine Revolution*. Quezon City: University of the Philippines Press, 1967.

Mangahas, Ma. Alcestis Abrera. "The Commecialization of Migration". *Asian Migrant* 2, no. 1 (January–March 1989): 9–16.

Martin, Philip. "Labor Migration in Asia". *Asian Migrant* 9, no. 3 (January–March 1996): 5–14.

May, Glenn Anthony. *Social Engineering in the Philippines: The Aims, Execution, and Impact of American Colonial Policy, 1900–1913*. Westport, Connecticut: Greenwood Press, 1980.

May, Ronald J. "Ethnicity and Public Policy in the Philippines". In *Government Policies and Ethnic Relations in Asia and the Pacific*, edited by Michael E. Brown and Sumit Ganguly. Cambridge, Massachusetts: The Massachusetts Institute of Technology Press, 1997, pp. 321–50.

McKenna, Thomas M. *Muslim Rulers and Rebels: Everyday Politics and Armed Separatism in the Southern Philippines*. Berkeley: University of California Press, 1989.

Omohundro, John T. *Chinese Merchant Families in Iloilo: Commerce and Kin in a Central Philippine City*. Quezon City: Ateneo de Manila University Press, 1981.

Scott, Joan W. "After History?" *Schools of Thought: Twenty-five Years of Interpretive Social Science*, edited by Joan W. Scott and Debra Keates. Princeton, New Jersey: Princeton University Press, 2001, pp. 85–103.

Shipper, Apichai W. "The Political Construction of Foreign Workers in Japan". *Critical Asian Studies* 34, no. 1 (2002): 41–68.

Smith, Anthony D. *Nationalism and Modernism*. London: Routledge, 1998.

Stanley, Peter W. *A Nation in the Making: The Philippines and the United States, 1899–1921*. Cambridge, Massachusetts: Harvard University Press, 1974.

Szporluk, Roman. *Communism and Nationalism: Karl Marx versus Friedrich List*. New York: Oxford University Press, 1988.

Tan, Antonio S. *The Chinese in the Philippines, 1898–1935: A Study of their National Awakening*. Quezon City: R.P. Garcia Publishing Co., 1972.

Taufik Abdullah. "Nation-Building: Indonesia". Workshop on Nation-Building Histories. Institute of Southeast Asian Studies, Singapore. 23–24 September 2002.

The Labour Trade: Filipino Migrant Workers around the World. London: Catholic Institute for International Relations, 1987.

Thongchai Winichakul. *Siam Mapped: A History of the Geo-Body of a Nation*. Honolulu: University of Hawai'i Press, 1994.

Vincent, Andrew. *Nationalism and Particularity*. Cambridge: Cambridge University Press, 2002.

Weiner, Myron. "Political Integration and Political Development". *The Annals of the American Academy of Political and Social Science* 358 (March 1965): 52–64.

White, Hayden. *Metahistory: The Historical Imagination in Nineteenth-Century Europe*. Baltimore: Johns Hopkins University Press, 1973.

―――. *The Content of the Form: Narrative Discourse and Historical Representation*. Baltimore: Johns Hopkins University Press, 1987.

―――. *Figural Realism: Studies in the Mimesis Effect*. Baltimore: Johns Hopkins University Press, 1999.

CHAPTER FOUR

Writing the History of Independent Indonesia

Anthony Reid

WRITING THE story of independent Indonesia has been a more than usually difficult enterprise, and particularly so for Indonesians. Very few have undertaken it, and most who did were either in the triumphalist semi-official school of Suharto's New Order, or were foreign political scientists or journalists telling a generally disenchanted story of failure. Before Taufik Abdullah's work, I know of no professional historian, Indonesian or foreign, who set out to tell the story of independent Indonesia as a totality, except as part of semi-official projects such as the national history or fiftieth anniversary celebrations. This chapter is designed to explain why it has been so difficult.

A Rupture with the Past

Revolutions have a way of breaking continuity with the past, as is indeed their intention. The normally fuzzy transition between the contemporary domain of the social scientists and the territory of the historian becomes a sharp break when marked by a revolution. While history is passionately important for revolutionaries, once in power they tend to make things difficult for historians of anything but ancient times. The past has to preserve a powerful myth, essential to the new way in which the revolutionary state sees itself. This is true even for the French, Russian, Chinese or Vietnamese revolutions, which explicitly sought a new beginning in which science and rationality would rule, in contrast with a discredited old order of oppression, hierarchy and privilege. Indonesian revolutionaries took the same view. Tan Malaka, the most cerebral of them, declared that "the true Indonesian nation does not yet have a history except one of slavery", while the leading professional historian of the 1950s titled both his first books in a way that consigned Indonesia's whole pre-independence past to a "feudal" category.[1]

Indonesia's revolution however brought a further discontinuity even more profound than these other revolutions. The language of the revolution was romanized Malay, renamed Bahasa Indonesia, and from the time of its triumph virtually all education was in that language alone. The languages of Indonesia's written past were Dutch (preeminently), and a range of vernaculars of which the most important were Javanese, Malay in Arabic script, Sundanese and Bugis, each written in a difficult script of its own, increasingly lost to the new educated generation. The first generation of nationalists who grappled with building a new past for a new country were all at home in Dutch, and could use a large body of Dutch historical writing for different purposes. Their students, however, lost contact with all the languages of their pasts extremely rapidly, and were put off history altogether by its arcane linguistic demands. In former colonies of the British, Americans, French or Spanish (and in a surprising throwback even the Portuguese in East Timor) the language of the colonizer remained useful and valued long after independence. But the dropping of Dutch as an internationally useless, even embarrassing, reminder of past subjection, was very sudden with the arrival in 1942 of the Japanese conquerors, who had absolutely no use for it. The new second language of the national education system after 1950 was English, and the overwhelming majority of Indonesian-educated students accessed international ideas in that language only. Bad to non-existent relations with the Netherlands in the 1950s and 1960s removed the possibility of maintaining continuities by pursuing higher education in the Netherlands.

The minuteness of the remnant truly comfortable with Dutch after the passing of most of the first generation in the 1960s helps to explain their crucial importance in Indonesian history. This applies especially to Sartono Kartodirdjo (b. 1921) at Gadjah Mada University, the only Professor of History in the country until the 1980s and therefore the supervisor of all the second generation of historians who could not study abroad. Among these the Menadonese maritime historian A.B. Lapian (b. 1929), the Ambonese historian of eastern Indonesia R.Z. Leirissa (b. 1928), and the aristocratic Javanese intellectual historian Abdurrachman Surjomihardjo (1929–94) moved easily with the Dutch sources as members of the tiny minority raised in Dutch–speaking families.

For the rest, however, Indonesian history since the 1970s has been written, taught and studied by people educated in Indonesian or in English (in the United States, Australia or Britain), for whom Dutch was a difficult foreign language only complicating the already substantial task of mastering English. The linguistic demands of the pre-colonial period — old Javanese, Malay in Arabic script, Sanskrit, classical Chinese, Portuguese and again Dutch — were still more forbidding. All of this served to accentuate the revolutionary doctrine that the past was a distant country of little real relevance. History students were always few in Indonesian universities, and their theses tended increasingly to concentrate on topics that could be dealt with in Indonesian and a little English. The Japanese Occupation and the Revolution of 1945-50 were favourite topics, since oral history could be combined with newspapers, and the general theme was widely agreed.

Studies of the 1950s, 1960s and thereafter ventured into more dangerous territory of many dark shadows. It was best left to officially-connected writers and foreigners. The fact that great emphasis in the school system was placed on an official version of history coloured more by nationalist and military myth than by contemporary concerns, added to its perceived low employment prospects, made history unpopular as a university subject. This may be part of the reason why historians played a relatively small part in debates on national issues even when these became vibrant again after 1987, and why such a large proportion of the history sold in Indonesian bookshops in the 1980s and 1990s was translated from foreign work.

National and Local

A second problem has been the disjunction between local histories and the national idea. The heroic ideals of the nationalist movement, sanctified during the revolutionary struggle of the 1940s, were about national unity in opposition to Dutch oppression. Since the most obvious common factor of the Netherlands Indies history they learned in schools had been Dutch rule itself, this became the dominant theme of the new Indonesian history, with suitable interchanging of heroes and villains. The nationalists of the 1920s and 1930s, raised on colonial textbooks about the rise of Dutch power over the archipelago, already decided that the most interesting characters of that story were the "rebels" who had opposed the Dutch, and in prehistory the builders of great "empires" which most nearly coincided with that of the Dutch. The moments of armed resistance were the best represented in the new textbooks, and their most appropriate heroes were those who had died opposing Dutch rule.

This theme created a point of contact between the separate histories of the archipelago and the new national myth. Those who had fought most passionately against incorporation into the national project, like the Acehnese resistance of 1873–1912, the Batak millenarian supporters of Sisingamangaraja XII, or the militant Wahabbi zealots in Minangkabau of the 1830s, were transformed into unwitting proto-nationalist heroes. A striking example of how this magic was effected was the twenty-three-year-old Hasan Muhammad Tiro, who in 1948 wrote what he claimed to be the first history of the Aceh war in "our language", Indonesian, to prove that the bitter Acehnese resistance was "one undivided part of Indonesian history".[2] This worked very well for the needs of the revolutionary struggle. As a permanent basis for understanding the diversities of Indonesian history, however, the formula was dangerously flawed.

For the majority of Indonesians whose rulers had made the necessary accommodations to Dutch commercial hegemony, this format either distorted or ignored their own history. Even the great liberator of the Bugis from their subjection to Makasar, Arung Palakka, had to be declared a villain or a nonentity because he allied with the Dutch. More sadly whole peoples (like the people of Flores or Nias, the Toraja, the Dayak) seemed to have no history unless or until they could find a rebel to fit the formula. Even Acehnese, who received far more than their demographic share of national heroes, increasingly failed to see the connection between what their ancestors fought for and the state that ruled them after 1950.

The initial nationalist writing of Indonesian history was of course questioned by many in the 1950s and 1960s, on local, Islamic or Marxist grounds. But the natural evolution towards a much more complex explanation with room for local stories was interrupted first by Sukarno's return to the old revolutionary themes in 1959, and then by the militarization of history in the Suharto era. In fact some valuable local histories were written in the 1950s, usually by journalists with some pre-war Dutch education.[3] But the Indonesian-educated generation who followed them had no such knowledge or motivation to retell the local stories.

The cult of national heroes was one of President Sukarno's principal initiatives to remake Indonesian memory around a revolutionary theme. In a set of decrees between 1957 and 1963 he laid down the procedure for declaring as national heroes people who had outstandingly resisted colonialism or served the cause of independence. Remuneration was arranged for the descendants of those so named (creating a small industry of lobbyists) and the manner of commemorating them through monuments, anniversaries, schools texts and street names was prescribed. Beginning in 1959, Sukarno proclaimed as national heroes the handful of anti-Dutch fighters of the nineteenth century already canonized by the nationalist movement, and added to it ever more twentieth century nationalist leaders and a few mighty kings (Iskandar Muda, Sultan Agung) who had entered the Dutch textbooks. Ninety-four heroes (only nine women) were declared between 1959 and 1992, although the two communists among them were removed from the list after the change of direction in 1965–66.[4]

The regime of Suharto was not at all interested in celebrating revolution, but did take over from Sukarno the theme of anti-Dutch struggle. The fact that many of those already declared heroes had died fighting the Dutch made it a small step to portray armed struggle as the *leitmotif* of national history, and the national army as its natural contemporary upholder. By 1992, twenty-three military officers had been added to the pantheon of national heroes, more than a third of the total declared under Suharto.

A key figure in the development of this official history was (Brigadier General) Dr Nugroho Notosusanto (1931–85), a capable professional historian who was convinced that history was the way to build an integral state with the army as its backbone. General Nasution brought him into the military in 1964 to set up the History Centre of the Armed Forces (Pusat Sejarah ABRI). He was asked to counter then dominant left-wing interpretations of Indonesia's past, and ensure in particular that the Communist Party (PKI)'s "treacherous" role in 1948, as the army saw it, was not forgotten. Once the military-backed Suharto regime was in place, Nugroho directed the centre to prepare "an integral history curriculum for the whole armed forces". He declared that *"history* is the most effective means to achieve the two [principal] goals, that is the goal of strengthening the spirit of integration in the Armed Forces, and the goal of perpetuating the precious values of the 1945 struggle."[5] Already then, in the late 1960s, he saw this project as a model for a true "history textbook that was systematic and integrated" for the whole national education system.[6] The latter task proved difficult, and Nugroho did not have things all his own way in the National History which was finally and controversially presented to schools in 1977.[7]

Nevertheless his was by far the most influential voice in establishing an official view of history in the 1970s and 1980s. As Minister of Education from 1983 he was able to ensure not only that the obligatory history subject in all schools served his objective of national unity, but also that an additional compulsory subject, "History of National Struggle" was added in 1985 — though removed ten years later. Together these two compulsory subjects represented a larger share of the primary and secondary curriculum than any other subject. As Jean Taylor put it, "The history classroom functioned to suppress knowledge of difference."[8] Dr. Nugroho was also the prime mover in the design in the late 1960s of the National Monument Museum and the Armed Forces Museum of the struggle of Indonesia, both showing the nation's history and identity as essentially a military struggle against enemies without and within.[9]

As Niels Mulder explained in a recent study, the textbooks used in all Indonesian classrooms up to the end of the Suharto regime expressed the meaning of Indonesian history in terms that projected modern boundaries back as a kind of past "given", with local kings acting always in a benign way to develop the people, while the outsiders come to oppress. Dutch oppression is given purpose, however, by the canonical series of armed actions against the Dutch, led by the established heroes Pattimura, Diponegoro, Tuanku Imam Bondjol, Teungku Chik di Tiro, and so forth. The events of 1945–50 and the abortive coup of 1965 are covered in exhaustive detail, but many other events are ignored, notably including the killings of 1965–66 and all other New Order violence. The two key themes hammered home about the independent period are the absolute centrality to Indonesian national identity of the *Pancasila* and the 1945 Constitution, both imposed by Sukarno's Guided Democracy, and institutionalized into national consciousness by Suharto's government. Rebellions and conflicts are explained as deviations from these two principles, requiring the military to act.[10]

This heavy national imprint certainly did not encourage the flowering of local, social, or alternative history. Most of those who continued to write history did so within the national paradigm, finding anti-Dutch, revolutionary, or military themes also in their own locality. Many of those most strongly connected to local pasts as aristocrats or intellectuals had supported the wrong, federal/Dutch side in the war of 1945–49, and therefore kept their silence if they remained in Indonesia after 1950. Partly because the case for continuity with a local past was so difficult to make within Indonesia in the 1950s and 60s, the most passionate arguments for autonomous histories were made by exiles outside Indonesia, especially from supporters of a separate destiny for West Papua, South Maluku, and Aceh.

Acehnese understandably felt they had the strongest credentials in terms of anti-Dutch struggle, including choosing the right, Indonesian Republican, side in 1945–49. They were therefore not intimidated by the new order after 1950, and produced the most frequent celebrations of a particular past. The most extreme was Hasan Mohammad Tiro, a descendant through his mother of the famous Tiro *ulama* who had led the last phase of resistance to the Dutch, and a passionate youth activist himself on the republican side in 1945, distinguished chiefly by his great interest in history. Once outside Indonesia, as a student and part-time assistant of the Indonesian mission to the UN, he gradually parted company with official history. The first step was his support for Daud Beureu'eh's 1953 rebellion, which led to the immediate cancellation of his Indonesian passport, permanent domicile in the United States (and later Sweden), and publication of a polemic for a less centralized Indonesia.[11] By 1973 he had studied enough Acehnese history to celebrate publicly in New York the centenary of Aceh's defeat of the first Dutch expedition against it in 1873. Three years later he returned to Aceh secretly and proclaimed its independence, in a declaration which set out his radically different ideas about the past:

> Our fatherland, Acheh,[12] Sumatra, had always been a free and sovereign state since the world begun (sic). Holland was the first foreign power to attempt to colonise us when it declared war against the Sovereign State of Acheh on March 26, 1873, and on the same day invaded our territory, aided by Javanese mercenaries.....
> However, when, after World War II, the Dutch East Indies was supposed to have been liquidated...our fatherland, Acheh, was not returned to us. Instead, our fatherland was turned over by the Dutch to the Javanese — their ex-mercenaries — by hasty fiat of colonial powers. The Javanese are alien and foreign people to us Achehnese Sumatrans. We have no historic, political, cultural, economic, or geographic relationship with them. When the fruits of Dutch conquest are preserved, intact, and then bequeathed, as it were, to the Javanese, the result is inevitable that a Javanese colonial empire would be established in place of that of the Dutch over our fatherland....
> 'Indonesia' was a fraud: a cloak to cover up Javanese colonialism. Since the world begun, there never was a people, much less a nation, in our part of the world by that name... 'Indonesia' is merely a new label, in a totally foreign nomenclature which has nothing to do with our own history, language, culture, or interests; it was a new label considered useful by the Dutch[13] to replace the despicable 'Dutch East Indies' in an attempt to unite the administration of their ill-gotten far-flung colonies...If Dutch colonialism was wrong, then Javanese colonialism which was squarely based on it cannot be right.[14]

Needless to say, this radically regionalist construction of the past was never debated inside Indonesia, where even federalism was difficult to raise until the late 1990s. Arguably, however, teaching millions of diverse schoolchildren a monolithic national syllabus bearing "no direct relationship to the lived history of their parents and grandparents"[15] made such extreme appeals as Tiro's more attractive to those who heard it.

Dealing with Democracy

The problems described above, the revolutionary break from the *ancien regime* and the Dutch language, do not explain the relative lack of interest by younger Indonesian historians in the democratic period, usually defined as 1950-57. This was the one period before the fall of Suharto in 1998 when fair elections were held, the press was free, debates were robust, and different parties contended to define the future of Indonesia. Although the first national elections were not held until 1955, in fact the previous revolutionary period (1945–49) had also been distinguished by a kind of parliamentary system, in which the great differences on the Republican side were managed by negotiations between their parties in a parliament. Governments were overthrown and replaced even more rapidly in the revolutionary period (ten cabinets) than the so-called "parliamentary" period (seven cabinets). The whole period 1945–57 should therefore serve as a particularly useful model for the new experiments with democracy since 1998.

Yet Sukarno, the military, and apologists of Suharto's government have been so successful in portraying the democratic period as "failure" that even democrats have been slow to redeem it. The army had always been uneasy with civilian and especially political party leadership, its first generation trained by the Japanese military to see "Western liberalism" as weakness. In the late 1950s, Sukarno was able to obtain the support of the army and enough other dissatisfied groups to have "parliamentary democracy" replaced by what he called "Guided Democracy" with himself at the centre. As he proclaimed in 1957:

I came to the conviction that we had used a wrong system, the wrong style of government, that is, the style which we call western `democracy…. We have experienced all the excesses which result from effectuating an imported idea…which is not in harmony with our national soul. … It is this idea of the opposition which has made us go through hardships for eleven years.[16]

The rhetoric of the Guided Democracy period which followed was increasingly shrill, as the economy collapsed, social tensions increased, and Sukarno professed "I am crazed, I am obsessed by the Romanticism of Revolution."[17] Despite the horrors that accompanied the army's ousting of Sukarno in 1965–66 (see below), many were relieved to be able to return to a calmer atmosphere under the Suharto regime. Those policies of Guided Democracy which were linked with the PKI, and notably the ruinous attempts at a command economy, were reversed by the new regime. But many of the political tactics that Sukarno had used to curb the parties were continued and developed by the New Order.

For our purpose it is important to note that Sukarno's negative view of the parliamentary period was continued and entrenched into the education system. Army strategists were determined not to return to a parliamentary system, and on the whole shared Sukarno's view about the divisiveness of party politics. The first of the textbooks produced by Pusat Sejarah ABRI declared that "As a result of the 'liberal' Western system which was applied in Indonesia, there was a rise of anarchy."[18] One analyst of Suharto-era ideology has concluded that by putting Dr. Nugroho in charge of developing an integral master text of Indonesian history, "the New Order leadership were doing their best to convince the public at large and the younger generation in particular that the only alternative to the present [Suharto] system of rule was anarchy."[19]

The school texts achieved this by portraying the 1945–49 period as essentially a military struggle in which party politics were a dangerous distraction and the skillful diplomatic negotiations of the civilian leadership were almost treasonous. The 1950s were then portrayed as dominated by regional rebellions. The junior high school text, for example, devoted twenty-three paragraphs to various regional rebellions suppressed by the military in the 1950s, and only two paragraphs to parliamentary politics.[20] Hatta's

3 November decree which in reality saved the republic by broadening its base beyond the Japanese-nurtured group who had set it up, was portrayed as a "dark day" when the republic went down the ruinous road of party politics. The 1950 "liberal" Constitution was portrayed as a fundamentally flawed document arising from the compromises of civilian politicians, and Sukarno's return to the authoritarian 1945 Constitution as a necessary step to restore an "Indonesian" spirit to the political system.[21]

While these views were of course contested in the universities by a broader range of views, there were good reasons not to try to build a history career by challenging the Nugroho format on the 1950s. Most serious historians avoided the period. In the battle over the authoritative resource-book for teachers, the six-volume *Sejarah Nasional Indonesia*, they had little choice but to concede to Nugroho the definition of what post-independence history was about.[22] Among the dissident voices that emerged in the 1990s, it was not historians but two lawyers who launched the most thorough critiques of New Order historiography. The pioneer of legal aid in Indonesia, Buyung Nasution, decided to write his dissertation in the Netherlands on the constituent assembly which Sukarno abolished by decree in 1959, revealing that it was the danger of its being close to success, rather than its failure, which had most troubled Sukarno and the army.[23] Democracy activist Marsillam Simanjuntak went further in his critique of the role of quasi-fascist integralist thinking in the minds of those who drew up the 1945 Constitution, subsequently sanctified under the New Order.[24]

The 1965 Trauma

Democracy at least was constantly talked about through the Suharto years. The violent events that began the New Order regime were covered by a deeper silence. An ostensibly pro-Sukarno coup attempt against anti-communist generals in the small hours of 1 October 1965 had misfired, and seven generals were killed instead of captured. The murder of these generals was blamed on the PKI by the military, and used as a justification for the subsequent destruction of communism through killings and detentions, and for General Suharto's seizure of power. As Suharto gradually drew all effective power into his hands, the military rounded up many of the 300,000 cadres of the Communist Party and encouraged Muslim and other youth groups to kill local leftist leaders and sympathizers. The PKI was completely eliminated as a factor in Indonesian politics, despites its claimed three million members and over six million voters (in 1955). Although nobody knows the full toll, military spokesmen later conceded that around a half million people were probably murdered in the violence between November 1965 and February 1966, and other estimates have ranged much higher. Around a million more were detained for periods of up to fifteen years, and permanently deprived of many of their rights as citizens.

These mass killings were much less documented and analyzed in the West than their importance justified, perhaps because they were not as explicitly state-directed as in Cambodia or Nazi Germany, perhaps because they made possible a change of direction welcome in Western capitals. Reportage was difficult, survivors were few and terrified. Moreover the issue was immediately caught up in Cold War polemics. One of the most careful studies of the 1 October coup attempt and the violence that followed, the famous "Cornell paper", was only published, its authors claimed, because anti-communist commentators were beginning to claim that it was being suppressed out of cold war motives.[25] Although the horrific events were known through newspaper and journal articles soon after the time, only in the 1990s did a few book-length studies begin to be published on them.[26]

Inside Indonesia the silence was much graver. In an atmosphere of great fear, the penalties for condemning or publicizing the killings seemed likely to be very heavy. Many of the elite who on other issues might be democratic and liberal believed that they would themselves have been killed if the communists had come out on top. Hostility between the two camps had become intense and bitter in the late Sukarno years. The now dominant Armed Forces put great emphasis on establishing their version of events in the public mind. The first step was to focus public attention on the killing of six generals (and one lieutenant) during the Untung coup attempt, and linking this with Madiun (1948) as evidence of the diabolical treachery of the PKI. October 1 became a national holiday as "Sanctifying *Pancasila*" (through the blood of these martyrs), and the site of the generals' death was built into a national shrine and museum of PKI treachery. An expensive feature film, "The Treachery of G-30-S" was prepared under the direction of Nugroho and leading film director Arifin C. Noer, and shown on television on every anniversary of 1 October.[27] All of this heavy-handed consciousness-building was designed to leave no room for memory of the hundreds of thousands of dead communists.

The official history of the textbooks was also guided very firmly on these issues. Nugroho began work immediately after 1965 on chronicling the attempted coup from the army's point of view, as PKI treachery. After the "Cornell paper" was circulated abroad, he was tasked also to produce an English-language rebuttal, published in early 1968.[28] These studies naturally portrayed the whole affair not as a massacre, but as a restoration of order by the military. The history textbooks Nugroho inspired made no mention of the mass killings, while carefully setting out the way in which the Armed Forces had rescued the nation from the PKI. Even the more academic and substantial National History, in the final volume edited by Nugroho, makes no mention of the mass killings that devastated Central and East Java and killed five per cent of the population of Bali.

Although the official myth of the Suharto era encouraged Indonesians to think that atrocities were committed only by colonialists and communists, in fact there was increasingly public debate about state violence in the 1990s, which became much more open after Suharto's fall. Islamic organizations tended to demand accountability for the bloody suppression of Muslim protestors in Tanjung Priuk and Lampung. Megawati's party demanded accounting for the violent break-up of a PDI-P meeting in 1996. Chinese Indonesians, and after 1998, church and women's groups and Chinese diaspora networks, demanded accounting for military-linked violence against the Chinese-Indonesian minority, of which the systematic rapes of 1998 were particularly emotive. Increasingly active, foreign-funded human rights groups drew attention to the much larger number of murders of alleged criminals, unionists, oppositionists, and others disapproved by the regime, including several thousand victims of "mysterious killings" (*petrus*) in the years from 1983. International pressure eventually led to Indonesian enquiries and trials of a few officers held responsible for atrocities in East Timor, and after 1998, also in Aceh and West Papua. Increasingly, in other words, there is public acceptance of the fact that the Indonesian military has used systematic terror against its opponents, and that its extra-judicial violence has been the chief obstacle to a rule of law in the country.

But few have spoken up for the victims of 1965. The destruction of the left was so total and so devastating that those survivors with a personal interest in rehabilitation have themselves scarcely dared to raise the issue, as other interested parties have done for less portentous crimes. Reducing the hold of government and army on power, moreover, leaves minorities prey to even more frightening intimidation. A brave little NGO was born in 2001, the Institute to Investigate the 1965–66 Massacres, but when it planned a religious reburial of twenty-six victims in one Central Java hamlet, death threats from the local Islamic solidarity front obliged them to call it off.[29]

Post-Suharto Reconsiderations

The pattern strongly established under Nugroho's guidance appears to have been little changed in the textbooks published since the fall of Suharto's government in 1998. While we might have hoped for an outpouring of questions long suppressed, the truth may be that thirty years of suppressing curiosity about the past have taken too heavy a toll.

Textbooks on sale in 2003 appeared to differ in no basic way from the established format described above. Colonialism and the long-established "Process of Resistance in various regions to foreign domination" remain the sole ways to understand national history in the period before 1900.[30] The 2003 edition of the history textbook for senior high schools claimed to have incorporated "new nuances" in response to a 2002 decree by the minister of National Education. "In some sections there were improvements, both editorially and in layout."[31] At least there was some revision of the uncomfortable inflation of Suharto's heroism in the revolution. The "six hours in Jogja" incident which became so prominent in the late Suharto period, because Suharto's role in it could be exaggerated to heroic proportions, is simply not mentioned in the 2003 edition. But it is fair to say that nothing has been done to reconsider what national history should be about. More worrying is the continuing absence of any invitation to critical thinking in discussing national history. Only foreigners may have honest debates, revisionism and tragedy. Indonesian states do no wrong.

The process of changing the history syllabus in a profound enough way to make it relevant, interesting and helpful to Indonesian students will no doubt take another generation. A beginning has been made in the customary top-down way. In 2001 the Minister of Education entrusted a team of eighty historians with the task of rewriting in eight volumes the six-volume *Sejarah Nasional Indonesia* of 1977. The large team and greater length already suggests the expanding number of regional and sectional points of view that now have to be accommodated. To judge by a recent press statement by Anhar Gonggong, a senior member of the team, some issues may be able to be treated as still controversial, suggesting alternative points of view. The chief incidents Anhar listed included three long-standing issues which might almost be called "official controversies" between the Sukarno and Suharto regimes:

1) *"Lahirnya Pancasila"*. Nugroho Notosusanto had disputed Sukarno's claim to be the author of *Pancasila*, preferring to give the credit to Muhammad Yamin. Sukarno's claim may be reasserted.
2) "Six hours in Jogja". Suharto's youthful role in the 1949 attack on Jogjakarta will certainly be reduced.
3) *"Supersemar"*. The Sukarno letter giving official authority to Suharto on 11 March 1966 has never been found, and the New Order's subsequent celebration of the decree as the basis for its constitutionality will be questioned.[32]

Two more fundamental issues were on Anhar's list, however. One was the responsibility for the Untung coup attempt of 1 October 1965, or the 30 September movement (G-30-S) as it is usually known in Indonesia. The new history promises to consider the line of argument long common outside Indonesia but banned under Suharto's rule, that the PKI was only marginally involved in what was essentially an internal army conflict, and that there is evidence that Suharto himself, the most senior general not targetted by the plotters, had prior knowledge that some kind of action was being planned. Since Anhar did not mention the much more difficult issue of the subsequent massacres in his interview, however, it may be left to readers to make their own inferences about responsibility for these.

The only regional issue mentioned by Anhar was the 1975 invasion and subsequent annexation of East Timor. The older version that had Indonesia selflessly bringing help to a grateful people certainly requires revision, if only for the sake of civil relations with a new neighbour. The term "annexation" will now be used.[33] Will the new treatment encourage discussion of other regional issues that trouble minorities, including different views on the incorporation of reluctant Papuans in the 1960s, or the reasons for Acehnese alienation since the 1950s? The new official history will at least need to allow for plural interpretations, and to acknowledge that Indonesians legitimately have different interests and aspirations, which need to be discussed and negotiated.

Younger historians, with no particular stake in the compromises of the Suharto period, are naturally more radical in their probing. Being now convinced that they were lied to about the events of the 1960s, before most of them were born, they want to know what really happened. The forbidden pre-1965 literature of the left is now being republished, and works by Pramoedya Ananta Toer, Tan Malaka, Njoto and Aidit, not to mention Marx, fill the university bookshops. The memoir of a doctor activist of the new left is selling well under the title, *I am Proud to be a Child of the PKI*.[34]

Meanwhile there has been debate in the press about how to reinterpret the past in an era of relative freedom, though it has to be said that the established historians have not been very prominent in it. Probably the most debated issue has been the 1965 coup attempt, and the way it was used to justify the military seizure of effective power (but not the massacres). The professional historian most tirelessly raising these issues has been Asvi Warman Adam of LIPI, perhaps significantly French-trained and outside the Gadjah Mada stable. Already in 2000 he was revisiting all the foreign theories about Suharto's and the army's responsibility for the coup attempt. He went further to demand the demiliterization of the history of the 1950s, where textbooks portrayed regional rebellion purely in terms of armed conflicts and the army's defence of the nation.[35] Even more strident was Slamet Soetrisno, a Gadjah Mada philosophy graduate and independent writer, who in 1999–2000 raised many of the issues referred to by Anhar Gonggong, but also others such as the silence about the military's attempted coup of 17 October 1952, and the intellectual support for Sukarno's 1959 shift to authoritarianism through the 1945 Constitution. The blurb on the back of these collected articles reads, "History has been used as a tool of power to legitimate a dictatorship. As a result, society has experienced amnesia towards important and meaningful historical events. The reconstruction of history is essential to awake from that amnesia." Though Soetrisno is by no means part of the professional history establishment, one of the leading Gadjah Mada historians did provide a preface welcoming the book.[36]

As if to demonstrate that the old tactic of ending debate with the "right" answer was still alive and well, President Megawati in 2003 appointed a three-man commission to investigate the 1965 coup attempt. Asvi Warman was the sole younger historian, balanced by the two most senior figures still active in A.B. Lapian and Taufik Abdullah, all three thus from the state research institute LIPI.

Of course more profound critiques are to be found. At the Seventh National History Conference in October 2001, Rommel Cumaring noted at least two of the hundred papers, by younger European-trained professional historians Mestika Zed and Bambang Purwanto, struck at the heart of the old nationalist format. Dismayed at the tendency to replace Suharto with some other hero figure in a basically unchanged format, they wanted to overthrow the "tyranny of national history" itself.[37]

The hundreds of thousands of victims of the 1965–66 killings are a harder issue again, only addressed obliquely by professional historians and journalists through their questioning of responsibility for the coup attempt. Even here however there are initiatives, like the Jakarta conference of 13 December 2002 at which victims of the violence were heard and recognized. There is a network of graduate students and young lecturers throughout Central and East Java, seeking to document the killings of 1965–66 by finding survivors and burial sites. If and when critical members of this generation grow to positions of influence the historiography will change profoundly. The centrality of the killings, as the basis for the Suharto government's unprecedented control of the population, means that painful rethinking will be required as to what truly constitutes the nation. Without the terror, how if at all is Indonesia's sprawling archipelago to cohere? Serious analysis will lead still further back to the very beginnings of the Indonesian military in the independence struggle, whence its claims to be entitled to act outside the law essentially derive.

As the colossus of New Order history is gradually chipped away, it is unthinkable that any single format will arise to replace it. Indonesia's histories will be plural as its people are plural. A new generation will learn to cope with difference and conflict in the past as in the present, and to draw inspiration from the way these differences have invigorated the nation.

NOTES

1   Tan Malaka, *Massa-Actie* (1926), as cited in Mohammed Ali, *Pengantar Ilmu Sedjarah Indonesia* (Jakarta: Bhratara, 1963), p. 145. Also Mohammed Ali, *Pengantar Sedjarah Feodal Indonesia untuk Tenaga Sosial* (Bandung: 1953) and *Perdjuangan Feodal* (Bandung: 1954).

2   Hasan Muhammad Tiro, "Perang Atjeh, 1873–1927 M" (stencilled, Jogjakarta: April 1948).

3   Aceh was over-represented with Abdullah Arif, *Tindjauan Sedjarah Pergerakan di Atjeh* (Kutaradja: 1950); Mohammad Said, *Atjeh Sepandjang Abad* (Medan: 1961); H.M. Zainuddin, *Tarich Atjeh dan Nusantara* (Medan: 1961); but note also Muhammad Radjab, *Perang Padri di Sumatera Barat (1803–1838)* (Jakarta: 1954); and Amen Budiman, *Semarang Riwayatmu Dulu* (Semarang: 1978). The official series of volumes on each of the then ten provinces, issued by the information ministry in 1954, also represented a remarkable embodying into the national narrative, largely by journalists, of distinct pre-war stories — *Republik Indonesia: Propinsi XX* (Djakarta: Kementerian Penerangan, 1954).

4   Klaus Schreiner, *Politischer Heldenkult in Indonesien* (Hamburg: Dietrich Reimer Verlag, 1995).

5   Nugroho Notosusanto, 'Pengantar Umum', in Drs Ariwiadi, *Ichtisar Sedjarah Nasional Indonesia (awal-sekarang)* (Seri Text-book Sejarah ABRI, Jakarta: Pusat Sedjarah ABRI, 1971), p. vi.

6   Ibid., loc. cit.

7   Sartono Kartodirdjo, Marwati Djoened Poesponegoro, Nugroho Notosusanto, eds., *Sejarah Nasional Indonesia*, 6 vols. (Jakarta: Balai Pustaka, 1977). The conflict between Nugroho's desire to push through an "integral" view, and the misgivings of the non-military historians led by his mentor Sartono, was an open secret.

8   Jean Taylor, *Indonesia: Peoples and Histories* (New Haven: Yale University Press, 2003), p. 362.

9   The most thorough account of Nugroho's role thus far is in Katherine McGregor, "Claiming History: Military Representations of the Indonesian Past in Museums, Monuments and other Sources of Official History from Late Guided Democracy to the New Order", unpublished Ph.D. dissertation, Melbourne University, 2002. McGregor published a brief overview as "A Soldiers' Historian", *Inside Indonesia*, July–September 2001.

10   Niels Mulder, *Indonesian Images: The Culture of the Public World* (Yogyakarta: Kanisius, 2000), pp. 36–44, 53–55, 72–83.

11   Hasan Muhammad Tiro, *Demokrasi untuk Indonesia*, (np: Penerbit Seulawah Aceh, 1958). This is the only one of Tiro's works to have been properly printed, which may suggest the often rumoured CIA assistance at this stage of his career.

12   Whereas I have followed Indonesian usage since 1974, which changed the Dutch 'tj' into 'c' in words such as Aceh, Hasan Tiro has consistently used an older English spelling "Acheh".

13   This is overstating the case. 'Indonesia' or 'islands of India' was first coined by European philologists in the mid-nineteenth century, and became gradually more useful as a way to describe the languages and peoples of the Archipelago. The high point of colonial acceptance may have been at the end of World War I, when the semi-official *Encyclopedia van Nederlandsch-Indië* used it as a linguistic category, and two men later to become influential officials — H.J. van Mook and J.A. Jonkman — both used the term in their theses. It was, however, the anti-Dutch nationalist movement which popularized and politicized the term in the following period, 1922–45. Only after the Japanese occupation and the proclamation of the Indonesian Republic in August 1945 did the term enter official Dutch usage.

14   The Declaration is in "The Price of Freedom: The Unfinished Diary of Tengku Hasan di Tiro" (stencilled, np [Stockholm?]: State of Acheh Sumatra, 1982), pp. 15–17.

15   David Bourchier, "The 1950s in New Order Ideology and Politics", in *Democracy in Indonesia: 1950s and 1990s*, edited by David Bourchier and John Legge (Melbourne: Monash University Centre for Southeast Asian Studies, 1994), p. 57.

16 Sukarno, "Saving the Republic of the Proclamation", speech of 21 February 1957, as translated in *Indonesian Political Thinking, 1945–1965*, edited by Herbert Feith and Lance Castles (Ithaca: Cornell University Press, 1970), pp. 84–85.

17 Sukarno, "Like an Angel that Strikes from the Sky", speech of 17 August 1960, translated in ibid., p. 114.

18 Ariwiadi, *Ichtisar Sedjarah Nasional Indonesia*, p. 122.

19 Bourchier, "The 1950s", p. 57.

20 Ibid., p. 54.

21 Ibid., pp. 51–57.

22 While the six-volume set was edited by a team of Sartono Kartodirdjo, Marwati Djoened Poesponegoro and Nugroho Notosusanto, the final volume of *Sejarah Nasional Indonesia*, covering the period since 1942, was edited by Nugroho, and apparently went to print without the blessing of Professor Sartono.

23 Adnan Buyung Nasution, *The Aspiration for Constitutional Government in Indonesia: A Socio-legal Study of the Indonesian Konstituante, 1956–1959* (Published Ph.D. dissertation, Utrecht University, 1992).

24 Marsillam Simanjuntak, *Pandangan Negara Integralistik: Sumber, Unsur dan Riwayatnya dalam Persiapan UUD 1945* (Jakarta: Grafiti, 1994).

25 Benedict Anderson and Ruth McVey, *A Preliminary Analysis of the October 1, 1965, Coup in Indonesia* (Ithaca: Cornell University Modern Indonesia Project, 1971 — first circulated 1966).

26 Robert Cribb, ed., *The Indonesian Killings, 1965–1966: Studies from Java and Bali* (Melbourne: Monash University Centre for Southeast Asian Studies, 1990).; Geoffrey Robinson, *The Dark Side of Paradise: Political Violence in Bali* (Ithaca: Cornell University Press, 1995).

27 McGregor, "Claiming History".

28 Nugroho Notosusanto and Ismail Saleh, *The Coup Attempt of the '30th September Movement' in Indonesia* (Jakarta: Pembimbing Massa, 1968).

29 Taylor, *Indonesia*, p. 359.

30 Nico Thamiend, *Sejarah 2 untuk Kelas 2 SMU: Pendekatan Kurikulum Berbasis Kompetensi* (Jakarta: Yudhistira, 2003), pp. 20–49.

31 Ibid., p. v.

32 *Jakarta Post*, 6 October 2003.

33 Ibid.

34 Ribka Tjiptaning Proletariyati, *Aku Bangga Jadi Anak PKI*, second edn., with preface by Abdurrahman Wahid (Jakarta: Doea Lentera Agency: 2002).

35 *Kompas*, 22 August 2003

36 Slamet Soetrisno, *Kontroversi dan Rekonstruksi Sejarah*, with preface by Suhartono Pranoto (Yogyakarta: Pressindo, 2003).

37   Rommel Curaming, "Towards Reinventing Indonesian Nationalist Historiography", *Kyoto Review of Southeast Asia* 3 (March 2003); on web.

SELECT BIBLIOGRAPHY

Curaming, Rommel. "Towards Reinventing Indonesian Nationalist Historiography". *Kyoto Review of Southeast Asia* 3 (March 2003); on web.

Klooster, H.A.J. *Indonesiërs schrijven hun geschiedenis: De ontwikkeling van de Indonesische geschiedbeoefening in theorie en praktijk, 1900–1980*. Dordrecht: Foris for KITLV, 1985.

McGregor, Katherine. "Claiming History: Military Representations of the Indonesian Past in Museums, Monuments and other Sources of Official History from Late Guided Democracy to the New Order". Unpublished Ph.D. dissertation, Melbourne University, 2002.

Mulder, Niels. *Indonesian Images: The Culture of the Public World*. Yogyakarta: Kanisius, 2000.

Proletariyati, Ribka Tjiptaning. *Aku Bangga Jadi Anak PKI*, second edition, with preface by Abdurrahman Wahid. Jakarta: Doea Lentera Agency, 2002.

Reid, Anthony and David Marr, eds. *Perceptions of the Past in Southeast Asia*. Singapore: Heinemann, 1979.

Schreiner, Klaus. *Politischer Heldenkult in Indonesien*. Hamburg: Dietrich Reimer Verlag, 1995.

Sartono Kartodirdjo, Marwati Djoened Poesponegoro, Nugroho Notosusanto, eds. *Sejarah Nasional Indonesia*, 6 vols. Jakarta: Balai Pustaka, 1977.

Soedjatmoko, ed. *An Introduction to Indonesian Historiography*. Ithaca: Cornell University Press, 1965.

Soetrisno, Slamet. *Kontroversi dan Rekonstruksi Sejarah*, with preface by Suhartono Pranoto. Yogyakarta: Pressindo, 2003.

Thamiend, Nico. *Sejarah 2 untuk Kelas 2 SMU: Pendekatan Kurikulum Berbasis Kompetensi*. Jakarta, Yudhistira, 2003.

CHAPTER FIVE

Ethnicity in the Making of Malaysia

Cheah Boon Kheng

THE WRITING of my book, *Malaysia: The Making of a Nation*, (published by ISEAS, Singapore, 2002) was not an easy task because it is primarily a book of contemporary history. Historians are usually more comfortable writing about periods further back in time than the ones they lived in. I lived through some of the major events in the 1945–2001 period covered by the book. It is possible that my present-day views and recollections of the events and personalities of that period may have influenced this study. This paper is to explain why I wrote the book the way I did.

First, I take comfort from what the Italian thinker, Benedetto Croce, has to say about contemporary history. "The practical requirements which underlie every historical judgement give to *all* history the character of 'contemporary history'," wrote Croce, "because, however remote in time events there recounted may seem to be, the history in reality refers to present needs and present situations wherein those events vibrate."[1] Croce was arguing that historians were guided in their judgment by present-day concerns as to what documents and events were important in the past, and what were unimportant.

All history was thus written, consciously or unconsciously, from the perspective of the present. Ideas and theories in the historian's own time are what allow a reading of a document in a such a way that may be contrary to the purposes of the people who wrote it. The historian, who believes that historians should reject present-day concerns when he researches the past, and merely engage in a dialogue with the past, is merely deceiving himself. He can no more escape from the past than from the present. All history thus has a present-day purpose and inspiration.

Writing about nation-building is very much like writing a biography. In the case of the latter, an author has to decide what are the key factors that shaped or made that person's personality and character. In the case of a nation, its origins, formation, development and identity are similarly crucial. Does such a nation exist, or is it still in the formative phase? The starting-point of my book is, therefore, the conscious creation of a "Malaysian nation". What are its features? How has it been shaped and formed? What were the forces contesting in the making of the nation? Who are the nation-builders whose policies or programmes have helped to mould the nation?

My approach in *Malaysia: The Making of a Nation* was to look at key developments in Malaysian politics and society from the perspectives of élite leadership, ideology, ethnicity and nationalism that were involved in the making of the Malaysian nation, or nation-state. Prior to this, I had studied history and society "from below". I preferred to view the role of social movements of the working class and the peasantry, as well as marginalized, subordinate groups and "losers" (such as the "communist insurgents" in Malaya and the rural bandits in the state of Kedah).

Some critics may argue that I have turned my back on these groups by writing an élite-based study in *Malaysia: The Making of a Nation*.[2] That was not the aim of the book. While it is focused on the four prime ministers of Malaysia, it has not left out the "losers", such as politicians like Datuk Onn Jaafar, Dr. Burhanuddin Al-helmy or the underground Communist Party of Malaya. The "losers" are still included in the history on nation-building as proponents of "failed" nationalist concepts or of "failed" political enterprises; their views are evaluated as having either directly or indirectly influenced nation-building policies. In writing a history of nation-building, it is impossible not to pay close attention to the ideas of political leaders, whether from the government or the opposition. If more attention has been focussed on the prime ministers, it is because they were given the mandate by the people to run the government. Their policies played a large part in determining the development and direction of the nation, or nation-state.

The aim of the book was to look at two main themes or issues running through Malaysian politics and society in the context of nation-building. These are: (a) the "social contract" formulated as part of the "informal bargain" in the 1956 UMNO-MCA-MIC Alliance Memorandum to the Reid Constitution and in Malaya's 1957 Constitution (which were originally meant to cover the three major communities in Malaya — the Malays, the Chinese and the Indians) and its extension later to the other communities in Sarawak and Sabah after the formation of Malaysia in 1963; and (b) Malay dominance, or *ketuanan Melayu*, the major demand of Malay ethno-nationalism. My study also focused on how the four prime ministers had handled these two issues in the context of power-sharing and nation-building in Malaysia.

What Kind of a 'Nation' or 'Nation-State' for Malaysia?

Since its birth, Malaysia has lacked a clear-cut national identity. From a statement made in 1991 by the Malaysian Prime Minister Datuk Seri Dr. Mahathir, a Malaysian nation (or *Bangsa Malaysia*) had not yet been formed even some forty years after independence. In putting forward his Vision for the year 2020, he accommodated the non-Malays as co-partners with Malays in the task of transforming Malaysia into a modern, highly-developed, egalitarian *Bangsa Malaysia* or Malaysian nation by the year 2020. He envisaged "a full and fair partnership", possessing "a sense of common and shared destiny", irrespective of race. This vision implies that such a nation does not yet exist; it also does not acknowledge that Malaysian multi-culturalism exists as a political practice. On 29 September 2001, he also declared Malaysia as an "Islamic state", which seems to contradict his *Bangsa Malaysia* concept. Some critics like the opposition parties, the Parti Islam (PAS) and the predominantly-Chinese Democratic Action Party (DAP), however, contested his "Islamic state" claim. They argued that Malaysia is still a secular state. Others say that Malaysia is already emerging as a multi-ethnic, multi-cultural nation, while yet others argue that it is still far from a civil society, that is democratic, just and egalitarian. These arguments form part of the ensuing discourse on nation-building.

Clearly, these competing notions represent what political scientist Benedict Anderson has called a nation, an "imagined community", reflecting the psychological needs answered by the sense of nationality, the personal and cultural feeling of belonging to or aspiring for a particular nation. "It is *imagined*," he says, "because the members of even the smallest nation will never know most of their fellow-members, meet them, or even hear of them, yet in the minds of each lives the image of their communion."[3] Most Malay nationalists aspire for a "Malay nation-state" exclusively for Malays, or almost entirely dominated by them, while the non-Malay communities desire some kind of a multi-cultural, egalitarian Malaysian nation or *Bangsa Malaysia* such as enunciated by Dr. Mahathir in his Vision 2020. Given the present political dominance of the Malays, Malay nationalism has been the most assertive in setting the national agendas and making its demands. The opposition PAS, on the other hand, conceives of Islam as "borderless and beyond ethnicity", says a Malay observer, "it preaches the unity of all Muslims who are principally bound by Islamic principles and values than narrow ethnic or national interests", but its objective in Malaysia is "an Islamic rather than a Malay state or society".[4] The DAP, however, wants Malaysia to be an egalitarian, multi-ethnic and multi-cultural "Malaysian Malaysia".

More non-Malays than Malays have accepted the idea of *Bangsa Malaysia*. Chinese social organizations, particularly the Suqiu (The Chinese Association Election Appeals Committee representing 2,095 organizations in Malaysia) have urged Dr. Mahathir to make his vision a reality by removing the differences between *bumiputra* (term for "indigenous people") and *non-bumiputra*. The ensuing debates showed that Malays generally were not yet willing to give up their special rights and privileges. Until Malays were themselves willing to do this, said Dr. Mahathir, the government would not take them away. Until then, it appears that the "full and fair partnership" that he envisioned in *Bangsa Malaysia* seems remote.

Homogenous or Multi-Ethnic?

While Benedict Anderson calls a nation an "imagined community", Cornelia Navari says it is a "fictional entity".[5] If we consider Malaysia as a new nation, it is, in reality, a multi-ethnic community made up of "citizens" of diverse ethnic groups and cultures, speaking different languages and living within a territory with fixed boundaries, which they regard as their legal home. Yet, in line with the modern notion that the state ought to serve the nation, or the ethnic communities that constitute a nation (an idea that first developed in the eighteenth century), nationalists in Malaysia, like those elsewhere, attempt to create what Cornelia Navari calls a "polity of *homogenous* people [emphasis added] who share the same culture and the same language, and who are governed by some of their number, who share their interests".[6] That is, they attempt to make the "people" or all the ethnic communities at least culturally the "same".

Herein lie the contradictions and paradoxes of "nation", "nation-state" and "nationalism". Everywhere ethnic pluralism rather than ethnic homogeneity seems the norm. Yet, nationalists try to create a homogenous "nation" or "nation-state" and very few succeed in doing so. Their goals remain imaginary, elusive. And this process of nation-building is dialectical. Every effort by nationalist leaders of a dominant ethnic majority, for instance, to integrate or assimilate other ethnic communities into their new "national" state meets or arouses ethnic antagonisms and highlights ethnic solidarities because most communities wish to remain separate and autonomous. Such efforts only reinforce ethnic cleavage, and sometimes foster inter-ethnic conflict. Most state structures take little cognizance of ethnic aspirations for greater autonomy, although some states have made provision for safeguarding the cultural rights of their ethnic minorities. Ethnicity, therefore, becomes an important factor in determining the shape of states.

If nations and nation-states are such fictional entities, why is it important to establish a "nation" or "nation-state"? The answer is that the notion that the government or state must serve the nation or ethnic groups is a recent invention. It has gained currency in the modern world and is now regarded as an essential pre-requisite of democracies today. The notion of "nation" or nationalism as an ideological movement really began with the French Revolution when "what was until then an isolated and reversible phenomenon came to be an almost irresistible and worldwide trend".[7] It helped to "spur ethnic nationalisms elsewhere, notably in the lands conquered by Napoleon; and it was the success of the French fusion of popular sovereignty, national unity and ethnic fraternity or identity that made it possible for other subordinated communities to entertain similar aspirations".[8]

The idea grew that ethnicity should determine the shape of states. The revolutions of 1830 and 1848 in Europe were the first to be undertaken in the name of ethnic groupings. By 1918 any government that called itself a nation-state had accepted this basic criterion of political legitimacy and as a basis for its relationship with other governments. In 1919 the League of Nations and in 1945 the United Nations emphasized ethnicity further by calling their world organizations "Nations" rather than "states". Nationalism is, therefore, the desire to create or establish a nation or "nation-state". It energizes and legitimizes the aspirations and discontents of ethnic communities, large and small.

Ethnicity in the Making of the Nation

In tracing the historical development of the nation or nation-state of Malaysia, I was keen to emphasize ethnicity and establish how the national leaders used it to determine its shape. As the nation is a community of ethnic groupings, it is important to show how the ethnic elements shaped the identity of the nation, and whether there was contestation. In the case of Malaya in 1957, there were three major ethnic communities (Malays, Chinese and Indians). Did the leaders combine the cultural and political aspects of the three, or choose only one to make it alone dominant? How did the various ethnic communities react to the proposals? Only after establishing this could I determine what type of nation or nation-state was emerging. It was clear that some of the shaping process had occurred in the last phase of British de-colonization from 1945 to 1957. It was necessary to show how both the British and the nationalist leaders had constructed or "invented" the future "nation" and "nation-state".

For the book, I had thought of starting the investigations far back into the nineteenth century to show the conditions that had first led to the emergence of the modern state. But the cut-off point for the book was the year 1957 when the state of the Federation of Malaya came into existence.

Since more emphasis was to be given to nation-building *after* 1957, the project group felt that not too much focus should be given to the origins of the state. However, looking back, I feel that a longer historical perspective back in time would have provided a sharper focus of how the colonial past had shaped the new state and "nation" that was to evolve. Britain's major contribution, it seemed to me, was to "invent" a civic and territorial state or nation where none had existed.

The previous colonial states of Malaya, Sarawak and North Borneo, that became the components of Malaysia, had all attempted to create a civic and territorial political identity. The colonial power, Britain, had destroyed the structures and privileges of the old Malay kingdoms, creating in their place new structures and a new administration. British capitalism also disrupted traditional society further. Sometimes the colonial state acted by sheer force of arms. As more and more of the states came to be governed by the colonial power, new laws and new institutions took the place of the old and knit society together in new ways. It created the conditions for mass migrations and mass communications among the people, such as the introduction of roads, railways, seaports, electricity and telecommunications. It created the idea of a state that exists to serve the people. It created common languages and common education systems, and enforced legal systems existing within clearly defined state boundaries. It created national bureaucracies and national armed forces that mobilized people from different regions, classes and races. In short, the colonial state created the basis of a modern state and a future nation-state. "The modern state and the nation-state are co-extensive phenomena," says Cornelia Navari. "In the process of development, modernization and nation-building imply the same programme."[9]

For most European imperial powers, there were two main ways to create civic, territorial nations out of their colonial states.[10] One was to follow the earlier pattern of late medieval kingdoms in Europe of building up the nation by "reconstructing" the major ethnic core, or *ethnie*, and integrating its "historic" culture with the requirements of a modern state and with the aspirations of minority communities. The European nations had been constructed around their ethnic cores and expanded to embrace adjacent lands and ethnic communities, which it then became necessary to suppress or accommodate. This dominant *ethnie* would become "the main pillar of the new national political identity and community, especially where the culture in question can claim to be 'historic' and 'living' among the core community, as with the Javanese culture in Indonesia".[11] The other way was to create new states, comprising a number of equally small ethnic communities in which no one *ethnie* was dominant and none of which can dominate the state, or new states of equal number of rival *ethnies*. Examples of the dominant *ethnie* model are Malaysia, Sri Lanka, Myanmar, Pakistan and Egypt. The "equal" *ethnie* model includes Tanzania, while the "rival" *ethnies* model comprises Nigeria, Uganda, Zaire and Syria.

At the end of the Second World War in 1945, Britain on its re-occupation of Malaya, however, chose to introduce the "equal ethnie" model. Based on population statistics alone, Malaya was predominantly non-Malay, while the major indigenous group, the Malays, was a minority. In 1945 "Malaya" was estimated to comprise 5.2 million people, of whom about 2.2 million were Malays and other indigenous races, while about 3 million were non-Malays. (The 1947 census confirmed these figures as follows: Malays 2.5 million, Chinese 2.5 million and Indians 0.6 million).[12] To transform the Malay community into an "equal" *ethnie* with the other ethnic communities, Britain adopted equal citizenship for all the communities and attempted to destroy completely the remaining vestiges of Malay kingship and Malay sovereignty by its introduction of a new constitutional plan for Malaya, the Malayan Union.

Under this plan, the Malay sultans would surrender their jurisdiction over the Malay States to the British Crown. The British Parliament would thereafter legislate on their behalf under the Foreign Jurisdiction Act. Malays in Malaya would no longer be treated as a special people or dominant *ethnie* who had sole proprietorship of the Malay States. They would share equal citizenship and status with qualified non-Malays, a reversal of their pre-war special status which had been recognized by treaties entered into between Britain and the Malay rulers since 1874. Under those treaties, British advisers "advised" the rulers in all matters except on Islam and Malay customs. It was on the basis of these treaties that British rule in the

Malay States had been established. The British had no such treaties with the non-Malay populations, who had emigrated in large numbers to the Malay States largely due to British policies of "opening up" the states for commerce and industry.

Thus, within the unitary state of the Malayan Union, Britain intended to create an equal citizenship-based nation-state for all the three major ethnic communities in Malaya, in which none would dominate. The Malay community would, however, remain the main "historic" community, with their traditional rulers as heads of religion, in each of the nine Malay kingdoms or "Malay States".

In *Malaysia: The Making of a Nation*, I regarded the colonial power Britain's role in creating and inventing a modern state as a "given". I went on to show how Britain then reversed its Malayan Union policies and "re-invented" a "Malay" nation and a "Malay" nation-state — the *Persekutuan Tanah Melayu* [Federation of Malaya] in 1948. Britain abandoned the Malayan Union, a nation-state without a dominant *ethnie* model, and instead adopted one with the Malay dominant *ethnie* model. The term, *Tanah Melayu*, in the name of the new nation-state, *Persekutuan Tanah Melayu*, literally means "Malay homeland". It assumes proprietorship of the Malay States. In this way Britain strengthened Malay ethno-nationalism, Malay ethnicity and culture and Malay sovereignty in the new nation-state. Though other cultures would continue to flourish in the Federation of Malaya, the identity of the emerging political community was to be shaped by the "historic" political culture of its dominant Malay *ethnie*.

Under strong Malay nationalist pressure, and due to the lukewarm support of the non-Malay communities to the Malayan Union plan, Britain had been forced to abandon the Malayan Union plan and to restore Malay political supremacy. Britain restructured the framework of citizenship and the future nation-state of Malaya to ensure that other communities would be incorporated and their cultures would continue to flourish. Britain initially negotiated mainly with the Malay rulers and the Malay nationalist leaders, ignoring the other communities until it had completed negotiations with them. Only then did it consult the other communities, but such consultations were confined only to the terms of their citizenship.

The decision to make the Malays the major *ethnie* in the new nation state was final and irrevocable when it was embedded in the Federation of Malaya Agreement of 1948. The document was officially signed by representatives of the British Government, the Malay rulers and the leading Malay nationalist party, the United Malays National Organization (UMNO). Malaya's pre-1948 colonial society had reflected a civic and territorial state and a society with a dominant British political culture under which cultural tolerance existed. The Malays were allowed to inherit this legacy of multi-culturalism by substituting British political culture with their political culture as the dominant culture.

The Federation of Malaya (the English title for *Persekutuan Tanah Melayu*) comprised the nine Malay kingdoms and the two British settlements of Malacca and Penang, which was similar in composition to the Malayan Union. Predominantly-Chinese Singapore was detached for the second time as a separate Crown Colony to provide for a more equitable population size for the dominant Malay *ethnie*. On 1 February 1948 Britain dissolved the Malayan Union, which had been constituted from 1 April 1946. On restoring power to the nine Malay rulers, whose states would constitute the core of the new federal state, the British Government acknowledged, in an explanatory text to the 1948 Federation of Malaya Agreement, that, "...these States are *Malay* States ruled by Your Highnesses, [and] the subjects of Your Highnesses have no alternative allegiance, or other country which they can regard as their homeland, and they occupy a *special position* and possess rights which must be *safeguarded* [emphasis added]."[13]

The 1948 Federation of Malaya Agreement, drafted in both the English and Malay languages, upheld the paramountcy of the nine Malay rulers and Malay political culture in the new federal state. The Agreement stated that the executive authority of each Malay State would rest with each Malay ruler.[14] The rulers could express their assent or refusal to any bill passed by either their State Council or the Federal Legislative Council.[15] In each Malay State there would be a *Majlis Mesyuarat Kerajaan*, or State Executive Council, comprising five ex-officio members, including the *Mentri Besar* [Malay title for Chief Minister] and each state would also have a *Majlis Mesyuarat Negri*, or Council of State, consisting of four ex-official members of which the *Mentri Besar* is the president.[16] The Council of State could pass laws on any subject, including the Muslim religion or the customs of the Malays. There would also be a Conference of Rulers [*Majlis Raja-Raja Negri Melayu*], which would bear a Rulers' Seal [*Mohar Besar Raja Raja Melayu*]. The *zakat, fitrah, Bait-ul-Mal* or other Muslim religious revenue could be levied under a state enactment.[17]

The Federation of Malaya Agreement 1948 clearly constructed each of the Malay States as a dominant Malay civic and territorial state within a federal structure. It was a two-tiered structure. It was not until 1956 [a year before Malaya's independence] that the major non-Malay political parties agreed to accept the dominant Malay *ethnie* model in negotiations with the major nationalist party, the UMNO. They accepted the British "invention" and the special rights that Britain had granted to the Malays. In their Draft Constitution to the Reid Constitutional Commission in 1956, the UMNO-MCA-MIC Alliance stated:

While we accept that in independent Malaysia, [sic],[18] all nationals should be accorded equal rights, privileges and opportunities and there must not be discrimination on grounds of race or creed, we recognize the fact that the Malays are the *original sons of the soil* and that they have a *special position* arising from this fact, and also by virtue of the treaties made between the British Government and the various sovereign Malay States. The Constitution should, therefore, provide that the *Yang di-Pertuan Besar* [sic] should have the special responsibility of safeguarding the special position of the Malays. In pursuance of this, the Constitution should give him powers to reserve for Malays a reasonable proportion of lands, posts in the public service, permits to engage in business or trade, where such permits are restricted and controlled by law, Government scholarships and such similar privileges accorded by the Government; but in pursuance of his further responsibility of safeguarding the legitimate interests of the other communities, the Constitution should also provide that any exercise of such powers should not in any way infringe the legitimate interests of the other communities or adversely affect or diminish the rights and opportunities at present enjoyed by them.[19]

The Reid Constitutional Commission, however, rejected the name of "Malaysia", as suggested by the UMNO leaders for the new nation-state and instead recommended that of *Persekutuan Tanah Melayu* or Federation of Malaya. The name "Malaya" had been suggested by the MCA. But whether "Malaya" or "Malaysia", either title clearly incorporated the ethnic identity of the dominant Malay *ethnie*. The final 1957 Federation of Malaya Constitution contained articles upholding the dominant position of the Malays and their rights, privileges and "special position". Constitutionally, by 1957, the federal state of Malaya was framed and "invented" as a Malay "nation-state", incorporating nine civic and territorial states which also reflected the dominance of the Malay *ethnie*.

But, from all outward appearances, it remained a "fictional entity". Malaya was "ruled" differently from 1957 onwards and not projected as a "Malay nation-state". A "Malay" or "Melayu" nationality had earlier been rejected. It had been mooted by a multi-ethnic coalition of leftwing parties and organizations, the PUTERA-AMCJA. Its proposal had been inserted within a package of recommendations, which included self-government and the establishment of a fully-elected legislature, but its proposals were found unacceptable by the British Government as well as by the Malay rulers and the representatives of UMNO. Consequently, the "federal" citizenship, which was adopted by independent Malaya, was not defined in terms of the identity of the dominant Malay *ethnie*. Neither was its nationality.

Under the administration of the first Prime Minister Tunku Abdul Rahman, political power in Malaya was shared by a multi-ethnic partnership. While multi-culturalism was never acknowledged publicly as a political practice, paradoxically, it was adopted as a government policy. Multi-culturalism has been described as a policy of cultural tolerance by a dominant ethnic group which is so confident of its own political position that it would tolerate and allow the cultures of ethnic minorities to co-exist with its own. However, multi-culturalism as practised in Malaya initially and in Malaysia subsequently never stressed full "equal status" and the "equal worth of citizens".[20] This was not done because citizenship was "exclusively" and "inclusively" defined, with Malays given more rights and privileges than the other ethnic communities.

Malaysia's multi-culturalism was different from multi-cultural discourse and practices, say in Australia and Canada, by putting the accent not on *minority rights*, but on the rights of the dominant Malay *ethnie* and the other indigenous peoples, or *bumiputra*, who together constituted the majority. The situation of the dominant Malay *ethnie* is somewhat comparable to that of the South African blacks, who constituted the majority but were treated like a *minority* during the white regime's policy of *apartheid*. Tunku Abdul Rahman's administration had argued that the economic backwardness of the Malays and the *bumiputra* conferred upon them the *privilege* to receive affirmative action in various areas ranging from holding administrative posts to scholarships to emplacement in educational institutions. The status of the dominant Malay *ethnie* and the other *bumiputra* reflected that of a "disadvantaged minority", in contrast to the Chinese and Indian "minorities" who were said to be more economically advantaged than the *bumiputra*.[21]

This policy of multi-culturalism "in reverse" continued in Malaysia, following Malaya's merger with Singapore, Sarawak and Sabah in 1963. While security and political considerations were uppermost behind the formation of Malaysia, ethnic considerations also played a crucial part. Only Malaya's UMNO leaders in the government were publicly conscious of the need to preserve the Malay dominant *ethnie* model in Malaysia. Guarantees were given to the ethnic communities of Singapore, Sarawak and Sabah to ensure that their rights would be protected. Interestingly, none of the Singapore, Sarawak and Sabah leaders raised any objections to the Malay dominant *ethnie* model. This meant that once Malaysia was formed, the Malays would continue to enjoy their "special position" and the Malay rulers would continue to uphold Malay rights. In fact, amendments to Malaya's Constitution, which enabled Singapore, Sarawak and Sabah to be merged with Malaya, ensured that the special rights of the Malays would also be extended to the "natives of Borneo".

However, after the formation of Malaysia, Singapore leaders were the first to challenge this dominant Malay *ethnie* image and to demand full parity of status between Malays and non-Malays. With Singapore's forced departure in 1965, the ethnic composition of the country shifted greatly in favour of the *bumiputra* [indigenous] communities. Despite the lopsided situation which they found themselves in, the Chinese, the Indians and the other non-Malay communities, aroused by Singapore's campaign, continued to press on for the creation of a more plural, more equal and more just society. This was a goal, which the moderate leaders of UMNO paid lip service to, in their earlier response to the Singapore leaders' demands. They held out the possibility that at some future date Malay special rights and privileges could be done away with, and everyone would share equality of status under the law.

The dilemma that Tunku Abdul Rahman and the Alliance leaders found themselves in was whether to maintain a multi-ethnic "nation" or forge a "homogenous" one. If a fully exclusive "Malay nation-state", or a "Malaya for Malays only" nation, were enforced, it would have to be done at the expense of the non-Malays, causing great discontent and opposition. But the Tunku and the other leaders of UMNO did not embark on this approach. It is the manner in which they attempted to compromise and accommodate the non-Malays that constitutes what I have described as the politics of nation-building. This policy worked remarkably well until the inter-racial conflicts broke out in May 1969.

Malay Ethno-Nationalism versus Multi-Ethnic Nationalism

The story that I have tried to present in my book *Malaysia: The Making of a Nation* is how an "exclusive Malay nationalism" transformed itself or had been transformed into an "inclusive multi-ethnic Malaysian nationalism". In the process, the original goals or objectives of Malay ethno nationalism were compromised by moderate Malay "inclusivist" nationalists. This ongoing struggle between the two forces constitutes the main struggles and themes of nation-building in Malaysia today.

"Malaysian nationalism" is an extension of an earlier so-called "Malayan nationalism", identified by several scholars as having emerged after the Federation of Malaya achieved independence in 1957. Professor Wang Gungwu, one of the earliest scholars to identify its features, in a very prescient analysis, in 1967, had described "Malayan nationalism" as comprising "a nucleus of Malay nationalism enclosed by the idea of Malay-Chinese-Indian partnership."[22] Since the formation of Malaysia, however, two political scientists Milne and Mauzy, have acknowledged Wang's definition as valid. They have modified it further by stating that "this outer ring would include contributions from Sarawak and Sabah."[23]

There are probably different versions or ways of seeing or interpreting this contest between Malay ethno-nationalism and Malaysian nationalism, from the perspectives of the Malays, the Chinese, the Indians and other ethnic groups. My book has only focused on how the national leadership as represented by Malaysia's four prime ministers had handled nation-building in the context of the 1957 "social contract" and Malay dominance. Undeniably, ethnicity became politically emphasized and a charged issue when Tunku Abdul Rahman unilaterally and unexpectedly made the distinction and channelled the various ethnic communities into two politically-constructed groups — *bumiputra* and *non-bumiputra*. The moral claim of *bumiputra* or indigenous status is legitimacy. Malays, once labelled as "indigenous", has claim to special consideration over others who were "non-indigenous".

Despite this official distinction, however, the Tunku later went on to curb Malay ethno-nationalism and worked to promote a multi-ethnic nationalism. It is this ambivalence, this tendency to flip back and forth between the two forces that has characterized Malaysia's nation-building. Malaysia's four prime ministers who began their political careers as "exclusivist" Malay nationalists transformed or re-invented themselves into multi-ethnic nationalists. They operated within an authoritarian/democratic framework to circumscribe ethnic mobilization and politics. This framework remains in place today. They manipulated Malay ethno-nationalism against multi-ethnic Malaysian nationalism, and *vice-versa*, by making compromises, and accommodating the interests and demands of the various communities to maintain racial peace and harmony.

As an example of this strategy, Tunku Abdul Rahman's administration showed that, from the time of Malaya's independence until the formative years of Malaysia in the early 1960s, Malay dominance was publicly masked. The cultures of other communities were allowed to flourish. The Chinese and Tamil schools were allowed to exist and to teach subjects in their own languages. Malays still continued to enjoy a more privileged status over all communities, but culturally, there was no attempt made at assimilation.

It was only during Tun Razak's administration that the Tunku's policy of multi-culturalism was slightly modified. Nationalistic policies were adopted promoting Malay political dominance openly, Malay culture was declared as the national culture, Malay history as national history and only literary works written in the Malay language were to be regarded as the national literature. But Chinese and Tamil cultures continued to exist. The "dominant Malay culture" policies held sway for about two decades, despite meeting strong opposition from the non-Malays, especially Chinese cultural groups. Yet even Tun Razak stopped short of full assimilation. He formed a national unity government of all ethnic groups. He is reported to have said, "The government policy on national unity is not by process of assimilation but by integration, that is, by mutual adjustment of diverse cultural and social traits, acceptable to all races in the country."[24] Later when it came to the turn of the administration of Dr. Mahathir Mohamad, many of these "dominant Malay culture" policies were allowed to lapse. Multi-cultural practices and policies were revived again.

Looking back, the failure of the non-Malays in 1948 to prevent Britain from making the Malays the dominant *ethnie* and granting them major political concessions proved politically disadvantageous to their future status. After 1948, non-Malay struggles became more uphill and difficult. They initially could only demand more liberal provisions of citizenship and more guarantees in respect of the practice of their religion, language, education and customs. Then, from 1963 onwards, Singapore's objections to "Malay rule" marked a high point in the open struggle against a "Malay nation-state". It was the most direct challenge to the "social contract" and to Malay dominance. Singapore wanted the creation of an egalitarian multi-ethnic "Malaysian Malaysia". But as the non-Malays had conceded to Malay sovereignty in 1948, in 1957 and again in 1963, they had little hope of reversing Malay dominance. A non-Malay challenge in the 1969 general elections led to bloody inter-racial riots, and the re-affirmation of the dominant Malay *ethnie* model.

The Role of the Prime Minister

In the contest between Malay ethno-nationalism and Malaysian nationalism, the role of the Malaysian prime minister is extremely important. He wields tremendous power, which is only circumscribed by communal interests. Frequently he practises the art of "divide and rule", of playing one race against the other. He oversees overall social and political development. He determines how much government funds and assistance are allocated to each of the various ethnic communities.

All four prime ministers upheld and worked the "social contract" of 1956 and 1957. All have attempted to juggle and balance the communal demands and interests of the respective communities. Each prime minister has been influenced, firstly, by the extent of political support he receives from his own party, UMNO. When his own position within UMNO is weak, he has had to rely on the non-Malay component parties in the Alliance or the Barisan Nasional (which replaced the Alliance) for support, as happened particularly to Dr. Mahathir when the UMNO was split into two factions and then was declared illegal by the High Court in 1987.

Since 1957 the prime minister has been a Malay, the elected president of UMNO. However, whenever he becomes prime minister, the UMNO president is transformed from being the head of a Malay party to that of a leader of a multi-ethnic nation. The fact that all four prime ministers have been Malays have led to an unwritten code that the Malaysian leadership of the nation is biased towards the Malay community. Yet the idea of a non-Malay as prime minister was bandied about in the 1999 general elections. Malay political leaders from the UMNO and the PAS stated such a choice could be decided by the people. The Malaysian Constitution does not bar any qualified citizen from holding the office. For at least two decades after the 1969 riots, the idea of a non-Malay prime minister was unthinkable. The situation has now changed because the Chinese voters have suddenly emerged as power brokers in the UMNO-PAS struggle for power.

Accommodating Ethnic Interests

In evaluating the roles of the four prime ministers, I have attempted to show that the prime ministers did not always act fully in the interests of the Malay community, but juggled policies in such a way to accommodate the demands of the other ethnic communities as well. This was part of their nation-building strategies. As a Malay politician, the prime minister has had an eye cocked not only on his own party's strengths and interests, but also anticipate the criticisms and comments of the opposition parties as well. He has also to build up overall public support for his ruling coalition parties.

In the contests between Malay ethno-nationalism and multi-ethnic Malaysian nationalism, for instance, Dr. Mahathir was expected to champion and uphold Malay nationalism. On the issue of Malay rights and privileges, he has refused to give in to non-Malay demands that differences between *bumiputra* and *non-bumiputra* should be eradicated. Following campaigns by Malay nationalist groups who opposed the non-Malay demands, Dr. Mahathir promised that so long as the Malays needed such rights and privileges, the government would not remove them. However, in subsequent speeches to UMNO and Malay gatherings, he berated Malays for their heavy dependence on such "crutches". He said that they would never progress unless they were prepared to compete openly with the other races. Such a public scolding of the Malays may be interpreted as an attempt to placate the non-Malays who might have been offended by his earlier rejection of their demands.

Often, too, the interests of Malay nationalism and those of the other ethnic communities may not be seen to be in the wider national interests. For instance, Dr. Mahathir's policy to revert to a wider use of English ran counter to the criticisms and fears of Malay nationalist groups as well as those of Tamil and Chinese educationalists. Malay nationalists feared that this would affect and compromise the role of the Malay language as the national language. In the past non-Malays had strongly supported the wider use of English mainly because more non-Malays had been educated in English. The implementation of Malay as the national language had benefited the Malays, while the non-Malays found the transition to a Malay medium a slow and difficult process. However, the government's reversal of the English language policy was in line with Dr. Mahathir's objective to move Malaysia into the world of information and telecommunications technology where the use of English was an essential prerequisite. Educationalists in Tamil and Chinese schools feared that if more subjects were to be taught in English, it would dilute the use and content of Tamil and Chinese languages in their schools.

Whenever his own position within UMNO is weak, and he lacks Malay support, the prime minister has had to rely on non-Malay support, especially those of the non-Malay component parties in the Barisan Nasional. This is a time for some horse-trading between him and these parties to accommodate the interests of their respective ethnic communities. The nature of the previous Alliance and the present Barisan Nasional coalitions has required compromises and concessions by the component parties. This is what happened to Dr. Mahathir when his UMNO party was split into two factions and then was declared by the court as illegal in 1987. He was a leader without a party, yet the non-Malay component parties rallied around him and to endorse his leadership and to re-appoint him as prime minister.

Within Malaysia's multi-racial politics most non-Malay political parties have refrained from militant alternatives. They adopt constitutional means of struggle to remove the barriers and hope eventually to obtain concessions and equality of status. By not denying them the right to make such demands, the prime ministers have gone along as part of a political game to maintain inter-racial peace and harmony. It was originally constitutionally stipulated that the Malays required a thirty-year lead after independence to hold on to such rights and privileges, but when the thirty-year deadline passed, they were still reluctant to give them up.

It has been shown time and time again that if a prime minister granted some concessions to the Malays, he would offset these later with some concessions to the non-Malays. Dr. Mahathir's strategy in this matter was very explicit: "You can say things are going well when everyone is unhappy with his lot. You cannot give everyone everything they ask for. You can only give a portion of what they ask for. If you find that a section of the people is extremely happy with their lot, you can be sure that you have been unfair. It is very important in a multi-racial country not to be seen to be favouring one race over another — you have to compromise."[25] It has to be borne in mind that such a strategy operates within the context of Malay political hegemony *via* UMNO in the political process.

Since Malay nationalism constitutes the more aggressive force in nation-building, its parameters will always be circumscribed by the forces of a multi-ethnic Malaysian nationalism. Like a yo-yo, the nation-building process will vacillate between these two forces, displaying both Malay and multi-ethnic features. Whenever either force weakens, the other is strengthened. They appear equally balanced largely because Malaysia's prime ministers have played the role of mediators, making sure that none is stronger than the other. How long this balancing act will continue remains to be seen.

The Dialectics of Malay and Malaysian Nationalisms

Malay political primacy rests on the assumption that the Malays are united and that Malay unity and Malay political strength would continuously reinforce Malay hegemony and Malay dominance. However, political differences and factionalism frequently break out within the Malay community and undermine this assumption. The UMNO-PAS split in 1976 and the UMNO split in 1987 reveal that the Malay community is unable to prevent serious divisions breaking out within itself due to intense political rivalry and the effects of globalization. Dr. Mahathir in appealing to PAS to come together with UMNO in the interests of Malay unity had warned that the non-Malays would take advantage of their disunity to press their claims. In making such statements, Dr. Mahathir wears the hat of a Malay nationalist and believes that Malay unity is to be strengthened at the expense of non-Malays and the wider interests of national unity.

The dialectics of Malay nationalism and disunity are to be found within the UMNO-PAS rivalry and the perennial competition for power and wealth among UMNO politicians. Increasingly, given Malaysia's rapid economic development and Malay advancement under the New Economic Policy, competition for power has been motivated by economic and material ambitions among the rising rich and middle class Malays. They are represented within UMNO and their aspirations and claims are manifested in the intra-party rivalries of UMNO. According to one Malay observer, Malay nationalism, while safeguarding Malay dominance, has been turned into "an instrument for the accumulation and concentration of corporate wealth in the hands of a few", and "in the process, compromised major symbols of Malay nationalism, such as Islam, the Malay-dominated education system, and the Malay language".[26]

Similarly, the material dialectics of unity and disunity also operate within the non-Malay communities. It is often assumed that they, too, could promote and safeguard their own communal interests and ethnic unity. But in the context of Malaysia's politics, however, the dispersal of their community members in different political parties and along class and linguistic lines have made them as unsuccessful as the Malays in achieving ethnic unity within their respective communities. Frequently, they do not speak with one voice.

Given this background of communal divisions and politics in Malaysia, the "social contract" and Malay dominance have become more problematic than ever. For the *bumiputra* communities of Sarawak and Sabah, the contract has not been very relevant, as they have been more concerned with safeguarding their respective state rights and their own status as *bumiputra vis-a-vis* other local *bumiputra*. While they generally accept Malay dominance at the federal level, they contest it at the state level in Sarawak and Sabah. The local *bumiputra* are in the anomalous position of being able to enjoy *bumiputra* rights and to align themselves either with the Malay or the non-Malay communities.

However, since 1999, religion has become another contentious element in the making of the Malaysian nation-state. It has figured prominently in the debates on the making of Malaysia as an Islamic state. As most Muslims in Malaysia are Malays, an Islamic state is actually another form of a "Malay nation" except that Islamic principles become the basis of its administration.

When Dr. Mahathir declared on 9 September 2002 that Malaysia was already an "Islamic state", this was contested by the opposition parties, the DAP and the PAS, and by some Roman Catholic groups. The PAS leaders said that until the Islamic *syariah* and criminal *hudud* laws were wholly incorporated into the Malaysian Constitution, Malaysia remains a secular state. A year later, on 16 September 2002, reflecting on his earlier declaration, Dr. Mahathir admitted that it was not stated explicitly in Malaysia's Constitution that Malaysia was an "Islamic state". "Even if it's not stated that Malaysia is an Islamic state, Malaysia is a model for other Islamic nations and has a responsibility to portray the religion as tolerant and moderate,"[27] he said, clearly indicating a change of mind on his part.

Ethnicity and Contesting Nationalisms

Contesting nationalisms is a common phenomenon of nation-building in most countries. The evolution of a nation or nation-state is a time-consuming process, with twists and turns, and ups and downs. While most developing countries are emerging as new nations, or have embarked on their mission of nation-building, it does not mean that older and well-established nations like the highly-industrialized nations of the West, or those like China and Japan in the East, have finished their tasks of nation-building.

In the 2002 French general elections, for instance, the French people still had to decide what kind of a French nation they wanted — a more racially exclusive and closed nation, that shut out all immigrant workers, or one that is continually inclusive and open? The election results showed that they chose the latter option. The French elections demonstrate that there is an ethnic revival in Europe that is related to the widespread acceptance of nationalist ideologies in the modern world. Nationalism endows the ethnic revival with a scope and intensity that have no parallel in previous ages. While nationalism is the driving force of ethnicity, ethnicity is the mother of nationalism.

To make any real headway in the modern world, ethnic movements, which include political parties and social organizations, will make demands in political and economic terms as well as cultural and religious ones. "Today, therefore, ethnicity is a 'total' phenomenon covering all aspects of social life," says Anthony Smith, "and this is largely due to the impact of all-embracing nationalist ideologies and movements."[28]

In Malaysia, which has attempted to become a civic and territorial nation, on the model of nations in Europe and America, the dominant *ethnie* is well entrenched, but will continually face challenge from the other ethnic communities. An ethnic revival occurs every now and then when the issue of ethnic rights, language, religion, minorities, poverty and nation-building are debated. The contesting communalisms and nationalisms in peninsular Malaya, Sarawak and Sabah present different problems and challenges in the making of the civic and territorial Malaysian nation or nation-state.

Anthony Smith, however, believes that, "it is where the new state is built up around a dominant *ethnie*, as in the West itself, paradoxically, [that] the best chance of creating a 'territorial nation' and a political community exists."[29] Sri Lanka as a dominant *ethnie* model, however, proves this statement to be not totally true. The other new nations, where there are no large ethnic communities to compete for domination, or where there are a number of equal rival *ethnies* as in Uganda, Zaire and Nigeria, have been even less successful models, with ethnic rivalries breaking out frequently into civil wars. Malaysia, like all the other new nation-states, contains within itself contesting nationalisms, behind each one of which is the force of ethnicity, and the illusion of a nation-state.

NOTES

1   Benedetto Croce, *History as the Story of Liberty*, Gateway edition (Chicago: Henry Regnery Company, 1970), p. 19. Emphasis added.
2   See especially the lengthy review of *Malaysia: The Making of a Nation* by Donna J. Amoroso in *Kyoto Review of Southeast Asia* 3 (March 2003), in which she compares it with Farish A. Noor's *The Other Malaysia: Writings on Malaysia's Subaltern History*, pp. 1–13.
3   Benedict Anderson, *Imagined Communities: Reflections on the Origin and Spread of Nationalism* (London: Verso, 1983), pp. 15–16.
4   Halim Saleh, "Globalization and the Challenges to Malay Nationalism as the Essence of Malaysian Nationalism," in *Nationalism and Globalization: East and West*, edited by Leo Suryadinata (Singapore: Institute of Southeast Asian Studies, 2000), pp. 132–74.
5   Cornelia Navari, "The Origins of the Nation-State", in *The Nation-State: The Formation of Modern Politics*, edited by Leonard Tivey (Oxford: Martin Robertson, 1981), p. 13.
6   Ibid.
7   Anthony Smith, *The Ethnic Revival* (Cambridge: Cambridge University Press, 1981), p. 23.
8   Ibid.
9   Cornelia Navari, "The Origins of the Nation-State", op. cit., p. 36.
10   Anthony Smith, *National Identity* (London: Penguin Books, 1991), p. 110.
11   Ibid.
12   M.V. del Tufo, *Malaya: A Report on the 1947 Census of Population* (London: HMSO, 1949).
13   See *Federation of Malaya, Summary of Revised Constitutional Proposals Accepted by His Majesty's Government* (Kuala Lumpur: Government Printer, 1947), p. 2. Emphasis added.

14 See *The Federation of Malaya Agreement 1948,* reprinted January 1956 (Kuala Lumpur: Government Printer, 1956), Article 87, p. 37.
15 See Articles 76 (1) and 76(2) and Articles 102 (2) and 102 (3) in ibid.
16 See Articles 89 and 97 in ibid.
17 See Article 112 (3) in ibid.
18 The title "Malaysia" for the new independent nation-state had been suggested by the UMNO leaders, but the MCA representatives had preferred the retention of "Malaya" or "Federation of Malaya".
19 See "Political Testament of the Alliance": Memorandum by Tunku Abdul Rahman for the Reid Constitution, enclosure dated 25 Sept. 1956, CO889/6, ff219–239, in *Malaya: Part III The Alliance Route to Independence, 1953–1957,* edited by A.J. Stockwell. British Documents on the End of Empire series, vol. 3 (London: HMSO, 1995), p. 315.
20 On the principle of "equal status" and "equal worth of citizens", the idea is explained more fully by Will Kymlicka, a major theorist of multi-culturalism, who has propounded a theory of minority rights. See Will Kymlicka, *Multicultural Citizenship: A Liberal Theory of Minority Rights* (Oxford: Clarendon Press, 1995).
21 I am grateful for these insights which emerged from several discussants at a seminar on "Malaysian Multicultural Policy and Practices: Between Communalism and Consociationalism", presented by Malaysian political scientist Professor Johan Saravanamuttu at the Centre for Policy Research, Universiti Sains Malaysia in June 2002 (publication forthcoming). In his paper, Professor Saravanamutu adds: "The argument [in favour of the Malays and *bumiputra*] perhaps is much like the feminist standpoint that women because of societal and 'structural' factors of discrimination should be accorded special treatment or positive discrimination in job emplacements. However the one major difference of the analogy would be that *bumiputeraism* also comes with *ketuanan Melayu,* the political hegemony of Malays via UMNO in the political process."
22 See Wang Gungwu, "Malayan Nationalism", in Wang Gungwu, *Community and Nation: Essays on Southeast Asia and the Chinese* (Singapore: Heinemann, 1981), p. 205.
23 R.S. Milne and Diane Mauzy, *Government and Politics in Malaysia* (Kuala Lumpur: Federal Publications, 1978), p. 366.
24 *Straits Times* (Malaysia), 16 May 1972.
25 Robin Adshead, *Mahathir of Malaysia* (London: Hibiscus Publishing Company, 1989), p. 2.
26 Halim Saleh, "Globalization and the Challenges to Malay Nationalism as the Essence of Malaysian Nationalism", in *Nationalism and Globalization: East and*

West, edited by Leo Suryadinata (Singapore: Institute of Southeast Asian Studies, 2000), pp. 132–74.
27 See *Malaysiakini* website, 17 September 2002.
28 Smith, *The Ethnic Revival*, p. 20.
29 Smith, *National Identity*, op. cit., p. 116.

REFERENCES

Anderson, Benedict. *Imagined Communities: Reflections on the Origin and Spread of Nationalism*. London: Verso, 1983.

Cheah Boon Kheng. *Malaysia. The Making of a Nation*. Singapore: Institute of Southeast Asian Studies, 2002.

———. *Red Star Over Malaya: Resistance and Social during and after the Japanese Occupation, 1941–1946*. Singapore: Singapore University Press, 1983.

Federation of Malaya. Summary of Revised Constitutional Proposals Accepted by His Majesty's Government, 21 July 1947. Government Printer, Kuala Lumpur, 1947.

Halim Saleh. "Globalization and the Challenges to Malay Nationalism as the Essence of Malaysian Nationalism". In *Nationalism and Globalization: East and West*, edited by Leo Suryadinata. Singapore: Institute of Southeast Asian Studies, 2000.

"PM Defends 'Islamic State' Declaration". *Malaysiakini* website, 17 September 2002.

Navari, Cornelia. "The Origins of a Nation-State". In *The Nation-State: The Formation of Modern Politics*, edited by Leonard Tivey. Oxford: Martin Robertson, 1981, pp. 13–38.

Smith, Anthony D. *National Identity*. London: Penguin Books, 1991.

———. *The Ethnic Revival*. Cambridge: Cambridge University Press, 1981.

The Federation of Malaya Agreement 1948. Revised January 1956, Government Printer, 1956.

Tufo, M.V. del. *Malaya: A Report on the 1947 Census of Population*. London: HMSO, 1949.

Wang Gungwu. "Malayan Nationalism". In *Community and Nation: Essays on Southeast East and the Chinese*. Sydney: Heinemann, 1981.

CHAPTER SIX

Historians Writing Nations: Malaysian Contests

Anthony Milner

A T FIRST glance the ISEAS project on nation-building in Southeast Asia seems dated — a hangover from an earlier scholarly preoccupation. In fact, the reverse is the case. In an era in which the nation-state is under attack from one quarter after another — with books bearing such titles as *"The End of the Nation State"*[1] — it is timely to review the processes which constituted the nation in the first place. Today we are getting the analytic distance to appreciate better the constructedness of the nation-state — to see it (as Wang Gungwu puts it) as an "idea".[2] The nation-state cannot now be seen as a taken-for-granted thing. It is a precarious structure, merely one of several options for organizing human communities, and a venture that has always been vulnerable to contest and subversion. In the early twenty-first century there seems nothing inevitable about the triumph of the nation-state. Now more than ever there is reason to identify the different elements in promoting the emergence of nation-states, if only to see more clearly the possible way or ways in which they might eventually fragment and perhaps disintegrate. In this nation-building, the element with which I will be concerned — influenced, as I am, by the writings of the ISEAS project — is the work of the national historian. My focus will be on Malaysia, where there has been exceptional interest in nation-building narratives. Examining this interest, and the different ways in which the "Malaysia" story is emplotted, throws light on the character of the Malaysian nation-state, and on the process of nation-building itself.

One of the gains of the ISEAS project has been to remind us of the plurality of forms in which nation states have emerged. This is not to deny the great, uni-directional historical forces that have acted across the globe to foster a nation-state architecture — the impact of European colonialism is one that has been recently reviewed.[3] But the differences in nation-state building, and between nations, are at least equally important. It is the specifics in each "national" situation that are likely to determine the shape and fate of one state or another, and that require the attention of political leaderships today, just as they concerned the founding architects in the past. The ISEAS project highlights specifics, drawing attention to the role of such potent phenomena as the national revolution in the Philippines, the plural society of Malaysia, the extraordinary diversity of Indonesia, the different political cultures operating in each Southeast Asian national situation, and the different colonial traditions (British, French, Dutch, United States) that have shaped constitutional, political and legal institutions across the region.

The Historian-Ideologue

A second gain of the ISEAS project — an endeavour of the historical profession, it should be admitted — is to highlight the role of history itself in the building of states into nations. I mean indigenous or local history, not that written by foreign analysts (who, of course, have their own different agenda).[4] To many readers it would seem to be the national historian as ideologue who is being profiled here, though some would consider the historian is always an ideologue. Such nation-builders as Thomas Babington Macaulay or Jules Michelet (or Manning Clark of Australia) would certainly be labelled ideologues. Such writers of national narratives have certainly worked shoulder to shoulder with other ideologues engaged in nation-building — an enterprise that engages also the surveyors, soldiers, police and diplomats who define and guard the territorial borders, and the loyalty of the citizen. There are as well the public servants and educationalists who create the state bureaucracies; and then the architects and road and rail engineers who create the physical structures — the monumental state buildings, the communication networks — which give an appearance of solidity to the state. But the historian-ideologues do not merely add a further dimension to this state creation. They also help to make all these building enterprises intelligible and convincing for people whose loyalty and commitment is vital to the nation project's success. They are nation-builders, but in addition they have often been in contest with one another, presenting rival versions of the nation — versions sometimes involving even competing geographic or ethnic definitions of the state itself. The historian-ideologues work in contexts — they respond in one way or another to often conflicting polemics; they seek to invoke or reject or explain away the different aspirations, fears and loyalties that operate in the community for which their national narratives are designed.

The project book that focuses most sharply on the role of the historian-ideologue as nation-builder is Rey Ileto's forthcoming study of the Philippines.[5] Ileto seeks to identify the "discursive threads" that run through Philippines' political events from the 1940s to the end of the century, and to show how their interaction "establishes the scaffolding of the nation-state" (p. 2). He focuses on "political oratory", noting that political figures are "the bearers of discourses" (p. 2), and analyses not only the political leaders themselves but also the "intellectuals behind the scenes", including the historians (p. 7).

In the case of the Philippines, the "common point of reference" of the oratory is the "nationalist movement of the late nineteenth-century, culminating in the revolution of 1896" (p. 3). Politicians of "all colours", he says, have spoken in "the idiom of radical nationalism" (p. 4), and writings from the period of the revolution have been viewed as "the foundational texts of the nation" (p. 50). The Philippines, he observes, lacks the Great Tradition, represented in "god-kings and sultans of a glorious past" and such monumental architecture as Angkor Wat that could be a focus of pride and, presumably, unity. It is the revolution that is the foundational experience in the Philippines, and lessons have constantly been drawn from the lives of the Filipino heroes of that time (p. 15). But importantly, the experience and the lessons are contested — and much of Ileto's book is concerned with following the different twists and developments of the ideological struggle, noting, in particular, the differences that have occurred in the historical "emplotment" (p. 44) of the Filipino past, and the way in which one protagonist, and then another, has been given hero status. In certain circumstances and for specific purposes, Rizal is heralded as the dominant figure of the revolution; in other cases, on behalf of different interests, there emerges a preoccupation with the role of Andres Bonifacio. Sometimes the same hero "might be appropriated for two competing causes"(pp. 61, 62). And the causes are presented as being only in part political in character. When a parallel is drawn between Rizal's death and that of Christ, we see a deeper current in the Filipino society, with the nation-building story being presented in a religious idiom.

The historians and other ideologues have given meaning to the Philippines nation, making sense of it in terms that the "national" community, or segments of it, could address. But while they draw time and again from religious and other imagery, and the revolutionary narratives and discourses that influenced (and often fragmented) the "national" community, the historian nation-builders have been as vulnerable as they are exploitative. A potent image or narrative, a potential "hero" figure, might be waiting in the wings — ready to be appropriated by a determined opponent. Thus, although some authors might seek to domesticate the plebeian revolutionary figure, Bonifacio, known for his radical Tagalog writings, he could nevertheless be a symbol of "violent class struggle" for the Huk guerrillas in the 1940s, and, in certain ways an inspiration for President Magsaysay in the 1950s and President Estrada in the 1990s.

The ideologues and intellectuals who have been building the Philippines nation know that Bonifacio is a figure, or rather an idea, that has to be "used or neutralised" (p. 62). In the terminology of Caroline Hau (see her Chapter Three in this book), "Bonifacio" might usefully be understood as "excess" with respect to some nation-building narratives. No writing programme (including a nationalist writing programme), she suggests, "can exhaust the possibilities of the social reality it seeks to engage".[6] The "space in which writing and action unfold is opened up…by the excess that slips their grasp".[7] "Excess" alludes, for instance, to those particularities in the "national" context that escape the grasp of the nation-building endeavour

— elements that may, in fact, have the potential to undermine or at least modify that endeavour. It is in this sense that "Bonifacio" has been a potent force that must be "used or neutralised", and Ileto's book on the Philippines explains the different ways in which both these objectives were attempted. Thus, Vice President Elpidio Qurino in 1947, in an extensive nation-building speech, highlighted the contribution of Rizal "the Christ like martyr" (p. 48) as an exponent of "peaceful and incremental change rather than the sort of violent movement that Bonifacio led" (p. 45). Five years later, Magsaysay's candidacy for the President was heralded in terms of his being a "new Bonifacio" who would be "truly sincere and patriotic" (p. 83). The influential historical text, Agoncillo's *The Revolt of the Masses*, which was published in 1956, focused precisely on Bonifacio's role in fomenting the 1896 revolution, and gave such stress to the class conflict that the book fell foul of the congressional Committee on Un-Filipino Activities (p. 63).

Reading Ileto on the Philippines immediately raises issues about national narratives in other parts of Southeast Asia. History seems to be so easy to harness to Thai nation-building. But what ideological skilfulness has there been in the construction of a unifying tradition in Thailand — from Sukhothai to Ayutthaya to Bangkok? One type of "excess" now being explored by historians (not always with political interests) is the counter narratives of rival courts or centres — narratives that tend to demand a more multi-centred account of the geographical region now claimed as national territory by the Thai nation state.[8] Just what role is given to kingship, race and religion is also a strategic interest in any historical emplotment of "Thailand".

Indonesia faces more serious problems in identifying a single Great Tradition. Nevertheless from the early twentieth-century there were attempts to construct a new "Indies kingdom, independent of any other kingdom" as a "new version of the kingdom of Majapahit" (to cite a Javanese intellectual of 1915);[9] and the idea of "Indonesia", as Taufik Abdullah will show in his ISEAS project volume, was well established by the 1920s.[10] Just why the idea of "Indonesia" had such wide and early success as a uniting concept for the extraordinarily diverse archipelago needs further exploration. The fact of this success may also help to explain why, compared to the situation in Malaya, there seems to have been comparatively little national history written in the early period of independent Indonesian history. It has been said that the "young republic had not much time to devote to historical research"[11] in that period. But there was perhaps a less urgent need for history work in the newly-independent Indonesia — where the idea of "Indonesia" was already firmly planted across the Dutch East Indies — than, for example, in the founding period of Malaya/Malaysia.

Malaysia

The founding narratives of Malaysia (which is my own research interest) have in fact never received the scholarly attention they deserve. In Malaysia the "social reality", as Caroline Hau puts it, is far from promising — and the history making is all the more interesting as a result. Malaysia is formed out of nine peninsular states — sultanates, or rajaships — and two British colonial settlements (which were combined together in 1957 to obtain independence as "Malaya"), as well as two large provinces on the island of Borneo (which were added to "Malaya" to create the expanded state of "Malaysia" in 1963). (Singapore was also a part of Malaysia from 1963 to 1965). It is difficult but not completely impossible to claim that all these territories share a common political or cultural heritage. No one kingdom or sultanate ever ruled over the entire territory; the Malay people for a time were actually an ethnic minority in the territories of the would-be nation-state, and in some states they were in a small minority. The Malay community, furthermore, has much more in common culturally with Muslim people in Indonesia, Southern Thailand and the Southern Philippines than with the other major races (particularly the largely non-Muslim Chinese) in their own country. Malaysia has no obvious single Great Tradition — indeed it even has a real lack of historical monuments when compared to Indonesia or the states of mainland Southeast Asia. What is more, unlike the Philippines or Indonesia, it has had no heroic anti-colonial revolution that might be a "common point of reference" for a large proportion of the would-be national community. The only common political experience across the Malaysian territories, apart from the spasmodic pressure of Malay, royal-court expansionism, was a relatively uneven subjection to British colonial control and the Japanese Occupation.

In the context of this unwieldy geographic, demographic, cultural and political substance, the writing of the nation state had an exceptional urgency, and the first question for the national historian was just how to emplot a narrative that supported a united Malaya (and later, Malaysia). Further questions concern how to resist other narratives (sometimes temporarily suppressed) that support other types of unity, and how best to construct the national narrative to reflect the interests and perspectives of one national group rather than another. There is no single issue on which the histories focus — such as the revolution in the case of the Philippines — but themes that are often encountered (and handled in competing ways) include: the role and problem of the plural society (a classic "plural society" with the Malays numbering only about half the population and differing in religion and lifestyle from the immigrant population), the handling of both the great fifteenth-century sultanate of Melaka and the British colonial administration as historical experiences with the potential to promote national unity; and the relationship between Malaya/Malaysia and the broader "Malay World" (including Indonesia) on the one hand, and the even broader Islamic world on the other. As in the case of the Philippines, there is also divergence over just who deserves greater credit in the making of the nation state, and the answer to that question makes demands on just how the nation state ought properly to be defined.

The practice of history, of course, was by no means entirely novel in mid-twentieth-century Malaysia. Those writing Malayan/Malaysian narratives would have had a familiarity with current European (especially British) practice, even if they read only the Malay language, and only Malay history. In 1918 Richard Winstedt had published his *Tawarikh Melayu*,[12] which the Malay scholar Za'ba later described as "the first scientific work on general Malay history ever produced in the Malay language",[13] and which "first opened the eyes of the average Malay to the meaning of history as distinct from legend".[14] Za'ba himself drew upon Winstedt's history for a series of modern historical essays in the Malay magazine, *Majallah Guru*, in the 1920s.[15] Although this work was not yet national history, the local national historians — usually products of the colonial education system — could turn to some of the great histories of England, such as Macaulay, or Trevelyan. Other practices of history writing which had the potential to influence national history in Malaya include the Malay and Chinese traditions. These display important contrasts with the British tradition, but in their own very different ways are also concerned to promote types of social unity. In the Malay case this unity focuses on a ruler rather than a state, but Malay *hikayat* tend to have the purpose of fostering loyalty and enunciating principles of hierarchy which form bonds across the community of the kingdom.[16] Using historical data for what we today would consider political purposes would cause no anxiety for the Malay or the Chinese chronicler of earlier periods, and the skills of these practitioners would be of real assistance to the nation-building historian of the twentieth century.

How, then, have historians constructed nation-building narratives on behalf of the Malayan/Malaysian state? Merely to ask this question adds interest to the many books and textbooks on the "History of Malaya", some claiming academic credentials, others seemingly prosaic and written for schools or the general reader. Reading and comparing these histories — and I will be examining just a small sample of texts in this essay — reveals elements of skilfulness in composition and, more important, draws attention to the interests and tensions that have been brought to bear in the nation-building itself. Moving back and forth between texts helps us to decipher the fault lines working through the nation itself.

My focus here will be on the initial state formation — particularly the period between the Japanese Occupation and independence itself, a decade in which there was disagreement and conflict between Malays and non-Malays, debate over the territorial scope of the new state and over what constitution it would be given (union or federation), a war against communism (the Emergency) and a dispute over how soon the country would receive independence. Although staying largely within the limits of a decade, this analysis will at least suggest the potential interest of a survey which would examine the ongoing national narrative, covering such formative experiences as the separation of Singapore, the 1969 race riots, the rise of Islamic "fundamentalism" in the 1970s, the constitutional crises involving government and the sultans of the 1980s and 1990s, the deep divisions developing within the ruling UMNO (United Malays National

Organization) party, and the impact of the long and creative prime ministership of Dr. Mahathir, ending in 2003.

The 'Historic Bargain'

The Malaysian volume sponsored by the ISEAS project, Cheah Boon Kheng's *Malaysia: The Making of a Nation*,[17] although of genuine academic interest, also provides a point of departure for a survey of nation-building narratives. Cheah identifies the plural society as the foundational issue for the Malaysian state, and in doing so, conveys that the structure of the constituted Malaysian nation state has much to offer the immigrant peoples of the peninsula. Central to the narrative presented in Cheah's account is the establishing of a "historic bargain" (p. 235) between the major ethnic groups of the peninsula — the Malays, Chinese and Indians. This "social contract" (p. 235), negotiated between political parties representing the three groups — parties that came together in the "Alliance" party that won government — "set out the rules or political framework within which the ethnic groups were to operate in Malaya..." (p. 235). It is a framework which entails the maintenance of the special position of the Malay community while offering citizenship to large numbers of non-Malays. In Malaysia, therefore, nation-building was "based on the theme of the making and sharing of the Malaysian nation among its multi-ethnic citizens" (p. 235). The "bargain", it is pointed out, "has remained the basis of the country's nation-building efforts" (p. 39).

Cheah's narrative gives emphasis to the role of the British colonial government which "compelled" the Malay nationalists to "work out a formula of inter-racial cooperation, unity and harmony among the various races in the country" before they were permitted independence (p. 2). It also examines changes to the "historic bargain": Lee Kuan Yew's demand for an "equality of status between Malays and non-Malays" (p. 54), and the subsequent expulsion of Singapore from the Malaysian Federation; the problem that arose in applying the 'bargain' to Sarawak and Sabah; the 1999 demand of the Malaysian Chinese Association's Election Appeals Committee that Malay special rights be brought to an end (pp. 66–72).

Much of the book is an account of the country's "four Prime Ministers as nation-builders" (p. 72), and the analysis refers back time and again to the 'historic bargain', and the problem of " juggl(ing) between 'pro-Malay' and 'pro-Chinese' policies" (p. 112). The first prime minister, Tunku Abdul Rahman, was the "Father of Malaya's Independence", and was known for developing policies "in the cause of racial harmony..." (p. 76). Apart from forging "the bargain" with the non-Malay representative parties, the Tunku attempted to "inculcate loyalty to the nation-state by promoting the Malay king, the Yang Di-Pertuan Agong (chosen every five years from among the state rulers) as the king of a multi-racial nation..." (p. 111), and also made use of sport (in particular soccer and badminton) as a source of unity in the nation (p. 111). The second prime minister, Tun Abdul Razak, was less sympathetic to the "historic bargain"; he was "a Malay nationalist at heart..." (p. 122). But he did not want to "dismantle (his predecessor's) national integration policies entirely" (p. 122) and therefore sought to strengthen "Malaysia as a plural, multi-ethnic nation" (p. 122). His Malay sympathies can be seen to some extent in the Malaysian Cultural Congress of 1971, which aimed to formulate a "National Culture" which would be "based on the culture of the Malays and other indigenous peoples", but would also include "suitable elements of other cultures" (p. 133).

The third prime minister, Hussein Onn — who ran a "phlegmatic administration" (p. 166), according to Cheah — "continued the national integration policies of Tun Razak", and with an element of political repressiveness maintained "political stability and racial harmony" (p. 159). Mahathir Mohamad, whose term of office began in 1981, used numerous "prestige projects" to promote national unity, including the new international airport, the new capital Putrajaya, and the world's tallest buildings (the Petronas Twin Towers) (p. 193). But the Mahathir nation-building on which Cheah focuses most attention was concerned with the "bargain" and the highlight of Mahathir's period is presented as being his commitment in 1991 (in his Vision 2020) to creating a "fully developed country" (p. 220) — a state in which both Malays and non-Malays would participate in a "full and fair partnership" (p. 221) and see themselves as being a "united Malaysian nation", a "*Bangsa Malaysia*", a Malaysian "nation" or "race" (p. 221).

Identifying discontents with the "bargain", Cheah's history recognizes the potency in the Malay community (and also in Mahathir's life) of Malay nationalism — which seeks to make Malaysia a " 'Malay' nation state" (p. 233). In addition, the book points to the aspirations of the Islamic party, PAS, to make Malaysia an Islamic state with foundations in Islamic law. In the final analysis, however, nation-building in Malaysia is "based on the theme of the making and sharing of the Malaysian nation among its multi-ethnic citizens" (p. 235). The Vision 2020 enunciated in 1991 by Mahathir, who had been described in the past as a "Malay Ultra", is therefore pivotal to Cheah's national narrative. It is in the idea of a *"Bangsa Malaysia"* that we see the non-Malays "firmly accommodated" as "co-partners with Malays in the task of transforming Malaysia into a modern, highly-developed, 'just and equal'...nation" (p. 240). In Cheah's book, this "bargain" between Malays and non-Malays — this focus on the ethnic pluralism which could conceivably have destroyed the unity of the country — is as central to the national narrative as the Philippines' revolution (in Ileto's analysis) is in the nation-making of that country.

The "bargain" (and to some extent the balance) is a theme in numerous other Malayan/Malaysian state narratives. As its presence in the recently published book by Cheah demonstrates, it continues to be a powerful ideal. But in certain cases historians have challenged the "bargain", sometimes in subtle but effective ways, and examining these contests can help to expose unresolved tensions that shape the ongoing process of nation-building up to the present day.

One early text that anticipates Cheah's positioning of "the bargain" at the core of Malaysian nation-building is Wang Gungwu's edited volume, *Malaysia*,[18] published soon after the inauguration of the new state. The brief introduction stresses that historically there never had been "a state, kingdom or empire known as 'Malaysia' or 'Melayu Raya' " (p. 16). There has "never been a political unit based on the idea of being Malay" (p. 16). Rather there were "old empires... based on...maritime power and the sovereignty of different ruling houses" (p. 16). The drive toward independence, to be sure, was "led by Malay nationalist leaders", but they "accepted the need to temper their nationalism with an appeal to the immigrant peoples to make their homes in Malaysia" (p. 20). Here is Cheah's "bargain", and the tone of even-handedness is continued in the expression of aspirations for the future. In the new Malaysia, the introduction explains, Indonesian as well as Chinese and Indian immigrants would have to prove their loyalty so that the "nation will emerge with a far more united people than was ever possible before" (p. 21). The "growth of a multi-racial nationalism" (p. 21) is represented as being the basis for Malaysian national development — a view from which, as we shall see, some Malay narratives diverge radically.

As the Wang Gungwu introduction formulates the "bargain" narrative, the new state had much to offer to Malaysians and others (including the British) who wished to uphold "freedom", "democratic representation" and "equality before the law" — what are termed "the finest ideals of modern history" (p. 22). These ideals have continued to inspire many Malaysians, but there were other, practical reasons for proclaiming them in the period of decolonization. At that time the elites of colonized countries were keen to demonstrate their credentials for establishing new states that would join the community of modern nations — a community which, at least in the non-communist bloc, was defined by the liberal value systems of the victors of World War Two. In later decades sectors of the Malaysian elite would speak eloquently of "Asian values", and mock the liberal heritage;[19] even in the 1960s, as certain Malay-language national histories will demonstrate, some were committed to establishing a non-Western heritage as the basis of the new state. In the 1950s and 1960s, however, the imprint of British ideals and institutions on the new Malaya/Malaysia was unmistakable, and the British themselves continued to exercise a vital economic and a substantial political influence over the country. Changing perceptions of the British role have been part of the "social reality" which any national narrative, in one way or another, had to engage.

The British Role

It is possible to portray the British period as a common, uniting experience that gave substance to national unity. The Wang Gungwu introduction noted that both the peninsular and Borneo regions had "come under British rule in one form or another" (p. 17). Some narratives have given the British almost the founding role in the creation of the Malayan/Malaysian state. The English-language *History of Malaya, 1400–1959*,[20] published in 1961 and written by Joginder Singh Jessy, includes a section entitled "Foundations of Modern Malaya, 1875–1941", with chapters covering the development of the British administration in the peninsular sultanates. An indication of the contents is the fact that there are five pictures of leading members of the British colonial establishment, two sultans and one Chinese. It was in this period, says Jessy, that "Malaya became the heir to the technical skill of the West and became a field for the investment of western capital" (p. xix). In examining the country's move toward political independence, he notes that in 1943 the British Government's aim was the "development of (Malaya's) capacity for self government within the Empire" (p. 301). The initial plan for post-war Malaya was to create a "Malayan Union", in which the sultans would lose their sovereignty and the "preferential status of the Malays was to come to an end" (p. 202). Here the issue of the plural society comes to the fore in respect to Malay rights *vis-à-vis* the non-Malays. The "Union" plan provoked strong Malay opposition and, as a result, it was agreed to establish a "federation" of the different states in which the "the position of the Sultans would be safeguarded and the political position of the Malays maintained" (p. 304). The communist insurgency (or the Emergency) followed, and the "armed forces under the leadership of General Sir Gerald Templer" put the communists " on the defensive, and paved the way for their ultimate defeat" (p. 306). The British now began to press forward with self-government and in the first federal elections of 1955, the "Alliance" formed in 1952 between the United Malay National Organization and the Malayan Chinese Association "swept to victory" (p. 307). To advance to full self government the chief minister and leader of the Alliance, Tunku Abdul Rahman, now headed the "*Merdeka* Mission" to London, where, in "an atmosphere of great cordiality" (p. 308), agreement was reached to achieve complete independence on 31 August 1957.

In this narrative the achieving of independence for the new state is certainly accompanied by tensions — in particular, those of race relations (defending Malay rights) and the communist insurgency (which the book does not analyse in any detail). But the formation of the Alliance and its election success carry the implications of a solution to the country's ethnic problems, and suggest the value of Cheah's "bargain". What we do not find in Jessy's account is the presence of strong anti-colonial sentiment, or even much sign of indigenous political agency. The British, who had laid the "foundations of modern Malaya" between 1875 and 1941, are presented as driving the move to independence and when British government leaders meet with the new Malayan leaders to discuss the final terms of independence their negotiations are conducted in "great cordiality". In Malaysia, following Jessy, there is nothing that could be compared with the Philippines revolution as a unifying movement. On the contrary, this "History of Malaya" is concerned to stress (and thereby assist) the smooth transition from the British to the independence period.

The book, it should be said, does not ignore the historic role of the fifteenth-century state of Melaka, which exercised an influence over a number of peninsular states and was admired as a great entrepôt by foreign traders. It says enough about Melaka, in fact, to suggest the possibility that this polity might be given the type of status in Malayan/Malaysian nation-building that is possessed by Majapahit in Indonesian history. The "period of the Malacca Sultan", it is observed in the first chapter of his book, "is often regarded as the golden age of Malayan history" (p. 3) and the sultanate "made a lasting impression on the development of Malaya" (p. 18). The port of Melaka continued to "act as the focal point of the international trade which passed through the Straits of Malacca" (pp. 18–19), and the empire of Melaka is described as "an inspiration to (later) Malay rulers" (p. 19). The administrative system and ceremonial of the sultanate certainly "served as models for later Malay rulers…" (p. 19). Jessy's account, however, does not emplot modern Malayan history in a way that draws upon Melaka's potential. For him, Melaka is only central to the story of the "old" Malaya. As we have seen, the "foundations of modern Malaya" are presented as a largely British story. Jessy's first chapter on "the Melaka Sultan" and the second on "Islam in South-East Asia", give a degree of dignity to the Malay population of the modern state, but after page 29 (in a textbook of 315 pages) the focus is on the creation of what he terms the "new Malaya", the British-created nation state that was constituted for "all people born in the Federation and their children" (p. 305).

Insisting on such a radical break between the "old" and "new" Malaya happened to have been quite consistent with British narratives on Peninsula history. Thus, the scholar-official R J Wilkinson, in the pioneering *"History of the Peninsula Malays"* (1908, 1923), saw the aftermath of the Pangkor Treaty of 1874 as the key turning point. The treaty had established a British administrative presence in the Malay states and was resisted in a small war in the state of Perak. Writing of the "rebels" who were hanged or banished, Wilkinson suggested that "Malay history proper ends with them".[21]

Such a nation-building narrative as Jessy presents — playing down the contribution of the old sultanates to the making of modern Malaya, identifying the British as the real founders and, furthermore, according no prominence to anti-colonial actors — contained little to offend the former (and still influential) colonial masters. An ultimately more important significance of such a stress on the break between the new and old (Malay) Malaya, however, is that it also gives no particular privilege to the Malays in the plural society. Like the "bargain", this break with the Malay sultanate past adds to the impression of a state narrative that has much to offer non-Malay people. At a time when there was a desire to win Chinese "hearts and minds" (away from communism), this strategy would have seemed wise. It would reassure non-Malays. But what did the Malays gain from Jessy's narrative? How did it accommodate specifically Malay anxieties and aspirations? These are what Caroline Hau termed "excess" in the Jessy narrative. Setting aside the "old" Malaya meant ignoring powerful Malay memories. Many Malays were hostile even to the word "Malaya", seeing it as a foreign idea which signified the claims of non-Malay people over the country.[22] They still thought of Malaya as *"Tanah Melayu"*, or the "Malay lands", and would see Jessy's stress on discontinuity as rejecting Malay ownership of the national story.

Building Ethnic Understanding

A Malay-language text of this period which is less accommodating of British colonialism, and would have satisfied some but not all Malay anxieties, is Shamsul Baharin's *Malaya dalam Tawarikh Dunia* [Malaya in World History] (1962).[23] This history, issued in three volumes, is also written in the idiom of the "historic bargain". It is explicit in seeking to promote inter-communal understanding. The three volumes begin with a chapter on "Malaya as the centre of Southeast Asia"; the chapters that follow cover early Indian, Chinese, Greek, Roman, Southeast Asian, and Mongol history, and then Christianity and Islam, finally coming to the issue of the arrival of Islam in India and Southeast Asia. The chapter on Melaka in Volume Two comes between chapters on the Holy Roman Empire and the Moghul Empire, and there is also coverage of the Renaissance, the Enlightenment and the French Revolution, as well as the rise of Germany. In Volume Three there is a chapter on *"Tanah Melayu* under the British" (note the use of *"Tanah Melayu"* — literally, the "Malay lands", rather than "Malaya"), and the final chapter of the volume is on "Malaya", beginning with World War Two and ending with independence.

For such an ambitious project, the justification is offered (in the preface of the first volume) that it is "very important for us to understand the background of our citizens who come from foreign countries like China, India, and so forth, and thus to strengthen the ties of understanding between us". Here is the spirit of the "bargain". The "us" in this quote is a multi-ethnic "us". Indeed the text states directly that the descendants of the people who brought the different cultures to Malaya "live together with us in Malaya and have become a part of us" (Volume 1, p. 2). It is necessary to know the story of these people, we are told, because they are "a part of us, and cannot be separated from us" (Volume 1, p. 2), and this explanation is repeated throughout the history. In the opening line of Chapter three (Volume 1), which is entitled "China", the point is made that the Chinese are a large part of the inhabitants of Malaya, and that they possess a culture that is "different from that of non-Chinese inhabitants" (1, p. 30). The opening of the chapter on India explains that it is important to study the history of India to understand the "background of a large group of inhabitants in Malaya", and also to understand the Indian influence on Southeast Asia (1, p. 15). Making such inclusive observations, it is significant also that the name used for the newly-independent Malaya in the title of the history is not the favoured Malay name, *"Tanah Melayu"* (the "Malay lands"), but "Malaya" — the term that many Malays disliked.

Even when the text focuses on the earlier history of the "Malay" regions — in the wider archipelago as well as on the peninsula — the stress on multi-culturalism or cosmopolitanism is present. The Sumatran-based empire of Srivijaya, described in some Malay writings as a "Malay" precursor to Melaka, is not explicitly called "Malay" in this history. What is drawn attention to is the similarity of Srivijaya and Singapore as entrepots on trade routes, the cosmopolitanism of the port and its role as a centre of Buddism (1, p. 97). It is not pointed out that Singapore and Srivijaya (with its capital in Palembang in Sumatra) differ in respect to the former being largely Chinese. With respect to the "Malay kingdom of Melaka", (*Kerajaan Melayu Melaka*) (2, p. 44), it is said to be only one of many Malay kingdoms (*Kerajaan Melayu*) at that time, but it was "important as the largest one" (2, p. 44). After the Portuguese conquest Melaka in 1511, its greatness was lost, "hidden behind the curtain of colonialism until this time" (2, p. 53). In this book, Melaka is not discounted as part of the national narrative. It is used to help explain the Malay background, as other pre-modern narratives are employed to help the understanding of the other peoples of the peninsula. The Melaka story is called "one hinge or facet of the history of our homeland (*Tanah Ayer*)" (2, p. 44).

In Volume Three of Shamsul Baharin's work, the history of *Tanah Melayu* (note the continued use of this term) is reviewed, stressing again the sultanate of Melaka; and when the book proceeds to take the narrative up to independence, the story is set in the context of international developments — the French Revolution, the American Revolution, the rise of Germany, European colonialism, World War I, the rise of Japan, the nationalist movement in China, the struggle for independence in India, World War II, and the emergence of independent states in Asia (the Philippines, Ceylon, Indonesia and so forth). The chapter entitled "*Tanah Melayu* under British Imperialism" covers the British founding and development of Singapore, the establishment of British control on the peninsula, the residential system of government, the "federation" of some of the Malay states in 1895, political and social change, and then a specific section with the heading "The Entry of the Foreigners". This section opens with the frank admission — a fact which provides the rationale for the entire scheme of the three volumes — that "now the Chinese inhabitants of Malaya and Singapore are almost the same in number as the Malay inhabitants" (3, p. 170). The final paragraphs observe that before World War II the inhabitants of "Malaya" were in three groups: Chinese, Indians and Malays — and they are described as living and working separately from one another. The government (and it is not clear whether this means merely the British administration or the sultans as well) is said not to have made an effort to "unite the people" who were living in separate races (*bangsa*) (3, p. 173). Writing in 1962, the author says that these racial problems were at last being overcome and people were beginning to " live as one family"; there is "more understanding than in the past" (3, p. 173). Such "understanding", as we have seen, is something the history itself was deliberately designed to foster.

When the text comes to the rise of independent Asian states, there is a brief assessment of "nationalist consciousness", noting its importance in Indonesia, the Philippines and India. Only in Malaya, it is observed, was such a consciousness not significant (3, p. 293). The text asks why this was the case, and notes that few Malays had a Western education (3, p. 294), and that despite the British colonial presence "they felt their states were still free", a feeling that was strengthened by a "close connection between the Rajas and the people, with the Rajas often visiting the kampongs" (3, p. 294). The Malay people were not conscious of the changes going on, especially the activities of the foreigners and the development in the main cities.

Concerning the move towards independence ("*Malaya*" not "*Tanah Melayu*" is used in the chapter title, which is reminiscent of Jessy's radical break), Shamsul's history sees World War II as having an important meaning. It was not just one colonialism replacing another, but rather it brought a "new wind" (3, p. 333). In describing the British return to Malaya, no mention is made of a warm welcome. Tension arose between the Malays and Chinese, largely over their respective roles in the Japanese Occupation and the identification of the Chinese with communism. The history's abiding concern about inter-communal understanding is evident when this tension is called "a very foul matter in our history" (3, p. 338). Nevertheless, it was not "hostility between two races but caused by opportunists who sought to control Malaya" (p. 338).

Discussing the Malayan Union, and the Malay opposition it aroused, the Shamsul text notes at last the appearance of a Malay "nationalist spirit" (3, p. 339) and that the United Malays National Organization (UMNO) was formed. It admits the Malay complaint that all people under the new scheme would become citizens and the *majlis ugama* (the religious councils) would now be under the governor (p. 340). But the text does not highlight the specific Malay anxieties about non-Malay influence in the new state, and the handling of the issue of citizenship is quite indirect; even when the emergence of a "Malay nationalism" is discussed, it is in a chapter headed "The rise of Malayan nationalism" not "The rise of Malay nationalism".

The history now relates that the British agreed to a new constitution (the Federation) and it is admitted that this constitution, which gave special rights to the Malays to help them to achieve "the same level with other races (*bangsa*)" (p. 342), was initially opposed by Chinese and Indians. A ministerial government was then established, and the Malayan Chinese Association formed. The leader of the latter was aware that "the Chinese must unite, and furthermore must unite with the Malays to achieve independence for Malaya" (3, p. 343) and, thus, in 1952 the Alliance between UMNO and the MCA was formed, and triumphed in the 1955 election. The "bargain" is certainly being announced here.

The final subsection of the narrative on the emergence of independent Malaya returns to the issue of the "unity of our people", which is said to be no less important than "our freedom" (*kemerdekaan*) (3, p. 350). Education, it is argued, is the method of achieving unity and, as noted already, the author tends to portray his own book as a tool to promote understanding. In this history, nation-building above all is a social rather than administrative or constitutional process.

Such seeming even-handedness — such balance — would have won favour with the statesmen creators of the "historic bargain"; but it inevitably neglected the powerful Malay aspirations which were an important feature of the "social context" in which the narrative was written. In laying out the historical background of the modern nation state, the text does reach back to the early kingdoms of the region, but they were depicted as "*Tanah Melayu*" not "Malaya" history. Again there is a narrative disjunction between the "old" and "new". The new "Malaya" nation is presented as incorporating many different histories. In this way Shamsul Baharin's nation-building history conveys a generous plurality — so generous, in fact, that it also communicates the sense of the Malays losing possession of the modern state.

A Malay Nationalist Version

A narrative construction that is more strongly Malay is presented in *Sejarah Tanah Melayu dan Sekitar-nya*[24] [The History of Tanah Melayu and its Region] published in 1964, soon after the creation of Malaysia, and written by Wan Shamshuddin and Arena Wati (who had migrated to Singapore from Makassar in Indonesia and became a well-known journalist and novelist in Malaya). As implied in the use of *"Tanah Melayu"* in the title, the book actually affirms the continuity of the modern nation state with the Malay past. In the words of the Preface, "the history of *Tanah Melayu* and its region begins in the fourteenth-century"(p. xii). Furthermore, the modern state is not presented in this book as a mere, impersonal entity — the creation of a foreign, colonial elite — but as "our homeland, which is cherished by our own race" (p. xii).

The British role in the making of the state is certainly acknowledged, and without antagonism — the founding of Singapore, the development of the Straits Settlements, the "origins of colonialism" in the peninsular states, the residential system of government, the 1895 federation, and then an examination of "Economy, Communications, and Industries" and, finally, "Treaties and important personages". A chapter on *"Tanah Melayu* from 1941 to 1961"* presents the usual story: Japanese Occupation, Malayan Union, Federal Constitution (suggested by the Malay leader, Dato Onn), the Emergency, the UMNO-MCA Agreement, and the "Steps toward independence". The attaining of *Merdeka* is pictured as a relatively smooth process, with little indication of British resistance.

The Malay sympathy in this narrative — the accommodation of Malay nationalist "excess" — is evident in the treatment of the Chinese and other non-Malay communities. There is no theme here about the need to "understand the background" of the different races. Also, this text (unlike that of Shamsul Baharin) does not hesitate to spell out the specifically Malay ethnic anxieties respecting Malayan Union, explaining the objection that the immigrant people would be given the same status and rights as Malays themselves in the latter's "homeland" (p. 276). The Malay perspective, however, is apparent most of all in the emplotment of the nation-building story — embedding it within a wider consideration of the development of the Malay race (*bangsa Melayu*), commencing in the twelfth-century (p. 295). Even the coverage of the colonial period gives less prominence to the British than the earlier histories offered, and conveys a sense of continuity in Malay/Malayan history. The chapter covering the Japanese occupation, the British return and the contests relating to independence is called merely "*Tanah Melayu* from 1941 to 1961".

The "Malayness" of Wan Shamshuddin's and Arena Wati's account is sealed in their decision to conclude the historical narrative with a chapter entitled "The Concept of *Melayu* or *Melayu Raya*". The term "*Melayu Raya*" (which might be defined as "greater Malaydom") is used to describe the expanded state rather than the now standard term "Malaysia", and this in itself had a "Malay" appeal. The phrase was certainly employed in the period when the new, expanded state of Malaysia was being forged. In his introduction to *Malaysia*, Wang Gungwu had noted this, commenting it was a "misleading translation" because it "led several political leaders to suggest that this Malaysia should embrace the whole of Indonesia and even possibly the Philippine Islands".[25] The term could certainly be used to invoke a rival state structure to that envisaged by the British, and, as we will see, some Malays viewed this as the preferred architecture for the new nation-state. A pan-Malay aspiration had an emotional appeal, and is "excess" in the UMNO national narrative. It might be argued that Tunku Abdul Rahman and his colleagues hijacked the potentially dangerous concept of "*Melayu Raya*" when proposing the more limited state of Malaysia — limited in the sense that it included only the formerly British-governed territories.[26] Appropriating the phrase in this way, they were countering their Malay nationalist opponents both within and outside Malaysia (and might be argued to have been provoking the "Crush Malaysia" campaign waged by the Sukarno government of Indonesia). In Wan Shamshuddin's and Arena

Wati's book we can see an example of such ideological work, using the expression "*Melayu Raya*" to enhance the "Malay" character of the expanded state. It is without doubt a far cry from the name "Malaya" which, as we have seen, was understood in some quarters to carry the implication of the dispossession of the Malays.

In other ways too the Wan Shamsuddin and Arena Wati book seeks to give Malaysia a cultural legitimacy. It quotes the Sultan of Brunei praising the Malaysia proposal because of the "the very close connections of religion, racial descent, customs and ceremonial and other culture" between the component states (p. 288). It notes as well the common colonial experience (p. 283), but the point is hammered home that the different states of "*Melayu Raya*" actually "share the same history from ancient times" and all felt "the same cultural influences" from China, India, Arabia and elsewhere (p. 294). Finally, they are all Malay, and are portrayed as beneficiaries of the heritage of the old empires of Srivijaya, Majaphit and "Melayu-Melaka" (p. 296).

This long (in time span) uniting narrative, it must be pointed out, is focused not primarily on kingdoms but on the "Malay race". Wang Gungwu had noted that there had "never been a political unit based on the idea of being Malay" (and I believe the historical evidence supports this view). But the history of Wan Shamshuddin and Arena Wati suggests that over many centuries the people themselves conceptualized their social/political condition in these terms. The topic of this history is the progress of a race that was to become the foundation of a nation-state. When these authors consider Portuguese and Dutch intrusion in the region, their concern is how the "Malay race" struggled to protect its freedom and its rights (p. 297). The attempt to snatch back Melaka from the Portuguese by Johor and Aceh is described not as a struggle by two sultanates but as "the struggle of the Malay race (*Bangsa Melayu*) to defend the homeland" (p. 298).

In this Malay race-based history, the significance of the non-Malays is only really revealed at the end of the final chapter. Here the authors produce the population statistics that indicate at the time of writing that the Chinese and Indians together equalled about the same number as the Malays in the peninsular states, and that the vast majority of people in Singapore were actually Chinese (p. 309). For some readers these statements would throw doubt upon the entire narrative strategy of the book, seeming to leave to the end the central issue — the plural society issue — faced in the making of the Malayan/Malaysian state. The "historic bargain" foregrounded in different ways by Shamsul Baharin, Jessy and Cheah Boon Kheng, is sidelined in this book. But can we conclude that Wan Shamshuddin and Arena Wati were less cognizant of the plural society issue? Or is the narrative responding to the issue in a more trenchantly "Malay" manner, downplaying the non-Malays and seeking to capture the story of the Malay people in a way that would have been reassuringly familiar to many Malay readers? This book addresses readers whom the other books largely ignored. Such Malays were waiting in the wings, just as they were in the political scene. Their anxieties and aspirations, it is well known, were taken far more seriously after some Malays expressed their frustrations with violence in the racial killings of 13 May 1969.[27]

The Treatment of Melaka

One aspect of the Wan Shamshuddin/Arena Wati Malay narrative that requires further inquiry is its handling of Melaka. It gives the fifteenth-century polity greater prominence than it receives in the other texts we have examined. Cheah's study does not reach back into the colonial and pre-colonial periods. Although Jessy begins his book with a chapter on Melaka he plays down its Malay character and conveys its irrelevance to the 1957 state. Shamsul Baharin does write in some detail of the "Malay kingdom of Melaka" but compares it with Singapore and situates it within the earlier history of *Tanah Melayu*, and not as an obvious foundation for modern Malaya. What Wan Shamshuddin and Arena Wati emphasize is Melaka's role in the long narrative of Malay history — commencing their book with a chapter called "The opening of the state of Melaka". This emphasis, however, could also be seen to exist in tension with the book's theme of a long "Malay" history that extends geographically beyond the peninsula. It is a tension that invokes a debate that was taking place in the Malay community itself — but this book does not spell out the opposing positions; the debate is merely implicit in its cautious narrative.

A focus on Melaka, of course, is not inevitable or necessary in a Malay national history. Melaka was only one of numerous royal centres based on the peninsula, Sumatra and other islands in the archipelago. One purpose a Melaka-centred history serves is that of concentrating attention on the peninsula itself, and thus helping to suggest the legitimacy of a peninsular polity in modern times. When the British and Dutch in the early nineteenth-century divided the archipelago into two broad spheres of influence — the British being now restricted largely to the peninsula — there was a potential strategic value in giving such an historic emphasis to Melaka. With the creation of "British Malaya" as a peninsular administrative unit, and as the leaders of the new independent state of "Malaya" sought historical justification for their nation-building, the profiling of Melaka gained added rationale. It was certainly heralded in early British histories, such as those by Swettenham (1907),[28] Wilkinson (1908)[29] and Winstedt (1928),[30] and a recent study of Malay historiography has noted how in independent Malaysia "the Melaka sultanate" became "an important component of the new history syllabus....".[31]

The Melaka-based construction of Malay history, however, did not go unchallenged. There were other versions of history available and potentially subversive. Although Melaka's importance had a basis in the chronicle of the Melaka/Johor Sultanate (which the British racialized by calling the "Malay Annals"),[32] other pre-modern royal texts advocated the importance of competing royal houses, many not based on the peninsula. With respect to modern history writing, a 1920s history that reaches beyond the Malay states that became a part of Malaya, and stresses the Malay race rather than Melaka specifically, is Abdul Hadi bin Haji Hasan's work, *Sejarah Alam Melayu*[33] [*The History of the Malay World*]. Beginning again with a consideration of the origins of the Malays, it then surveys the Malay world, giving particular but by no means sole attention to the peninsular states including Melaka. The term *"Melayu"* is given a very broad definition in this text, the "Malay World" including Java. The author was a teacher at the Sultan Idris Training College in Perak and his History is consistent with the aspirations of the Malay elite from that college — aspirations that would later be "excess" for Malayan/Malaysian nation builders, and which included the vision of a new nation that would incorporate not just the British-controlled peninsular states but also the Dutch East Indies.[34] Such an archipelago-wide aspiration, of course, would have been hindered rather than helped by an insistence on the centrality of Melaka in "Malay history". Another aspiration of even wider scope that was resisted in the peninsular political vision — an aspiration that will be considered at the end of this chapter — is that of the Islamic community that transcends all national borders.

Hearing Malay Radicalism

The particular way in which Melaka is accommodated in a nation-building text, therefore, is one indication of contrasting visions; the treatment of the "historic bargain" suggests another. These and further splinterings of the "Malay" perspective are evident in Maswari Rosdi's and Suhara Salim's *Sejarah Malaysia Moden*[35] [*A History of Modern Malaysia*] — a book first published in 1984, in a new political context, and adopting a frankly sceptical view of the UMNO élite that established the inter-communal bargain with the major Chinese and Indian parties. Unlike the other narratives we have scrutinized, this narrative is explicit in giving space to a radical Malay alternative (including the archipelago-wide ambition), and does so in part by recalling an often-neglected history of violent opposition to British colonialism. Commencing with a discussion of "The origins of the Malays", and a brief survey of early kingdoms (including but not dominated by Melaka) and involvement of the Europeans and Chinese in the Malay States, the text goes on to examine anti-colonial action in the Naning war of 1831–32, the Perak War (including the killing of British Resident Birch in 1875), the uprising in Pahang in the 1890s, the Kelantan uprising of 1915 and the Trengganu uprising of 1928. Collected together in this way, these narratives of Malay resistance undermine the view of pre-World War II Malaya as a peaceful territory, and the Malays as being passive toward (and perhaps not conscious of) the various changes imposed. The Malays are given greater agency in this book. In the Pahang Uprising, they learnt the lesson that with the spirit of struggle it was possible to defy the English despite their superior weaponry (p. 125). In Trengganu, the rebels had "the objective of chasing away the English and forming a Malay government (*pemerintah*) (p. 129).

Linking this early resistance to what the book calls (in chapter 12) "The nationalist movement in *Tanah Melayu*, 1900–1945" (p. 166), this account also counters the view that nationalism was only a post-World War II development. If nationalism is understood more broadly as "the love of the mother country and opposition to colonialism" then the nationalist movement began in the nineteenth-century with the Naning war (p. 166). The Maswari and Suhara book admits nationalism moved slowly in *Tanah Melayu* compared with the Philippines and Indonesia, and attributes this to the plural society in which the component groups differ so greatly with one another in their attitudes to life, customs and culture. The Chinese and Indians, it is explained, "extended their emotion and loyalty to China and India" (p. 166). There were in fact "three types of nationalism" (p. 166) in *Tanah Melayu*, although, in surveying the first half of the twentieth-century, this history devotes most attention to the Malay community, examining Middle Eastern influences, the emergence of a number of periodicals, and educational developments (including the creation of a "*radikal*" (p. 169) elite at the Sultan Idris Teachers Training College). This elite, influenced by the nationalist movement in Indonesia, fostered the creation of various Malay nationalist organizations (in both Malaya and Borneo) which called for unity with Indonesia (p. 170). The book mentions but gives less emphasis to another leadership group — that is, the Western educated, who were more willing to co-operate with the English government. This latter elite included such leaders as Rajah Chulan and Dato Onn, and presumably the later UMNO leadership. Regarding the radical elite, the Maswari/Suhara account examines in considerable detail (for a general history) the pre-war emergence of the radical organization, *Kesatuan Melayu Muda* (KMM). Led by such figures as Ibrahim Yaakub and Ishak Haji Muhammad, the authors insist on its anti-colonial credentials and its "great influence on Malay society" (p. 176). The foregrounding of these radicals, and the disclosing of the longer history of resistance, distinguish this book from those of Shamsul Baharin or Wan Shamshuddin and Arena Wati. It is evident that it also takes a more critical view of the British.

In discussing the Malayan Union issue, the British are given the objective of "obstructing the emergence of greater Indonesia (Indonesia-Raya)" (p. 180) — a potent detail certainly neglected in our other narratives. One of the Malay radical supporters of Indonesia-Raya, Dr. Burhanuddin, is quoted as declaring that "we Malays in *Tanah Melayu*, with a loyal spirit, fully support the idea of one homeland, with *Tanah Melayu* being a part of Indonesia-Raya" (p. 180). When the book turns to the activities of the UMNO élite — the future leaders of the country — the treatment is less detailed. In discussing the massive Malay opposition to the Malayan Union, for instance, the leadership of Dato Onn is mentioned, but the text does not take pains to describe the way he emerged as leader of so important a movement. The non-Malays are also viewed with more explicit harshness in this book. The reasons for Malay opposition to the Union are stated with little diplomacy. The Malays were "worried about foreigners especially Chinese who controlled their economy" (p. 184).

A negative and even pessimistic attitude toward non-Malays is maintained in the narrative. In the case of the Emergency, this book stresses that the communists tended to be Chinese (p. 194). In the process leading to independence the text gives attention to "the bargain", but the tone suggests a continuing suspicion. With respect to the UMNO-MCA alliance, it is observed that "faced with the election" the MCA leaders co-operated with UMNO out of self interest. They believed the two parties would achieve compromises concerning the problems of the Chinese people, and that it would also be possible to strengthen the position of the MCA itself (p. 209). The final chapter of the book places the Malay-Chinese relationship in a broader economic and social context. Explaining it was "a consequence of the development of the tin and rubber industries" in Malaya that the Malays lost their majority position, the history comments that the Indian and Chinese immigrants tended to be "still loyal to their original residence" (p. 227); when the immigrants did eventually become permanent settlers, they were "not able to assimilate with Malay society" (p. 228).

Such comments, which reflect disappointment and anxiety existing in the Malay community — sentiments that had been expressed with ferocity in the race riots of 1969 — challenge the optimism in UMNO toward "the bargain" as a step toward effective nation-building; their tone also contrasts with the book's continuing sympathy toward the alternative radical Malay leadership. Thus Maswari Rosdi's and Suhara Salim's book profiles the post-war Malay Nationalist Party (MNP), led by the radicals Ishak Haji Mohammad and Burhanuddin — a party that viewed UMNO as being "soft and conservative" (p. 188); and it also takes a favourable view of the co-operative plans which developed in the immediate post-war period between the radical Malay leadership and the "All Malayan Council of Joint Action", a gathering of radical non-Malay parties. A "Peoples' Constitution" was proposed — one that would insist on all citizens being called "Melayu", and without the religious connotations of that word. The text comments that "unfortunately" this peoples' constitution was not supported by the Malays (p. 190). At an earlier point in the narrative it is noted that "unfortunately" the hopes of Ibrahim Yaakub and other KMM leaders to achieve independence together with Indonesia were destroyed "because of the Japanese surrender and the sudden return of the Allies" (p. 175).

Observations of this type — particularly set in the context of the longer history of anti-British resistance — suggest a lament for the lost opportunities of the radical Malay elite. While ensuring that this group is recognized in the narrative of nation-building, the text's forbidding portrayal of the plural society, and the mention of the existence of alternative possibilities and strategies in the past, suggest to the reader that the process of nation-building is incomplete; the "excess" that is concealed or sidelined in our other accounts has its potential exposed in this book.

The narrative strategy of the Maswari Rosdi and Suhara Salim text — particularly its different approach to Malay radicalism compared with other accounts that we have examined — must have been influenced by the changing political situation; in particular the impact of the 1969 riots as strong Malay condemnation of the "historic bargain". Also, the British were no longer major political players in Malaysia — by the 1980s the prime minister himself (Dr. Mahathir) was willing to tell his people to "buy British last".[36] But the Maswari/Suhara narrative is also better appreciated if we see it as responding to the views expressed by certain members of the radical elite itself — powerful writings that were available to the broader

Malay community, and helped to sustain memories that (in Caroline Hau's words) were part of the "social reality" which the authors were compelled to engage. For instance, Ibrahim Yaakub, the former leader of the KMM, who went into exile in Indonesia after the war, wrote a number of books about "the history of the struggle to achieve a free Malaya". According to his *Sekitar Malaya Merdeka*[37] [*Concerning Free Malaya*], the Malayan state led by Tunku Abdul Rahman had not obtained a "full freedom" (pp. 7–8). Written just after the celebration of "*Merdeka*" in 1957, it notes the country had recovered only "independence within the commonwealth" and that this independence was a "gift given by the English government to the bourgeois-feudalist group in Malaya which had compromised and cooperated with that government" (p. 17). This is the "incomplete" independence that is derided in the Maswari/Suhara text.

"National consciousness" (*kesadaran nasional*) in Malaya, Ibrahim Yaakub's book comments, was divided into two streams (*aliran*) (p. 21). The first advocated "Malaya for the Malays", and was supported by the bourgeois-feudal leadership which was willing to accept less than a complete independence for the country. The second group was concerned about the rights of everyone who is oppressed and desires freedom. This latter group was influenced by the idea of an "Indonesia-Raya" in which all the peoples of the archipelago would become members of one great *bangsa* ("race" or "community") (p. 22). The book admits that in the period of opposition to the Malayan Union "all groups" had come together, but the co-operation soon foundered; the radicals departed, and UMNO was left in the hands of feudal groups, led by "Dato Sir Onn bin Jaffar, the Chief Minister of the Sultan of Johor" (p. 44). The British gave up their plans for the Union, recognized as their true enemies the Chinese communists and the nationalist movement of Indonesia, and worked with the UMNO group to create a federation which would restore the rajas.

Reading Ibrahim Yaakub's book, it is clear that although the second group — the radical nationalists — were in retreat, they include national heroes who "cannot be forgotten in the history of attaining freedom" (p. 51). The Malay Nationalist Party (MNP) had been the "first political party to oppose colonialism after the English army returned at the end of

1945" (p. 53), and it was a continuation of the radical movement of the 1930s. According to Ibrahim even the successor to Dato Onn, Tunku Abdul Rahman, acknowledged these radicals. Coming to Jakarta in November 1955 to meet Ibrahim, the Tunku sought his support, arguing that the "struggle of the Alliance follows the plans of the Malaya Nationalist Party" (p. 57). Ibrahim replied that there could be no compromise with England and that he continued to seek "full freedom for Malaya" (p. 57). The closing passages of the book affirm that this would involve the national unity of all the Malay race in Island Southeast Asia (p. 76). It invokes the aspiration that continued to operate beyond the ideological boundaries of the new Malayan state, and would only be partially incorporated in the new "Malaysia": that is, a Malay state incorporating both Malaya and Indonesia.

A further book that claims space for Malay radicals in the national narrative is the former KMM activist Ahmad Boestaman's *Merintis Jalan ke Punchak* [*Carving the Path to the Summit*] (1972).[38] The "summit" is "independent Malaysia" (p. vii), and the author says he wants the pioneers of independence to get the credit due them. (The word he uses for "credit" is *"nama"*, a term that for centuries had conveyed the powerful Malay concern about reputation). Like Ibrahim Yaakub's book, this one discusses the MNP, noting its early popular support, its opposition to feudalism and its commitment to "full independence" (p. 56). Before the MNP left UMNO, it pressed for the organization to use the "Red and White flag", an obvious reference to Indonesia (p. 82). Losing by one vote, the MNP members withdrew. The "peoples'constitution", which the MNP later supported, also called for the red and white flag. Toward the end of the book it is explained how the Malay radicals were suppressed by the British, along with the Chinese communists, during the Emergency. Although the narrative does not continue up to 1957, as in the case of Ibrahim Yaakub's book, the message is clear: the radical struggle requires recognition and, also, its aims have not yet been achieved.

The accounts of Boestaman and Ibrahim Yaakub, and the national narrative of Maswari Rosdi and Suhara Salim, are not flattering to UMNO. The radicals, who claimed to be inheritors of an anti-colonial tradition going back to the Naning wars of the early nineteenth century, continued to offer an alternative way forward in the nation-making process. They branded those Malays who saw themselves as recognizing the reality of having to accommodate a large immigrant minority population as merely "bourgeois feudalists". In later years Tunku Abdul Rahman wrote memoirs, seeking to restore his own reputation as a player in the gaining of Independence. In the tradition of "the bargain", when he described the "men who helped to shape the nation"[39] he took pains to include Chinese and Indian leaders as well as Malay ones. He constructed his memoirs in a way that gives scant attention to his radical rivals; his biography[40] (based largely on extensive interviews with the Tunku) admits only that in the immediate post-war period "groups of young Malays" had talked of independence. The Tunku, in fact, was actually back in England when the early struggle took place against Malayan Union. After returning, he opposed the leader of UMNO, Dato Onn, and in his reminiscences he explains how Onn had begun to promote a "Malayan" rather than a "Malay" identity. The Tunku himself asked: "who are these Malayans that Dato Onn speaks of?" And then emphasized that "this is a Malay country. The Malays will decide who should be included in the term Malayan".[41] That is, in his view Malay unity needed to be achieved in the first place, and then the "historic bargain" with the parties representing the broad Chinese and Indian communities. It was a bargain that he and many other commentators portrayed as being necessary not only to establish the credentials to set up a new state independent of colonial power, but also to ensure that this state was not destroyed by inter-ethnic conflict over the coming decades. The "bargain" recognized the demographic imperatives of Malaya/Malaysia and, as we have seen, it was reaffirmed in Mahathir's Vision 2020 and celebrated in so recent a national narrative as that of Cheah Boon Kheng.

Accommodating Monarchy

The main features in the Tunku's account of his own role in the independence process are his successful convincing of the sultans to accept the ideas of independence and democracy (an achievement that is neglected in many radical narratives), his demand that the British give Malaya independence some years earlier than they had proposed (again often ignored), his negotiations with the communists, and his contribution to the ceremony of the nation state. The Tunku, as a royal prince from Kedah, "had been surrounded by royal pageantry since his birth",[42] and the state anthem, the titles, the royal regalia, and the official music of the new nation all owe much to him. The Tunku's narrative brings home the extent to which the Malaya/Malaysia nation state was constituted as a monarchy — it is a warning that the negotiations between the UMNO leadership and the sultans must have achieved gains for both sides. It is a reminder that the sultanates themselves, despite their continued potency, have often been neglected in national narratives.

Standing back from the to-and-fro of narrative and counter narrative, it does seem surprising that the sultans have continued to have the status of "excess" in many foundation accounts. Until the Japanese Occupation they had remained sovereign and prominent, even in states where there was a relatively large, British-administered bureaucracy. As prime minister, Mahathir once observed that large numbers of Malays had relatively little preparation for the transition from a collection of sultanates to an independent state with a common citizenship — a state led by people who invoked Malay nationalism, not loyalty to a royal house.[43] The sultans clearly retained support among sections of the Malay people, and this support must have been grounded in notions of allegiance that preceded any modern concept of racial or national loyalty. It might also be asked what a monarchical Malaya/Malaysia offered to other interests. Has it offered specific reassurance, for instance, to non-Malays who would be anxious about an ethnicity-based nation? Also, holding a position at the apex of the religious establishment in the polity, was monarchy seen to provide a means of incorporating or moderating Islamic aspirations in the independent federal nation? In the light of these questions, just which groups influenced (or at least supported) the creation of the new state as a monarchy?

Historical research supports the Tunku's insistence that the sultans themselves were far from being automatic supporters of the new nation: the negotiations with the rulers on the eve of independence were demanding and risk-laden,[44] and even today the rulers have not been completely transformed into "constitutional monarchies".[45] The old and extraordinary claim that "a people cannot exist without a Raja" can still be found in publications issued by a Malay royal court[46] and, at least in a small section of the Malay community, there continues a belief in the "elements of sovereignty in a spiritual form".[47] Certainly, in the constitutional confrontation between the UMNO-led government and the sultans in 1983–84, large crowds gathered to support not only Mahathir but also some of the sultans. As the Tunku's own nation-building account makes clear, the rulers contributed to the construction of the Malaysian state with its king and national ceremonial but, like the proponents of the Indonesia-Raya, they could (and can) also draw upon an ideology that is inimical to the existing modern state system. They have subversive potential. And whether or not a national narrative stresses the nation-building capacity or subversive potential of monarchy will depend on context — on the penumbra of events and polemic in which the narrative is composed.

Moving from the "historic bargain" interpretations of Malaysian nation-building to different Malay nationalist versions; noting the competition between the peninsular state and a broader archipelago vision; examining the way different constructions highlight or downplay the British contribution; and then returning to the "bargain" interpretations of the former Alliance prime minister (Tunku Abdul Rahman) himself, and what he opens up regarding the sultans — such shifts in perspective suggest the tension and contest in the task of nation-building. Although only focusing on the national story up to the 1960s, the ever-present difficulty of incorporating varying forms of "excess" in a coherent national narrative is evident. Memories and aspirations — alternative possibilities — that are harboured or emerge in the "national" community make demands for new interpretations as well as new futures. And demands change over time.

The Malayan/Malaysian narrative, of course, did not stop with the celebrations of 1957 and 1963. The writing up of such later defining events as the separation of Singapore, the 1969 riots, the Islamic fundamentalism (or Islamism) of the 1970s and 1980s, the constitutional crises over the sultans, and the UMNO divisions of the Mahathir period (1986–87; 1998), is necessarily a continuing ideological activity, and riven with contest. The different ways such events are experienced, however, also influences how the founding of the state in the post-war period is viewed and formulated in retrospect. The foundation story — the specific problems and achievements that are identified — will go on being shaped and re-shaped by events as well as potent visions.

Other Fissures

What other sympathies or identities, then, have the capacity to compete with the Malaysian national? Malayness, as an identity and a commitment, as we have seen, is capable of undermining nation-building — although one cause that might seem to have been lost over time is that of Indonesia-Raya, the Malay archipelago-wide state which would incorporate both Indonesia and Malaysia. The creation of Malaysia in 1963 seems to have helped this outcome, giving the impression of taking over the idea of a broader single "Malay" grouping, and in the following years much ideological work was put into creating the Malaysian state with a separate identity from Indonesia. Despite these moves, however, the aspiration of a greater Malaydom is there in the wings, from time to time attended to by state ideologues. Its presence can be felt in apparently innocent observations. Thus, when a national historian writes of the "origins of the Malay race"[48] there is an inevitable allusion to the idea of a larger Malay entity. When the Malaysian Government set up an "International Malay Secretariat" in 1996,[49] holds numerous conferences on the "Malay World",[50] or supports a school textbook dealing with "Malay civilization",[51] these initiatives draw the eye across the political spectrum, recalling the ongoing need to incorporate or at least engage with the powerful pan-archipelago project of the Malay radicals. It is a project that would be revived as a result of new developments in the social (or international) context, and would be likely to call for even more new interpretations of the Merdeka period.

Is state (*negeri*) loyalty a further cause of fissure within the Malaysian, and "the Malay", narrative? If nation-building in Malaysia continues to be compromised by monarchy, does it also compete with a potentially separatist loyalty to the state (*negeri*) of say, Kelantan or Kedah? There is a need to distinguish between sultan and *negeri*. In the late nineteenth-century some states began to be defined in a territorial way, and not essentially as a network of relationships around a ruler. Johor continue to have a sultan, but by the end of the nineteenth-century it had been surveyed and defined as a territorial entity, and it had a constitution (described in Malay in a way to suggest that the laws themselves gave "body" to the kingdom).[52] In earlier years allegiance had been to the person of the ruler: the great courtier, Hang Tuah (in the opening sentence of the *Hikayat Hang Tuah*) was said to be a man who "showed loyalty to his lord and great service to his lord".[53] By the late nineteenth-century another senior courtier, in writing about his life, compared himself to a plant living on a giant tree, "spreading myself over it and winding myself around every branch and fork".[54] But his words make clear that the tree to which he was bound was by then not the person of the ruler but rather the state of Johor.

Just how many Malays began to shift their loyalty from ruler to state is difficult to determine. By the 1980s, the Perak sultanate was explaining that the titles of that state were given for service "either to the state (*negeri*) of Perak" or to the state (*negara*) of Malaysia.[55] It is not service to the sultan that is mentioned. In another modern royal text, the sultan is described as a "symbol of the unity of the people" of a state, and as himself working for the progress of that state (*negeri*).[56] That is, in these formulations it is to the state, not the ruler, that priority is given. The degree of emotive power invested in the *negeri*, however, is less clear.

Histories are written of the individual states (*negeri*) of the federation, but most of the post-Merdeka texts I have seen merely highlight the special characteristics and achievements of a particular state, and do not suggest that the state can compete with the nation-state as a focus or source of identity. Even in a history of Johor written a century ago, the ruler is praised for being "energetic" in "raising the reputation" of both the *negeri* and the Malay race.[57] The mention of the Malay race suggests a larger context than the *negeri* itself and, as has been observed, the nation. In the post-independence *negeri* histories, the setting is often revealed to be the larger nation-state — the "federation" in which the individual *negeri* is located —

or the Malay race. Such local histories tend to celebrate the specific role of their state, but they do not challenge the nation state itself. They merely present their own angle on the national narrative. A 1971 history of Kelantan, for instance, is explicit about not studying Kelantan for its own sake. Although the author hopes it will "benefit the people of the state", he stresses that Kelantan is a "centre for the development of the spirit and culture" of the Malay *bangsa*.[58] In the closing chapter of the book, the themes covered are exactly the ones we find in most national histories: the Japanese occupation, the threat of Malayan Union, the Emergency, *Merdeka*. The author notes with pride the Kelantan contribution to a national festival in 1955, displaying Kelantan kites, tops and music.[59] After 1959, he notes, Kelantan is governed by the Islamic party, PAS, and not the governing party of the Federation.[60]

Some local histories are more explicit in signalling the nation state context. Haji Buyong Adil's *Sejarah Johor* [The history of Johor] (1971) is one of a series of state histories, and in the introduction the author hopes that his history, like that of other Malay states, will act as a "mirror for comparison" for all the inhabitants of Malaysia in protecting the "freedom and the sovereignty of the state of Malaysia over the centuries".[61] The author of a further state history (of Trengganu) argues that the study of the 'homeland' has a "natural place in the society, race and nation which we love".[62] But one of his history volumes also includes an introduction by the Mufti of Trengganu, who takes the implications of the study in another direction — in fact, he invokes the final form of "excess" that we will consider in this essay. He is concerned not about nation or race, but about the Islamic community (*umat*). He praises the author for studying a "portion of the history of Islam in the state of Trengganu" and he complains that no one yet has published a general history reflecting the life of the "*Umat Islam* on the Malay Peninsula".[63]

Looking at these local state histories, we see little repetition of the passionate loyalty to the *negeri* which was expressed by the Johor courtier a century ago. The individual states are not presented as rivals to the nation state. Their treatment even suggests a certain lack of substance in the idea of the *negeri* — at least as an entity considered independently from the raja or sultanate. The state histories do not circle around the state as court texts once circled around the sultan or ruling family. The nobility of the narrative seems to come from being part of something larger — the nation-state itself, the Malay race, or the Islamic community. In the case of the Islamic vision — or certain, specific Islamic visions — there is again the continuing possibility that that larger context might subvert the entire Malayan/Malaysian nation-building process.

Islamic Claims

The drive toward a broader religious allegiance — toward loyalty to an Islamic community (*umat*) that transcends membership of a Malaysian or even a Malay community — tends to be either absent or suppressed in the narratives we have considered. A recent textbook[64] on "Islamic Civilization and Asian Civilization", used in Malaysian schools, suggests one way in which Islamic claims are acknowledged but then subtly blunted. Although highlighting "Islamic civilization", the book is in fact written from the stand point of Malay civilization and Malaysia. Features of Islamic civilization are certainly surveyed, including its impact on Malay culture (161ff), Malay education and Malay nationalism (241ff). But the volume concludes with a long section on "Malay Civilization" (pp. 257–378). The section does touch upon the rise of the Islamist movement in Malaysia in the 1970s (pp. 322–23), with the challenges it brought to the constitution, economy and so forth. It also notes that Nik Abd. Aziz Hj. Nik Hassan, the Kelantan PAS (Islamic party) leader, has said that a large proportion of the historical writing on Malaysia follows a Western style, and that the history of Malaysia needs to be written again from an Islamic perspective — one that does not ignore the spiritual (p. 376). Although the potential of a rigorously Islamist perspective (even in the writing of history) is acknowledged, however, the book manoeuvres back in its final chapter to the task of foregrounding the Malays and Malaysia. The achievements of Malaysia are listed in the last paragraphs; then, the final sentence of the book asserts the continuing importance of the Malay people and the Malay language, underlining their significance within Southeast Asia, and quoting the Malay hero, Hang Tuah, as saying that "the Malays will never disappear from the world" (p. 378).

The potential for an *umat* focus actually to challenge the nation-state (and nation-building narratives) is obvious — but not fully realized — in a range of books that analyse one aspect or another of the progress of the religion in the Malaya/Malaysian context. A subversive agenda can be detected in the way some describe their subject of study not as "Malaysia" or "Malay" but as the community of Islam (*"umat Islam"*, *"masyarakat Islam"* or *"orang Islam"*). We see this, for instance, in surveys of the advance of Islamic law (and the frustrations of colonialism),[65] and in studies of society,[66] education,[67] literature and thought.[68] In some cases, the Malaysian situation is discussed in a wide "international" context, in others a book or monograph is focused just on Malaysia. In either situation the real concerns are revealed as transcending the nation-state — they are focused on the fortunes of the *umat Islam*, one portion of which only happens to be located in that particular part of the globe.

The Islamist vision — promulgated today by a number of political groups in Malaysia, most prominently the opposition party, PAS (and sections of UMNO) — can be revolutionary in its aspirations to overturn the constitutional, legal and political structures of the Malaysian state, as well as a wide range of social attitudes. It has the potential to demand a sustained re-examination of the nation-forming period. Some Islamist narratives, one could imagine, would be nation-critiquing not nation-building accounts — they would be likely to examine the concerns of certain key Islamic leaders (Zulkiflee Muhammad, the vice-president of PAS, is one possible example[69]), who were sceptical of the entire political programme for a post-independent Malaya/Malaysia, and certainly expressed frustration regarding the very limited impact of the Islamic critique on the making of the new state. A reconstruction of nation formation from an Islamist perspective may demand a new assessment of the British role, focusing on the way in which British rather than Islamic institutions were built into the constitutional, legal and political foundations of Malaya/Malaysia. For the Islamist, perhaps more than any other historian ideologue, the task of writing the nation would seem to be ongoing and far from complete. From the perspective of most of the national narratives considered in this essay, this Islamist "excess" will need to be acknowledged and, then, in some way or another, tempered and accommodated in the "Malaysia" story.

Historical Work/ Unfinished Business

Identifying possible future as well as current emplotments, commencing with Ileto's Philippines and then concentrating on a few examples of narratives of Malaya/Malaysia, we see how analysing national narratives helps to reveal the different elements of the "scaffolding of the nation-state": in Malaysia's case the plural society (balancing the divergent interests of communities having little in common), the experience of British colonialism, the "Malay" vision (including the archipelago-wide "Malay" vision) of radical nationalism, the autochthonous sovereignty of the sultanates, and the transcendent claims for the Islamic *umat*. Each of these issues, as will be evident by now, represents in one form or another, an unresolved tension in nation-making. Dissecting national narratives enhances the sense of the nation state as an ongoing and contested project, formulated and re-formulated over time, never permanently anchored, always vulnerable — a project in constant demand of attention, including that of the ideologue. What we also acquire, however, is a closer scrutiny of the actual ideological work of the national chronicler.

Just how critical this historical work happens to be, of course, will depend on historical context. We have seen that in Malaysia more than other Southeast Asian contexts the geographic, demographic, cultural and political substance of the intended nation-state was so unwieldy as to place a high premium on the task of writing the national narratives. For this reason it is surprising that the role of the Malaysian national historian has received so little recognition.

In this chapter I have not had room to explore in real detail — as Ileto has in his Philippines study — the relationship between the historian-ideologues and the political leaders of the country. The role of intellectuals and think-tanks in Malaysia has in fact been the subject of recent research,[70] and it would be fruitful to examine the relationship (of people and ideas) between specific historians and such political leaders as Tunku Abdul Rahman, Tun Razak and Dr. Mahathir. In general, a full-scale study of Malaysian national history writing should not only examine more texts than I have examined, but also investigate far more thoroughly the context in which they were written. I have done little more than allude to the significance of British colonialism (and its passing), the demographic structure of the country, the May 13 riots, the growing mainstream respectability of Malay radicalism, the rise of Islamism and so forth. Yet even in this preliminary survey of a small sample of national narratives, when we investigate the work of the historian-ideologues — proposing and defending such constructions as the "historic bargain", or one of the Malay nationalist emplotments we have considered — we have seen that they have to make sense of what has been happening, have to spell out what the nation-state entails in ways that will be understood and attractive to the local population. They must convince the "national" public that the territorial and perhaps ethnic scope of the state they support has a greater legitimacy than other counter proposals, and that in general the "national" type of social organization is more appropriate than alternative possibilities (monarchical, religious or any new concept of community) that may emerge.

The narrators need to be able to refine or modify their formulations to account for the often changing data at hand (the "social realities"). Their ideological work must be sensitive to context — especially, to the different types of alternative and competing projects that are specific to the would-be "national" community. In giving meaning to a novel nation-state, the question will always be asked: how is it possible to neutralize the potency of other different narratives that privilege competing forms of allegiance, organization and identity? How can one incorporate or negate powerful fears, desires and memories? How does the historian-ideologue cope with excess? Like other ideologues, he or she must deal with the particularities. The stakes are high, and we have seen how a number of histories — some seemingly commonplace school texts — not only help to disclose the "scaffolding" of modern Malaysia; they also exhibit a particular ideological skilfulness in narrative construction that is seldom valued by academic analysts, but crucially significant in the building of a nation-state.

NOTES

For assistance of various types with this chapter, the author would like to thank Tony Day, John Funston, Rey Ileto, Claire Milner, Craig Reynolds, Sharon Siddique and Wang Gungwu.

1   Kenichi Ohmae, *The End of the Nation-State: The Rise of Regional Economics* (New York: Free Press, 1995).
2   Wang Gungwu, "Political Heritage and Nation Building", *Journal of the Malaysian Branch of the Royal Asiatic Society (JMBRAS)* 73, no. 2 (2000): 5.
3   Harry G. Gelber, *Nations out of Empires: European Nationalism and the Transformation of Asia* (Basingstoke: Palgrave, 2001).
4   See, for example Robert Young, *White Mythologies: Writing History and the West* (London: Routledge, 1990).
5   Reynaldo Ileto, "Nation-Building: The Philippines", draft manuscript.
6   Caroline S. Hau, *Necessary Fictions: Philippine Literature and the Nation, 1946–1980* (Manila: Ateno de Manila Press, 2000), p. 7.
7   Ibid.
8   See, for example, Sunait Chutintaranond and Chris Baker, eds., *Recalling Local Pasts* (Chiang Mai: Silkworm Books, 2002). See also, Chris Baker, 'Introduction', in Prince Damrong Rajanubhab, *Our Wars with the Burmese* (Bangkok: White Lotus, 2001), pp. x–xxxix.
9   Gunter Bergerak, 25 September 1915, quoted in Bijage 4 of "Nota Over Tjipto Mangoenkoesoemo", MR 2198/1915, V 26 January, 1916/32, AMK, NADH. I am grateful to Professor R.E. Elson for this reference.
10 Taufik Abdullah, "Nation-Building: Indonesia", draft manuscript.
11 J.G. de Casparis, "Historical Writing on Indonesia (Early Period)", in *Historians of South East Asia*, edited by D.G.E. Hall (London: Oxford University Press, 1961), p. 148. See also Bambang Oetomo, "Some Remarks on Modern Indonesian History" in the same volume, p. 82.
12 R.O. Winstedt, *Kitab Tawarikh Melayu* (Singapore: Kelly and Walsh, 1921).
13 Za'ba, "Modern Developments" *JMBRAS* 17, no. 3 (1940): 151.
14 Ibid.
15 Republished as Za'ba, *Sejarah Ringkas Tanah Melayu* (Singapore: Pustaka Melayu, 1961).
16 I have discussed this issue in a preliminary way in *Kerajaan: Malay Political Culture on the Eve of Colonial Rule* (Tucson: University of Arizona Press, 1982). Among many other works on Malay approaches to History, see O.W. Wolters, *The Fall of Srivijaya in Malay History* (Ithaca: Cornell University Press, 1970).
17 Cheah Boon Kheng, *Malaysia: The Making of a Nation* (Singapore: Institute of Southeast Asian Studies, 2002).

18   Wang Gungwu, ed., *Malaysia: A Survey* (London: Pall Mall, 1964).
19   Noordin Sopiee, "The Development of an East Asian Consciousness", in *Living with Dragons*, edited by G. Sheridan (St. Leonards: Allen & Unwin, 1995), pp. 180–93; Anthony Milner, "What Happened to 'Asian Values' ", in *Towards Recovery in Pacific Asia*, edited by Gerald Segal and David S.G. Goodman (London and New York: Routledge, 2000), pp. 56–68.
20   Joginder Singh Jessy, *History of Malaya 1400–1949* (Penang: Peninsular Publications and United Book Company, 1964 orig. pub. 1961).
21   R.J. Wilkinson, "A History of the Peninsular Malays with chapters on Perak and Selangor", in R.J. Wilkinson, *Papers on Malay Subjects* (selected and introduced by P.L. Burns) (Kuala Lumpur: Oxford University Press, 1971), p. 118.
22   Cheah, *Malaysia*, p. 7.
23   Shamsul Baharin, *Malaya dan Tawanikh Dunia*, 3 volumes (Penang: Sinaran, 1962).
24   Wan Shamsuddin and Arena Wati, *Sejarah Tanah Melayu dan Sekitarnya 1400–1963* (Kuala Lumpur: Pustaka Antara, 1964).
25   Wang Gungwu, *Malaysia*, p. 16.
26   I examine this point of view in " 'Malayness'. Confrontation, Innovation and Discourse", in *Looking in Odd Mirrors: The Java Sea*, edited by V.J.H. Houben, H.M.J Maier and W. Van der Molen (Leiden: Rijksuniversiteit, 1992), pp. 43–59
27   John Funston, *Malay Politics in Malaysia. A Study of UMNO and PASS* (Kuala Lumpur: Heinemann, 1980), 223ff.
28   Frank Swettenham, *British Malaya* (London: John Lane. The Bodley Head, 1907)
29   Wilkinson, "History" (orig. pub. 1907).
30   Winstedt, *Kitab Tawarikh*.
31   Abdul Rahman Haji Ismail and Badriyah Haji Salleh, "History through the Eyes of the Malays", in *New Terrains in Southeast Asian History*, edited by Abu Talib Ahmad and Tan Liok Ee (Singapore: Singapore University Press, 2003), p. 186.
32   Virginia Matheson Hooker and M. B. Hooker, "Introduction", *John Leyden's Malay Annals* (Kuala Lumpur: Malaysian Branch of the Royal Asiatic Society, 2001), pp. 35–36.
33   Abdul Hadi bin Haji Hasan, *Sejarah Alam Melayu*, 3 volumes (Singapore: Malaya Publishing House, 1925–29). Khoo Kay Kim has commented: "This was Malay history which tended to cut across state boundaries because the author focussed on the existence of a Malay world and its glorious past"; *Malay Society: Transformation and Democratization* (Petaling Jaya: Pelanduk 1991), p. 287. The book was "used in Malay schools until the early 1950s"; Khoo Kay Kim, "Local Historians and the Writing of Malaysian History in the Twentieth Century" in

Perceptions of the Past in Southeast Asia, edited by A. Reid and D. Marr (Singapore: Heinemann, 1979), p. 305n33.

34 W.R. Roff, *The Origins of Malay Nationalism* (Kuala Lumpur: University of Malaya Press, 1967), pp. 222–26.

35 Maswari Rosdi and Suhara Salim, *Sejarah Malaysia Moden* (Kuala Lumpur: Adabi, 1987).

36 Khoo Boo Teik, *Paradoxes of Mahathirism* (Kuala Lumpur: Oxford University Press, 1996), 54ff.

37 Ibrahim Yaacob, *Sekitar Malaya Merdeka* (Djakarta: Kesatuan Malaya Merdeka, 1957).

38 Ahmad Boestaman, *Merintis Jalan ke Punchak* (Kuala Lumpur: Pustaka Kejora, 1972) The book is translated as *Carving the Path to the Summit*, translated with an introduction by W.R. Roff (Athens: Ohio University Press, 1979).

39 Tunku Abdul Rahman Putra, *Looking Back* (Kuala Lumpur: Pustaka Antara, 1977), p. 162.

40 Tan Sri Dato Mubin Sheppard, *Tunku. A Pictorial Biography 1903–1957* (Petaling Jaya: Pelanduk, 1984), p. 103.

41 Ibid, p. 117.

42 Ibid, p. 157.

43 Mahathir Mohamad, *The Challenge* (Pelanduk, 1995) p. 155.

44 Simon C. Smith, *British Relations with the Malay Rulers from Decentralisation to Malayan Independence 1930–1957* (Kuala Lumpur: Oxford University Press, 1995), Chapter 6; T.N. Harper, *The End of Empire and the Making of Malaya* (Cambridge: Cambridge University Press, 1999), pp. 343–43; Mohamad Noordin Sopiee, *From Malayan Union to Singapore Separation* (Kuala Lumpur: Penerbitan Universiti Malaya, 1974), 80ff.

45 See Anthony Milner, "How 'traditional' is Malaysian Monarchy" in *Malaysia: Islam, Society and Politics*, edited by Virginia Hooker and Norani Othman (Singapore: Institute of Southeast Asian Studies, 2003), Chapter 9.

46 Mohd. Zain Salah, *Keluarga Diraja Kelantan* (Kota Bahru: Musium Negeri Kelantan Istana Jahar, 1987), p. 14.

47 Muhammad Yusoff Hashim, *The Malay Sultanate of Melaka* (Kuala Lumpur: Dewan Bahasa dan Pustaka, 1992), p. 281.

48 See, for instance, Hj. Md. Sidin b. Hj. Md. Resad, *Asal Usul Alam Melayu* (Pinang: Sinaran, 1954); Omar Amin Husin, *Sejarah Bangsa dan Bahasa Melayu* (Kuala Lumpur: Pustaka Antara, 1962).

49 A, Rahman Muda, "Sekretariat Melayu yang Menatah Harapan", *Dewan Masyarakat*, May 1996, 38ff.

50 See, for instance, Ismail Hussain et al., eds. *Tamadun Melayu*, vol. 3 (Dewan

Bahasa dan Pustaka, 1995). See also Mohd. Taib Osman, ed., *Islamic Civilisation in the Malay World* (Kuala Lumpur: Dewan Bahasa dan Pustaka, 1997).

51 See, for instance, Azhar Hj. Mad Aros et al., eds., *Tamadun Islam dan Tamadun Asia (Titas)* (Shah Alam: Fajar Bakti, 2002), Part C: "Tamadun Melayu".

52 Milner, "Malaysian Monarchy", pp. 176–77.

53 Kassim Ahmad, ed., *Hikayat Hang Tuah* (Kuala Lumpur: Dewan Bahasa dan Pustaka, 1968), p. 1.

54 Cited in Milner, "Malaysian Monarchy", p. 176.

55 Ibid, p. 190.

56 Ibid, pp. 188–89.

57 Cited in Anthony Milner, *The Invention of Politics In Colonial Malaya* (Cambridge: Cambridge University Press, 2002), pp. 201–2.

58 Sa'ad Shukri bin Haji Muda, *Detik-detik Sejarah Kelantan* (Kota Bharu: Pustaka Aman, 1971), p. 5.

59 Ibid, p. 193.

60 Ibid, pp. 201–2.

61 Haji Bujong Adil, *Sejarah Johor* (Kuala Lumpur: Dewan Bahasa dan Pustaka, 1971), p. xiv. See also his *Sejarah Pahang* (Kuala Lumpur: Dewan Bahasa dan Pustaka, 1972), p. x.

62 Haji Muhammad Saleh bin Haji Awang (Misbaha), *Terengganu dari Bentuk Sejarah* (Kuala Lumpur: Utusan, 1978), p. vi.

63 Yusof bin Ali Al-Zawawi, Forward, in Misbaha, *Sejarah Trengganu* (Kuala Trengganu: Mansor, 1966). For further discussion of "local history" writing in Malaysia see Khoo Kay Kim, "Panji-panji Gemerlapan: Satu Pembicaraan Pensejarahan Melayu", in Mohd. Abu Bakar et al., *Historia: Essays in Commemoration of the 25th Anniversary of the Department of History, University of Malaya* (Kuala Lumpur: Malaysian Historical Society, 1984), pp. 175–92.

64 Azhar Hj. Mad Aros, *Tamadun.*

65 See, for example, Abu Bakar Abdullah, *Ke Arah Perlaksanaan Undang undang Islam di Malaysia: Masalah dan penyelesaiannya* (Kuala Trengganu: Pustaka Damai, 1981); Mahmood Zuhdi Hj. Abdullah Majid *Ke Arah Merealisasikan Undang undang Islam di Malaysia* (Sungei Tua: Thinker's Library, 1988).

66 Ismail Awang, *Adat Orang-orang Melayu yang bertentangan dengan Akidah Islam* (Kota Bharu: Pustaka Aman, 1983).

67 Mohd. Kamal Hassan, *Pendidikan dan Pembangunan* (Kuala Lumpur: Nurin, 1988); Sabri Salamon and Haron Din, *Masalah Pendidikan Islam di Malaysia* (Kuala Lumpur: Al-Rajmaniah, 1988).

68 Abdul Rahman Haji Abdullah, *Pemikiran Islam Masa Kini* (Kuala Lumpur: Dewan Bahasa dan Pustaka, 1987); Siddiq Fadil, *Kebangkitan Umat* (Kuala Lumpur:

Yayasan Dakwah Islamiah Malaysia, 1978).

69 Funston, *Malay Politics*, pp. 121–22; Mokhtar Petah, *Zulkifli Muhammad dalam Kenangan* (Kota Bahru: Pustaka Aman, 1966).

70 Johnson, D.A., "The Malaysian Intellectual: In Thought and Context", Ph.D. thesis, Australian National University, 2002.

CHAPTER SEVEN

Writing Malaysia's Contemporary History

Lee Kam Hing

A RECENT DISCUSSION on nation-building in Southeast Asia steered participants to look into the broader questions of what indeed is the region's contemporary history and how it should be approached. It is striking, as Professor Wang Gungwu has noted, that the early study of nation-building has been done largely by political scientists and not by historians. If the process of nation-building in the region is still on-going, as is generally acknowledged, and if the study of nation-building then is considered as falling within contemporary history, it may then be asked whether historians are able to offer an approach that is new or different from what have been applied so far by social scientists.[1]

The historian distinguishes his work by an adoption of a narrative form. This presentation of an unfolding of events requires the searching and collection of data, critical evaluation of evidence, and assembling them into a coherent and accurate account. The historian retrieves facts that are of historical significance and draws attention to these in his careful and accurate recording of what happened. More importantly, the historian offers chronological depth in explaining and analysing features and issues that may be contemporary or otherwise. The product stands, at the least, as a faithful and well-documented chronicle of a particular period of the past.[2] It is upon the historian's detailed and well ordered data that many social scientists eventually draw upon for comparative studies across time and place.

The historian, however, goes beyond a narration of the sequence of events. He may suggest how the distant past continues to have an influence on his unfolding story and might discover that amidst the changes taking place today are elements of continuity. Among these enduring features are ideas and institutions that have survived the past and have, in modified forms perhaps, persisted to shape events in contemporary history. Furthermore, the historian is sharply aware that how the country's past is recalled and reconstructed has a bearing on the thrust and direction of nation-building. Nowhere is this most evident than in the drawing up of school history syllabus which is seen as an essential strategy in inculcating a sense of loyalty and patriotism.

Thus far the number of published works on Malaysia's contemporary history are few. Several general histories do bring the story right up to very recent times. There are, for example, monographs on the immediate post-World War Two reconstruction period and the Emergency years. But large areas of Malaysia's recent history have yet to be researched into.

One of the areas in contemporary Malaysian history that presents great scope for research and writing is biographical studies. Serious and scholarly attention on the lives and times of early leaders who played major roles in recent history has still to receive adequate and scholarly attention. Published titles on the less prominent leaders representing various interest groups and non-state organizations are even sparser. Well-researched biographical studies offers a most promising and yet challenging area of contemporary Malaysian history. The lives of leaders and of ordinary Malaysians is a story of the times they lived through. It provides colour and texture which becomes a helpful context for others more interested in political policies and economic programmes. Until then, evaluation of the politics and policies of prime ministers and other political leaders is difficult.

The case of Dato Hussein Onn, the third prime minister, illustrates this point. Reports so far of him is mixed. He is depicted in some news reports and general studies as authoritarian and repressive. Other studies portray him as timid and indecisive. These assessments arose because earlier he had been undecided as to who he would appoint as deputy prime minister and that during his administration there was a spate of detentions under the Internal Security Act. Yet records also noted his determination to prosecute Dato Harun Idris, a very influential UMNO leader then on corruption charges, declaring a state of Emergency in Kelantan to resolve the problem of PAS within the ruling coalition, and insisting on revised quota for university admission against the sentiments of sections within his party. Certainly the circumstances and the man himself is more complex as to deserve several fuller and more careful research in order to arrive at a confident judgement of him. Such studies on the prime ministers are urgent since they are initiators of so much of the policies and thrust of nation-building.

This neglect of biographies extends even to the histories of major political institutions and organizations. There are very few histories of the larger and more important political parties. Surprisingly, full historical studies of UMNO, the DAP, and PAS have yet to appear. Even less attention has been shown to smaller ones such as the Labour Party and the Parti Rakyat. A major difficulty in research into Malaysian party histories is that the passage of time has made retrieval of information, much of these often being of back-room manoeuvrings and therefore mainly non-documented, even more difficult. There is also the political parties' reluctance to delve into past periods of fractious splits which could stir unhappy and what they deem as unproductive memories. Effort is required to gain the trust of political parties in order to gain co-operation and access to sources. Efforts to fill these research gaps are now being made at the universities, and some of the graduation exercises and theses are of promising quality.

The proximity to events may be one reason why so little has been written on Malaysia's contemporary history. Events are too recent to allow for deep reflection and analysis. It is also not easy to adopt detachment and distance to evaluate the often fast tempo of developments that had taken place. Conclusions and interpretation arrived at are sometimes overtaken by opening of new documentary records or disclosure of fresh information. Former participants are still around and out of respect to sensitivities, there is usually reluctance to open up issues and episodes which might be of embarrassment to them.

There is also the matter of materials. Access to official records is still difficult. The Colonial Office records in London on Malaysia are helpful up to about 1963 but new sources, particularly those of the Malaysian Government, have yet to be made available. Cabinet papers and those in the Prime Minister's Office are not opened to researchers yet. Published government reports such as those of Bank Negara and the Finance Ministry have proved fairly useful particularly in tracking economic performance of the country. But the twenty-five year ruling on opening of departmental files as well as the effects of the Official Secrets Act offer little prospect of a rich corpus of primary materials ready for the use of historical analysis. Furthermore, non-state records such as those of the chambers of commerce as well as of voluntary associations are still largely unavailable, unorganized, and their quality unknown.

The memory and recollection of those who participated in events that were turning points in the country's recent past have largely still to be retrieved and recorded although the national archives has made some efforts in that direction. Few of those who took part in recent momentous events have kept diaries or private papers. So much has been lost, and the war years especially have resulted in the destruction of valuable private and officials papers that could have helped to explain or to provide fuller account of recent history.

Newspapers remain an easily available source to help document recent Malaysian history in a systematic and chronological manner. Accounts of journalists may lack the analytical depth and balance. Often, they reflect the bias of the authorities or the papers' owners. But still, only the newspapers carry daily reports of happenings in the country as well as the speeches of leaders. At the least, these accounts set a straightforward chronicling of events. The historian could still cull useful data out of them and this could go towards giving some insight into official thinking. Publications belonging to critics and opposition, to some extent, can correct the deficiencies of mainstream media.

Newspapers, as a source, highlight the language requirements of researchers covering a multi-ethnic society such as Malaysia. Fujio Hara in his study of the Malaysian Chinese Association showed how important

Chinese documents and newspapers are as references. He pointed out that Henry Gurney, the British High Commissioner is generally regarded as the man who was responsible for getting Chinese leaders to set up a Chinese organization as an alternative to the Malayan Communist Party. However, Hara pointed out that even before Gurney's move, Chinese newspapers had carried reports of the various initiatives taken by influential Chinese to form the MCA. Hence, the voice of the different communities in this nation-building process can only be captured through their press and publications.

This present paucity of studies on contemporary history poses difficulties for historians. Lacking a broad and detailed canvas of Malaysia's contemporary history and without complete access to documents, the historian venturing into the field finds it difficult to set his subject against a perspective that has width and depth. Without biographies of the leading personalities, it is difficult to locate the thoughts that went into shaping the country's recent political developments. Without study of the organizations, it is not possible to determine how the broader society was mobilized. On nation-building and of the men who provided direction, the historian must be able to draw upon a rich and diverse body of literature to offer a more nuanced and multi-layered analysis.

Proximity to events must, in fact, be a reason why there should be historians willing to engage in the study of the contemporary history of Malaysia. Such historians, present in the politics of their times, have knowledge of the key players, organizations, and the issues to an extent that a scholar of a much latter age will not have. Such a historian senses the swift shift of events, of varying mood, and of nuances in statements and sentiments of his time not captured in a document or a newspaper report. He has access to participants and even of materials which, over time, may be lost or irretrievable. This is particularly important in Malaysia where memoir writing has still to be widely practised. A well-written contemporary history is also a commentary of the period for this will reflect the thoughts of the writer as a product of his times. The biographies and histories written today will be a voice to the future. This, as well as the data assembled, is what later historians build upon.

The Beginning of Contemporary History

One of the first tasks in embarking on a study of contemporary history is in marking out the period. G. Barraclough held that "contemporary history begins when the problems which are actual in the world today first take visible shape". It is "a distinct period of time, with characteristics of its own which mark it off from the preceding period".[3] This delineation is not easy in Malaysia as is also the case elsewhere. So many ideas and institutions that are important today have virtually a seamless connection to the past. The multi-ethnic character of society, the changing status of the monarchy, and resurgence of Islam for example could be traced back over several centuries.

Using nationalism and nation-building as a theme might help define a more specific and separate period for Malaysian contemporary history. No other topic so dominated the thinking as well as of events in recent years. It is also sufficiently broad to cover a wide range of important concerns. Nation-building, being not only about politics, encompasses social, cultural, and economic aspects of an evolving process. It also provides a confluence or meeting point where the different forces operating within Malaysian society responded to.

But the narrative of nation-building is multi-layered and the task of the historians is in peeling these out in his analysis. There is, for instance, the difficulty in distinguishing ambition driven more by party or personal interests than from commitment to nation-building. Symbols and rhetoric of nation-building are often wielded to couch less elevated intentions. Narrow communal sentiments are thinly veiled with nationalist goals to mobilize electoral support. Yet those seeking power, positions, and patronage could well have some adherence, perhaps of varying degree, to nation-building.

If nation-building is understood, as often suggested, to be a conscious effort to create a sense or an "imagining" of a nation among the citizens in Malaysia, it is the debates among the major communities as to the kind of nation they aspire that one could use as a start to the study of nation-building and also of Malaysian contemporary history. The Second World War then has often been taken as a significant event to mark the beginning of de-colonization and the creation of a new nation. The military reverses of

Western powers encouraged Malayans to believe that a new political order was possible.

But it could be pointed out that many of the thoughts among political activists concerning the impending nation had in fact taken shape long before World War II and the ideas quickened in the immediate post-war when leaders of the different communities sensed the possibility of accelerated political change. Scholars can point to the important strands of Malay nationalism and Chinese political consciousness of the early decades of the twentieth century and that these remained influential right up to the independence period. Discernable in these emerging expression of early nationalism were elements of Islam, socialism and communism. Individuals and groups used these to formulate a nation-state which they believed could carry out programmes to uplift their communities. Pre-war radical political activities, for instance, laid the groundwork for the communist challenge to the British in the late 1940s and it was the communist insurrection of 1948 that remained in the Malaysian political consciousness for a long time.

The legacy of the past weighed heavily in the early discussion on independence and nation-building. How the different communities viewed their past as they tried to define the nation they wanted was reflected in the different arguments during the 1956 to 1957 constitutional negotiations. Each side believed history as lending authority to the political demands of their communities. The Malays saw the country's history as of early antiquity, tracing it back to the fifteenth century Malacca sultanate. The Malays envisaged political independence then as a return to historical continuity and therefore to past and future political preeminence. The Malacca sultanate provides the symbols for the new state with Hang Tuah and Tun Perak evoked as cultural heroes. It was this history, a distinctive culture, and a sense of solidarity of the archipelago people upon which the idea of *Bangsa Melayu* had evolved.

For many Malay nationalists, history was also a cautionary tale. The lesson from history is that disunity among the Malays allowed the West to colonize them. The coming of the West was seen as having led to the loss of Malay political power and a decline in economic welfare. Colonialism also brought a large influx of immigrants who consolidated a strong position in the economy and able thereby to compete for political power. It was important then that the Malays be united, and this became a regular clarion call even after independence. Historical memory then was to create communal cohesiveness, to rally support for UMNO and its leaders, and to warn the nation to be on guard against foreign interference.

For the non-Malays, their understanding of the country's past goes back to the mid-nineteenth century. The arrival of the British and immigrants during this period was seen as the start of modern Malaysia and the beginning of all the modern institutions.[4] They see the opening of tin mines and rubber estates as key to early economic development, a process which they were part of. Upon this was based their expectation to parity of rights. This interpretation of Malaysian history yields its own cultural figures such as Yap Ah Loy and Loke Yew.[5]

Tan Liok Ee in her study argued that *Bangsa Melayu* or Malay nation was consciously developed through this historical understanding. *Bangsa* has the culture of *Melayu* as its core and seeks to assert dominance by insisting that all citizens embrace this definition. The Chinese, on the other hand, saw themselves as a *minzu* or community. The *minzu* was culturally defined while the nation was a political construct. The Chinese *minzu* claims equal status with other *minzu* within a nation. In such an understanding, the culture and language of the *minzu* are protected within the political framework of a nation.[6]

But a desire to gain early independence persuaded elites of all sides to compromise on the contentious issues. The inter-ethnic negotiation produced what has now become popularly referred to as the social contract. This has been described variously as a bargain, an agreement, or an understanding of what the rights and interests of the various communities were. The basic meaning of the social contract provided for Malay political preeminence while assuring continued and unhindered non-Malay commercial opportunities. The "contract" is elaborated subsequently to include Malay special rights in exchange for granting of citizenship to non-Malays on liberal conditions.

It is not clear if the social contract was accepted by participants in the discussion, including the non-Malays, as providing for Malay political dominance or that the new nation should be a Malay state as suggested by some observers today. Such views would have to account for leaders such as Tunku Abdul Rahman and Tan Cheng Lock who were men influenced by the notion of democracy and equality, and of the fundamental rights of the individual. The non-Malays accepted provisions in the contract as temporary measures to correct prevailing imbalances in economic, social, and educational positions. Tan Cheng Lock in 1949 declared that "the people of Malaya can only constitute a nationality if the different communities making up its mixed population are united among themselves by common sympathies and fellow-feeling and reconcile themselves to living together in peace and harmony under equal rights and laws."[7]

The architecture of today's largely ethnic based politics has probably obscured the alternative visions of the nation that were non-communal. There is a risk that historians read the UMNO and Malay dominance of today into the discussions held during the period of political transition. Among the alternative visions was one presented in 1948 by the Putera-All-Malayan Council of Joint Action which attempted to forge links among different ideological and ethnic groups. It questioned the narrower definition of nation held then by UMNO. This was an early expression of Malayan nationalism supported by Malay radicals.

If nation-building eventually took a route of increasing Malay dominance in the form it assumes today, that was certainly not anticipated or accepted by all at the start. Rather, there was agreement among early leaders that the agenda in nation-building was to promote unity of the people and to inculcate a sense of a common identity, to push for economic development so as to reduce poverty and social distance, and to have an independent Malaysia take its place in a community of nations. Attaining all these would create conditions of social and political stability, and thereby ensure prospects of greater freedom and rights for all.

In the implementation of the nation-building agenda there were divergent views. There were those who wanted a strong and interventionist role for the state. Others, particularly non-Malays, preferred a minimalist and less intrusive government. In the years that followed, the dynamics and discourse of Malaysian politics centred largely on the evolving and expanding role of a powerful state.

Malay nationalists looked to the state to implement a common language and a uniform education system as a first and necessary step towards nation-building. They argued that only through Malay culture and language would there be created coming generations of young Malaysians having shared outlook and identity. An even more interventionist state was sought by Malays who believed that the economic imbalance and social disparity existing then was a hindrance to unity and nation-building in Malaysia. It was a view influenced by a perception that the past was a cause of the weak economic position of the Malays. Given the resulting absence of a strong and independent entrepreneurial class, Malays looked to the state to advance their economic position. Some Malays saw historical justification for this particularly in the distant, pre-colonial past which they nostalgically depicted as one where the ruler owned all economic activities and was protector of his *rakyat*.

Non-Malays, on the other hand, were worried about too strong a role for the state and preferred a *laissez-faire* approach. They were particularly apprehensive that if the state regulated the economy too much in order to address imbalances in equity and participation among the ethnic groups, costs of business would go up and economic opportunities restricted.[8]

The Malays and the non-Malays also differed in their expectation of the state's role in religion. The Malays see Islam closely associated with the traditional state. The sultan was the centre of Islamic knowledge and he occupied the apex of the religious hierarchy. With the coming of colonialism which resulted in the state being controlled by a non-Muslim power, the *ummah* became weak and divided. It is contended by some Muslims that freedom for the individual is possible only in a free community, and that such a community is free when it exists within a society untainted by idolatry or foreign divisive forces. Religious freedom has come to mean unity of the *ummah* where only one God is worshipped and where the *ummah* dominates society. The state has to protect the community of believers against external threat that could oppress. Through attaining freedom and fulfillment of religion for the *ummah*, the state reaches its perfection. On the other hand, non-Muslims came from societies which were generally secular in character. Non-Malays such as the Christians place strong emphasis on the individual as the subject of true faith. There is separation of religion and the state, and religious liberty is freedom from state interference of private belief and practice.[9]

Change and Challenge

The constitution that was agreed upon in 1957 set out a secular and multi-ethnic nation. It provided for special status of the Malays and safeguarded the rights of non-Malays. Nevertheless, the terms in the constitution did not please all sides. Non-Malays contended that the state was too Malay while Malay nationalists were aggrieved that their aspiration were not fully met within the proposed format of a multi-ethnic society. And already then, Islamic groups were beginning to call for the implementation of religious laws. In the years after independence, the character of the new nation was questioned. The debates led to tension, the splitting away of Singapore, and a bout of racial violence.

The need to respond to the aspirations of the different communities and maintaining an acceptable inter-ethnic balance was therefore a challenge to nation-building. The process has led to a concentration of power in the executive, particularly the prime minister and resulting in what some scholars described as a semi-democratic or soft authoritarism political system in Malaysia.[10]

The semi-democratic style of government has been defended on grounds of stability and order. This has also been explained against a background of feudalism and colonial experience during which power was concentrated in the ruling class. Memory of inter-ethnic violence in the immediate post-period and a communist insurrection has also led the elite not to trust a completely free and open political system. Such a system, they argue, could be misused to threaten the security and stability of the nation. They were also of the view that the inter-ethnic equilibrium is too finely poised and fragile to cope with unrestrained public debate. Issues deemed too sensitive have therefore to be resolved behind closed doors. But this risks having the direction of nation-building being decided without full consultation among the leaders of the inter-ethnic coalition or broad consensus of the people. The declaration in late September 2001 of Malaysia as an Islamic state is cited as an example.

The administration of Malaysia's first four prime ministers could be studied as a distinct phase of nation-building and of contemporary history. For Tunku Abdul Rahman, the first prime minister, the task was to weld together an inter-ethnic coalition and to negotiate independence for the country. The approach taken was to build unity through a national language and a common education. But unity among the different communities remained fragile. The second prime minister saw the prevailing social and economic disparity among the various races as a cause for this lack of social cohesion and therefore embarked upon a re-structuring of society. The New Economic Policy was introduced and seen as fundamental to the nation-building process. It was a programme continued by the third prime minister, Hussein Onn. The fourth prime minister, Dr. Mahathir, pursued NEP-like goals such as promoting a Malay capitalist class and Malaysian-owned large scale enterprises, embarked on heavy industrialization, privatization, and offered a new vision of a Malaysian nation.

This period of nation-building witnessed the transfer of power from London to Kuala Lumpur, the introduction of modern political institutions and a bureaucracy, the ending of an insurgency that was costly, the maintenance of territorial integrity in a Malaysia enlarged in 1963, *Konfrontasi* with Indonesia and the Philippines, construction of impressive physical infrastructure, economic growth through industrialization and export, and the dramatic reduction of absolute poverty and an increase in per capita income.[11] In this period of contemporary history there are also the broad trends of change. Some of these can be noted through observing of key features in society and a tracking of their development over the period under study. This, however, may not be easy for the historian who must then turn to the research findings of other disciplines. All these serve as a context within which nation-building in Malaysia can be studied.

By the end of Dr. Mahathir's administration, it could be claimed that there had been put in place a number of essential institutions to integrate a diverse community of people. There have been significant changes in Malaysian politics to encourage an optimism that there will be greater acceptance in society of common goals and symbols of nation-building. There is now a national educational system at all levels. Since independence the number of schools and universities have greatly increased. Proportionately, more young people are now in tertiary education. In addition, there is the introduction and development of Malay medium education. An entire generation of Malaysians, including those attending the national-type schools in Chinese, is educated almost entirely in Malay and fluent in that language. They have also been brought up with a Malaysian-oriented curriculum.

Nation-building in Malaysia has been accompanied by high economic growth. There is construction of infrastructure such as ports, airports, and highways that has facilitated development. Malaysia, in particular, also benefited from large inflow of foreign direct investments and transfer of technology. The economy of the country has progressed impressively from largely agriculture towards one that is industrial and service based. Exports of manufactures goods are driving economic growth. Malaysia is seeking in the coming years to move into a digital and knowledge-based economy.

The economic growth of the country strengthen and legitimizes the government, provides it with resources to gain political support, and contributes to stability and social order. The standard of living has improved and there is greater prosperity than before independence. Malaysians see themselves as better-off than most other countries emerging out of colonialism. They see as an indicator of this in the entry of thousands of immigrants in search of work and better opportunities. The Kuala Lumpur Petronas Twin Towers, the national car project, the F-1 races, and its futuristic-like Multi-media Super Corridor are not only a source of pride but also give confidence to its people that the country will continue to move ahead.

Ethnic concerns have since become less divisive than in the early years of independence. Racial divisions remain but communal issues are not driving the political discourse in the 1990s. There is a broader common ground within which the various ethnic groups are working together. And while major parties remain ethnic-based there are token gestures to open up membership including UMNO accepting non-Muslim *bumiputra* in Sabah and Sarawak. The major opposition political parties such as PAS, Keadilan, and the DAP in programmes are non-communal. Issues such as re-introducing English as a medium of instruction, national service and meritocracy once deemed controversial issues are now openly discussed and even accepted. It shows a society confident in its inter-ethnic relations.

This continued acceptance of a multi-ethnic society for nation-building is an achievement of the first four prime ministers. The view that the multi-ethnic character of society is a hindrance to nation-building has since been reworked to one that sees strength in diversity. Celebration of the different community's festivals through open-houses are embraced as a distinct Malaysian feature. Leaders now take pride in the plural character of the nation and they are further encouraged when overseas leaders praise Malaysia as a model for other nations with troubled experience in racial experiment. There is also a realization that a condition of multi-ethnic harmony is necessary for continued inflow of foreign investments.

That ethnicity is less a defining factor in political debate is also an outcome of the social and economic transformation that the country has undergone. Through affirmative action and expansion of educational opportunities, a large Malay middleclass is created and one that is more urbanized. Social and economic restructuring under the NEP has corrected the major income and occupation imbalances between Malays and Chinese that gave rise to racial tensions in the past. Where they were once a minority, Malays now dominate the public service and many sectors of profession. The NEP has created a large Malay corporate and middleclass which share the experience and expectation of the non-Malays.

Mahathir made an effort to develop a Malay middleclass able to compete not only locally but also overseas. Khoo Boo Teik suggested that this ambitious effort could be viewed either as a nationalist project driven by capitalist impulses or that of a capitalist project imbued with nationalist aspiration. It could also be interpreted as the continuing dynamics of Malay nationalism which having been expressed within the borders, is seeking a global profile. Globalization offers new challenge and opportunity, and it is the intention to create a new Malay capable of global achievements. And hence the effort to build up Malay tycoons and Malay international business. Indeed, only when these elements were finally in place, particularly where there is a Malay middleclass capable of competing with the non-Malays, did the Malay leadership felt confident about a multi-ethnic society.

There are the demographic changes. The country's population has grown from 5 million in 1957 to 23 million today. At the time of Malaysia's independence no ethnic group was overwhelmingly the majority. It was this finely balanced ethnic ratio that influenced the terms of the political bargain reached. Since then the Malay population has grown at a rate faster than the other groups. In 1974 the Malays for the first time formed more than 50 per cent of the population and today it is 60 per cent. This, together with the electoral weightage that favours rural Malay constituencies, has resulted in smaller non-Malay parliamentary representation, and even in Kuala Lumpur half the parliamentary seats are Malay majority. There is also the presence of a very large number of Indonesian and Filipino immigrants where estimates put it at more than a million, many of whom have become permanent residents. These have implications on population balance and therefore of new power equilibrium and direction in nation-building.

Non-Malays are now politically a minority and unlikely to seek combative politics along ethnic lines. The MCA which was a founder member of the ruling Alliance, now Barisan Nasional, cannot even claim the fiction of political parity. Even the post of opposition leader, long held by a non-Malay, passed on to PAS' parliamentary leader after the 1999 elections. Nevertheless, while the political balance has tilted towards the Malays, the views of other communities have been heeded. But while the non-Malays may not be politically large enough to have all their demands considered, they are significant enough to insist that their important concerns such as education, language and business participation be taken into account.

The political and economic climate has become more accommodating to Chinese interests since 1987 when Mahathir liberalized and deregulated state involvement in the economy in efforts to pull the country out of the recession. Growth and income-raising policies over income redistribution programmes are emphasized. And while policies aimed at creating a dynamic *bumiputra* commercial and industrial class are still pursued, Chinese business have benefited from the large inflows of foreign investments in the period between 1987 and 1997. The area of small and medium-size enterprises offer opportunities for strong Chinese participation. And with the Malay political constituency today deeply divided, non-Malay support is pivotal and therefore courted.

There are the external forces that exert upon the political process in Malaysia and influencing the course of nation-building. External factors, particularly the Cold War, created conditions that aided rapid economic development. More specifically, rising commodity prices during the Korean War provided resources to the Malaysian Government to battle the Emergency. Again it was improved revenue from commodity exports that enabled a relatively painless restructuring of the economy under the NEP.

Ben Anderson argued that the Southeast Asian region benefited from the United States' Cold War largesse as Washington sought to hold the line against communism.[12] Also, with communist China closed to Japan, Tokyo expanded its trade and investment to Southeast Asia including Malaysia. Thus for most of the post-war period, Southeast Asia benefited from the presence of the world's two largest economies, that of the United States and Japan. The Cold War also isolated China from playing a significant economic role that could have been in competition with Southeast Asia. Increased investments from Japan in the 1980s and from Korea and Taiwan in the 1990s assisted the industrialization drive of Malaysia. Malaysian businessmen are today plugged into this expanding network of regional and international trade. However, Malaysia has also been alert to a China now opening up its economy. Developing trade with new regions such as China and the Middle East creates new opportunities and allow local businessmen to expand their business. It is prepared to see China as a partner rather than a threat and this policy overrides initial apprehension arising from domestic inter-ethnic relations. The broadening of Malaysia's economic and diplomatic horizons encourage a widening of perspective beyond narrow communal issues. These shift attention and interest of Malaysians beyond the narrow domestic concerns that are liable to be divisive.

This energetic engagement in international economy and diplomacy serves as a further basis in the nation-building process. In adjusting to an evolving regional and international politics, Malaysia has moved towards a more independent and assertive posture. Mahathir gave voice to Malaysia in international forums and the country joined in United Nations peace-keeping roles. He had since set nation-building against the broader international context.

Under Mahathir this international role is to secure for Malaysian and Malay Muslims a rightful and respected place in international forum. All these instil a sense of pride among its people. There is memory of an age of the sultanates when the Malay world was an emporium of world commerce in spices and much later, as producer of tin and rubber vital to an industrializing world. More than that, it was a regional centre of Islamic learning and expansion. Today leaders seek to recover some of that past role by enhancing the status of Malaysia in the Islamic world, its international standing as a nation of moderate Islam, and its success in multi-ethnic experiment.

Globalization and increased international trade, while opening up opportunities, also pose challenges to nation-building. The risks of a broader engagement in the international economy was underlined when there was a global recession in the mid-1980s and Mahathir had to rescind some of the NEP conditions in order to stimulate both local and foreign investments. Then there was the regional financial crisis of 1997/98 that led to an economic and political crisis in the country. These underlined how vulnerable the economies of nation-states, including those of Malaysia, are to larger international forces.

But the events following the financial crisis is illustrative also of the shift Malaysian politics has taken. The severe recession in 1997 which saw the collapse of companies, pull-out of foreign investors, and loss of jobs did not lead to any communal tension as might have been feared in an earlier period. The results of the NEP was a positive contributing factor for this.

But Mahathir in attacking currency speculators and foreign economic threat whom he blamed for the sharp ringgit depreciation, successfully turned the crisis into a rally for unity and support from Malaysians. In turn, the Chinese responded to the crisis by launching a Love Malaysia Buy Malaysia campaign. It was a show of support for Mahathir's leadership and an opportunity for the Chinese to demonstrate their patriotism.

No less significant has been the part played by mainstream and alternative media in nation-building. The role of the media in promoting a national identity and in nation-building should be evaluated. Until the introduction of satellite television and the internet, the state had almost a monopoly of the media through which news and entertainment were disseminated. They helped, for instance, popularize the cry of *Malaysia Boleh* [Malaysia Can] when Malaysian competitors are treated either with unalloyed pride by supporters or cynicism by critics.

There are also alternative sources of nation-building. These compete with and complement the state. There have therefore been new arts, literature, and the theatre such as Instant Café which offer new expression and interpretation of national identity and integration. These have extended the parameters of social consciousness of ordinary citizens and encouraged new voices that have a bearing on state policies and action. Large numbers of young Malaysians especially Malays have been sent overseas to study and this has ensured a diversity of educational exposure. Technological transformation in this digital and IT age has rendered not only economies borderless but also culture and information. Satellite television, while threatening to homogenize culture and even life-style, has at the same time encouraged cultural plurality in states like Malaysia which once monopolized information and entertainment. This new technology has in recent years spawned alternative media such as the Internet.

The process of nation-building has also been reflected in the rewriting of the country's history. More than just the desire to expunge colonial reminders and to install in their place features appropriate to the new nation-state is the effort to have a more Malaysian-centric history. At the same time the lives and deeds of men and women who fought for the ideals of communities or the nation were held up as worthy to be honoured. Portraits of national heroes emerge from accounts of national struggle and from the collective memory. This use of national heroes is more immediately evident in the replacing of road or town names that were colonial in origin with nationalist ones. This was followed by revision of school text and curriculum.

Seeking to establish a history and a gallery of national heroes has not been uncontroversial in Malaysia, and the exercise has been entangled in the politics of the country. Attention is now given to retrieving the history of indigenous society and people. There is the question of integrating the story of immigrant communities and of new regions such as Sabah and Sarawak into the Malaysian story.

The retrieval of heroes from history or the recasting of figures from the past reflects changing values and attitudes particularly among the Malays in the years since independence. This was most striking in the early 1970s when younger Malays revised their views of Hang Tuah and Hang Jebat of the fifteenth century Malacca sultanate. Hang Tuah had for long been extolled for his quality of absolute loyalty to the ruler while Hang Jebat was depicted as a traitor for going against the sultan. In the early 1970s of Malay student activism and criticisms of the establishment, Hang Jebat emerged as the new Malay hero while Hang Tuah was seen as a defender of an old order.

The fate of modern leaders is reflected in the rewriting of history. The Tunku, the target of much later criticism found that his nation-building role was ignored among sections of the Malays after he retired as prime minister in 1971, and later he was aggrieved that no reference of his independence role was made in a history book that was used in Malaysian schools.[13] The fallen hero is both a political reality and a historical construction, and this loss of support underlines the political difficulty of trying to be both a Malay and a national leader. In becoming a national leader, a prime minister risks accusation of betraying the community as he balances competing ethnic demands. The Tunku was not the only Malay leaders to encounter a fall from grace in the community's esteem. So did Dato Onn Jaafar, and after the case of the Tunku, Dato Hussein Onn and Dr. Mahathir all suffered a drop in popularity within their community.

The End of Contemporary History

The retirement of Dr. Mahathir probably marks the end of one phase of nation-building and of Malaysia's contemporary history. The life and political career of Mahathir overlapped with much of this period of contemporary history. Mahathir was a young student in the immediate post-war years and wrote letters to the press as C.H.E. Det.[14] He debated with Lee Kuan Yew in the Malaysian Malaysia years, was a critic of the Tunku in the 1960s, a cabinet member in the administrations of Razak and Hussein Onn, and then became prime minister. He served for almost half the time of Malaysia's independence and left what is likely to be the widest impact on the country. More than that, Dr. Mahathir's career embodied the transition in nation-building. The political era of Dr. Mahathir extended beyond his own generation of political leaders. There were those ahead of Mahathir such as Dato Onn Jaafar, Tunku Abdul Rahman, and Tun Tan Cheng Lock. Then there were those almost contemporaneous to him such as Tun Hussein Onn, Lim Chong Eu and Tan Chee Khoon. They expressed their hopes of a new nation. Some of these were later taken up by Dr. Mahathir in his policies and in the vision he came to articulate in *Bangsa Malaysia*.

The recording of the lives of these men and women will add further to the narrative of what happened over the last forty-five years. And this offers a valuable area of contemporary studies that deserves attention. The life and times of Tan Chee Khoon, once described as Mr Opposition, as an example will give a perspective of a non-Malay and an opposition leader. Interestingly, his take-off point in Malaysian politics was not too different from that of Dr. Mahathir.

Dr. Tan entered parliament in the same year as Dr. Mahathir did after the 1964 elections. Like Mahathir, Tan was active at the University of Malaya in Singapore in the immediate post-war years. They, as with others such as James Puthucheary and John Eber, were already seeking to shape the future of Malaya. They lived through momentous times and sensed the significance of events taking place around them. They also had a quiet confidence that they were destined to play meaningful and decisive roles in the independence and nation-building process.

In the 1960s amidst the loud ethnic rhetoric of his times, Tan came out as one of the few moderate forces. Tan spoke out against those in his Labour Party whom he described as extremists for making unreasonable demands in a multi-ethnic society. He was fully conscious of the fine equilibrium of balancing Malay assertion of political dominance and of non-Malay insistence on parity. He put across his views in parliament and subsequently in a regular newspaper column. He belonged to a disappearing generation of Malaysians who entered politics out of a sense of public duty. Tan's style gained him acceptance among those even in UMNO. He came to be accepted by many non-Malays and Malays as a voice of reason in the quest of a truly Malaysian outlook. His story will be a counterpoint to that of the prime minister and as one on the outside.

The retirement of Tan from politics represented a shift in generational outlook. The Tan Cheng Lock and the Tan Chee Khoon type has since been replaced in the 1970s by mostly those who see politics as a career or a step towards rewards. There are still those from the old clan-association but they are no longer in the mainstream of politics.

Prime Minister Mahathir himself signified a shift in social origin of new political elites. While the first three prime ministers were linked to the royal courts, Dr. Mahathir has a commoner background. In his times, a new urban Malay middle-class, professionally trained, is replacing the aristocrat-bureaucratic led UMNO party supported by rural Malays and mainly *guru*. UMNO today reflects in membership and leadership the new Malay middle and professional class that Mahathir had a major part in creating.

This generational shift within the Malay community is marked by three occasions of mass Malay political protest, all of which had major political repercussions. Significantly, as noted by Khoo Boo Teik, Mahathir was situated within all three events. He was a young nationalist in Singapore during the opposition to the Malay Union in 1946 that led to the formation of UMNO. He was a Member of Parliament and an UMNO leader when the May 1969 riots occurred and Malay anger was directed against the Tunku. In the third mass Malay protest in 1998 he was prime minister and this time he was himself the target of strong criticisms.

The third Malay mass protest directed against Mahathir signified the success and the failings of Mahathir's efforts in nation-building. Mahathir who served as leader for almost half the time of Malaysia's independence, without doubt, left a major impact and a legacy. But the 1998 crisis expressed the alienation of a generation of young Malays many of whom grew up in the years of Mahathir's premiership and the product of his policies. Critics point out that over the years since independence there has evolved a bureaucracy-party-corporate tripartite that wielded most influence in state policies. The power of this tripartite had greatly expanded under Dr. Mahathir. It has been the excesses of this tripartite that much of the anger and alienation of the new middle-class was directed against. There were accusations of growing corruption, of cronyism where selected business groups were favoured with contracts, and the limiting of democratic space. There are complaints of persistent poverty in rural stretches and urban slums, corruption, social problems such as incest, domestic abuse, and high divorce rate, weakening of the judiciary's independence, and abuse of human rights. Many young Malaysians, largely professionals and middle level business groups, viewed these weaknesses as arising from a development which was too uneven. Many of them wanted to address new concerns they regarded could have a more positive consequence on nation-building.

In his last year in office, Mahathir re-visited the agenda of nation-building first set out by the founding leaders. In his speeches he lamented the lack of inter-ethnic integration and he called for national unity. He proposed a return to the use of more English in schools. The strategy in the restructuring of the economy remains but with globalization and the need to be internationally competitive there is a re-look at the meritocracy-affirmation action options. More than any leader, in government or in opposition, he has offered a vision of a Malaysian nation. Malaysia must be, according to him, a country that is "ethnically integrated, living in harmony with full and fair partnership, made up of one *Bangsa Malaysia*, with political loyalty and dedication to the nation".

That he should, at the end of his career be criticizing the Malays and himself be attacked by the community he had sought to help, illustrates the remarkable shift of political discourse over nation-building. And because it encapsulated all the stages in the present nation-building process, his leaving the scene appropriately marks the end of contemporary history. As he retires, several major studies on his politics and policies have appeared. Written largely by economists and political scientists, these promise to be the basis upon which attempts at offering not only a biographical study of Dr. Mahathir but also a contemporary history of Malaysia could be made.

The leadership of Badawi that has since taken over represents a different generation. It is one that grew up after the war. They are mostly men and women who had not been involved in the nationalist and independence struggle. His deputy Dato Seri Najib Tun Abdul Razak, was born long after UMNO was set up. And so is the case with the two leaders in the MCA, Dato Ong Kah Ting and Dato Chan Kong Choy, both of whom grew up after the forming of the Alliance coalition. Both are also the first Chinese-educated leaders who went through a university education that was already Malay-medium. It is a generation of leaders who lived through the early experiment in nation-building but who are now entrusted to take the nation to the next phase.

Conclusion

There is a sense of this period of contemporary history as being transitory, one of moving away from colonial rule towards being a nation set out in Vision 2020. So far, the economic and social development part of nation-building has been impressive. But in other areas there is some distance still to be covered. Hence, while new institutions such as parliamentary democracy and the modern judiciary are functioning, there are citizens who worry that their performance is falling short of the promising start they made.

On unity and integration, some surveys report that the young see themselves as Malaysians and that there is greater consciousness and sensitivity to the aspiration of the various communities. However, unity as aspired by the early leaders remains as elusive as it had been. Ethnicity continues to be evident at all levels and in all sectors, and its use for categorization hinders a speedier process in nation-building.

Historians and those from other social science disciplines would need, therefore, to investigate the extent to which the new national education has created a common outlook and a sense of national identity. While Malay is now widely and fluently used, there are reports of ethnic polarization in schools and universities. There is also a trend that more parents are sending their children to the national-type streams or to Islamic schools. Chinese parents, some 85–90 per cent, are not enrolling their children in national schools. And at tertiary level, non-Malays attend private colleges or go overseas while local public universities are predominantly Malay.

The continued ethnic dimension in Malaysian politics contributes to what some scholars noted as a drift towards soft authoritarianism in the political system. It has been argued that communities rally in unquestioning loyalty behind those individuals seen as protecting or advancing the communal cause. This loyalty has greatly increased the power of the leader in UMNO. With UMNO dominant within the ruling coalition and with the executive branch of government overshadowing the legislative and judicial, the position of the prime minister has become very powerful.

Hence, more than any other institution, UMNO dominates the nation-building process. Its formation and rise is prominent in this period of contemporary history. For this reason, it is the power competition in UMNO that has the most serious implications upon national politics. But once power is consolidated, the leader of UMNO is moderated by his position as national leader. However, whenever the party experiences a factional conflict, the political instinct is to utilize ethnic issues to mobilize support.

Standing out also as a significant feature of the period is the inter-ethnic coalition of the Barisan Nasional. It could be argued that the inter-ethnic coalition of the Barisan Nasional worked because it drew on the old pattern of political relationships. In the pre-colonial days, traditional rulers relied on Chinese *kapitan*, usually wealthy merchants, to represent their community. This co-operation has re-emerged as the Alliance (now Barisan Nasional) with UMNO replacing the rulers as protector of the Malays and the MCA seen very much in a role of a Chinese *kapitan*.

The BN's early success came out of a unique set of circumstances in Malaysian political history during the 1950s and unlikely to be replicated.

Competing ethnic demands continue to be negotiated within the mechanism of Barisan Nasional. Equilibrium is maintained through consultation and consensus, and this has ensured low level of conflict in situations of dangerous multi-ethnic tension .But this mechanism of inter-ethnic co-operation has weakened, and there is a concern whether nation-building is a continuing process of multi-ethnic negotiation or that it has become predominantly a nationalizing process by the state. Reality in Malaysia dictates that the expectations of multi-ethnic society in nation-building be accommodated through some form of consensus while recognizing that only the state has the resources and the capability to bring change and transformation.

A new generation of Malaysians born after independence has grown into adulthood. Their expectations of a nation have increasingly taken on different expressions. There are those more concerned about the integration of marginal communities, of religious and cultural pluralism within a more democratic system, of preserving the country's environmental and cultural heritage, and of more equitable sharing of the gains from development. There are others who, inspired by international religious resurgence and dissatisfied with domestic direction, seek a more Islamic definition of the nation.

Growing globalization, with its accompanying change and uncertainties, has partly contributed to a worldwide religious resurgence. The rise of Islamic fundamentalism in Southeast Asia, largely urban centred but expanding into rural constituencies, is challenging the earlier secular character of nation-state in Malaysia. It is a resurgence that draws inspiration from the larger international *ummah* but derives strength from local aspirations and grievances. UMNO-PAS competition for votes is a political manifestation of the deeper struggle in deciding how nation-building should now proceed.[15] Mahathir's declaration in September 2001 of Malaysia being an Islamic state is an attempt at appropriating the demands of the more radical religious groups.[16]

It is difficult to anticipate how historians of a later age will assess the significance of the present period of contemporary history of Malaysia. It is possible the dates of major events which our period consider as historic turning points, such as 1946 when UMNO was formed to fight the Malayan Union, or 1957 when the country achieved independence, may be replaced by new ones. And nationalist leaders of today will have to compete for ranking in importance with later leaders. To help later scholars therefore, historians of today writing of their age have the responsibility to capture in their balanced and accurate historical narratives the dynamics and complexities of the period. Their works are also commentaries of the times.

NOTES

1   Wang Gungwu, "Political Heritage and Nation Building", *Journal of the Malaysian Branch of the Royal Asiatic Society* 73, Pt. 2 (2000): 5–30.
2   Stephen Ellis, "Writing Histories of Contemporary Africa", *The Journal of African History* 43 (January 2002).
3   G. Barraclough, *An Introduction to Contemporary History* (New York: Basic Books, 1964), p. 4.
4   Wang Gungwu, "1874 in Our History", *Peninjau Sejarah* 1 no. 1 (June 1966): 12–16.
5   Sharon A. Carsten, "From Myth to History: Yap Ah Loy and the Heroic Past of Chinese Malaysians". *Journal of Southeast Asian Studies* 19, no. 2 (September 1988): 185–207.
6   Tan Liok Ee, *The Rhetoric of Bangsa and Minzu: Community and Nation in Tension, The Malay Peninsula, 1900–1955* (Clayton, Australia: The Centre of Southeast Asian Studies, 1988).
7   Address of Tan Cheng Lock at inaugural general assembly meeting of the Malayan Chinese Association, 27 February 1949, Tan Cheng Lock Papers (TCL.26.6-6a), Institute of Southeast Asian Studies, Singapore.
8   Sharon Siddique and Leo Suryadinata, "*Bumiputra* and *Pribumi*: Economic Nationalism (Indiginism) in Malaysia and Indonesia", *Pacific Affairs* (1982): 662–87.
9   Robert Hunt, "Individual, Community, State and Perceptions of Human Rights and Religious Freedom", *Trinity Theological Journal* 5 (1995): 15–30.
10 Harold Crouch, *Government and Society in Malaysia* (Cornell University Press); William Case, *Elites and Regimes in Malaysia: Revisiting a Consociational Democracy* (Clayton: Monash Asia Institute, 1996).
11 T.M. Harper, *Malaya: The End of Empire and the Making of Malaya* (Cambridge: Cambridge University Press, 1999).
12 Benedict Anderson,"From Miracle to Crash", *London Review of Books* 20, no. 8 (16 April 1998).

13 Tunku Abdul Rahman Putra Al-Haj, *Looking Back: Monday Musings and Memories* (Kuala Lumpur: Pustaka Antara, 1977), p. vii.

14 Khoo Boo Teik, "The Legacy of C.H.E. Det: Portrait of a Nationalist as a Young Man", *Kajian Malaysia* 11, no. 2 (1993): 28–43.

15 Hussin Mutalib, *Islam in Malaysia: From Revivalism to Islamic State* (Singapore: Singapore University Press, 1993).

16 Zainah Anwar, *Islamic Revivalism in Malaysia: Dakwah amongst Students* (Petaling Jaya: Pelanduk, 1987).

CHAPTER EIGHT

Forging Malaysia and Singapore: Colonialism, Decolonization and Nation-Building

Tony Stockwell

Colonialism and State-Building

Nations have been compared with organisms. Metaphors of growth and evolution, of life and death, have been used in their depiction. They have alternatively been seen as constructs, or products of a political process characterized as "nation-building". This process is sometimes described as "forging a nation". It suggests feats of engineering and conjures up the heat of the workshop and the strength and skill of the craftsman. Yet fabrication also suggests falsification. Indeed, as Avi Shlaim has commented, "it is interesting to note how frequently the phrase 'forging a nation' is used, because most nations are forgeries. Indeed, some nations are based on little more than a mythological view of the past and a hatred of foreigners".[1] Post-colonial nations have been deliberately and artificially shaped to fit nationalist agendas, but they also bear the hammer blows of colonialism which over the years worked against the grain of national self-determination and only in its last phase hastily cobbled together successor-states that might pass for nation-states.

While nation-building has been the principal task of political leaders, economic planners and social engineers in post-colonial Southeast Asia, the foundations of their states were laid during the colonial period. Colonialism demarcated territorial boundaries, established institutions of centralized government, developed primate cities, served as a conduit for global influences, and bequeathed models for modernization. In so doing, colonialism was responsible for the integration of communities within larger government structures and economic systems. Moreover, the capacity of colonial administration for ruling and the costs of doing so led to its greater intervention in indigenous societies as heads were counted in the census, as land ownership was determined, and, most importantly, as taxes were collected. At the same time, the long reach of the colonial state contributed to individuals' consciousness of being members of a larger community. Thus colonial rule provoked resistance from those whom it dispossessed and sharpened the aspirations of others whom it benefited. Unwittingly fashioning the political identities of subject peoples, the colonial state not only provoked demands for self-determination but also provided the mould for its successor, the nation-state.[2]

If the foundations of the nation-state derived from colonialism, so, too, did many of its structural flaws. The tendency of colonial administrators to compartmentalize ethnic groups according to social and economic functions the better to control them led to virulent communalism. The development of plantations, mining enterprises and infrastructural programmes brought in immigrant labour, thereby emphasizing inequalities between communities or regions and challenging indigenous cultural assumptions. Colonialism aggravated differences within society and between peoples to spawn a variety of competing nationalisms that would later threaten the integrity and jeopardize the stability of nation-states. In addition to these enduring, systemic effects of colonialism, ephemeral relations between rulers and ruled together with superficial resolutions of their profound differences embittered the struggle between competing heirs to the colonial state. Thus, as one group gained political advantages or consolidated its status as the result of constitutional reforms, so others either sought similar recognition or contested the very basis of such collaborative arrangements.

Nowhere is the dual impact of colonialism — consolidation and fragmentation — more glaring than in the case of Malaysia. On the one hand, a new state was constructed from previously disconnected parts which lacked an integrating, pre-colonial core and whose commonalty at the time of Malaysia's formation rested merely on experience of various forms of British rule. On the other hand, the colonial legacy of racial divisions, economic inequalities and local autonomies meant that the legitimacy and very survival of the new state were vulnerable to challenges both from within and from outside. This chapter examines Britain's contribution to the formation of Malaysia in the context of its post-war strategy of de-colonization. It argues that, notwithstanding its commitment to nation-building, Britain's declining power constrained its capacity to influence developments, let alone to integrate the components into a nation-state. What was inaugurated on 16 September 1963 was a state without a nation. Whereas proof of nationhood had formerly been the pre-requisite of independence — the very talisman without which decolonization could not proceed — now nationhood became the goal to which post-colonial leaders aspired and without which they would be in danger of falling.

Decolonization and Nation-Building

That Britain contributed to the making of Malaysia there is no doubt, but the nature and extent of its role have been the subject of conflicting interpretations. Some have stressed Britain's impact in terms of neo-colonialism, while others have focused more on the aspirations and actions of indigenous leaders, on, for example, the independent vision and statesmanship of Tunku Abdul Rahman or the determination and brinkmanship of Lee Kuan Yew. Leaving on one side episodes such as the Brunei revolt of December 1962 or Singapore's operation "coldstore" in February 1963, the making of Malaysia has generally been presented as a collaborative exercise rather than as a bi-polar struggle. Take, for example, Lee's own account which is informed by contemporary documents as well as memory. Notwithstanding the steadfast commitment to independence expressed in the book, the principal target is neither the colonial government (with whose ministers and officials Lee appears to have got on well) nor his vacillating Malayan partners (with whom he would later fall out with such acrimony) but the enemy within: Singapore's communists and their fellow-travellers who subverted trade unions, mobilized student protest and penetrated government. In *The Singapore Story*, the battle for independence was also the battle for merger; independence through merger is presented here, as it was fervently advocated by Lee at the time, as the only way to defeat communism and secure the peace and prosperity of the island.[3]

Another perspective and a different emphasis are provided in the memoir by Tan Sri Ghazali Shafie who, as permanent secretary of the Malayan Ministry of External Affairs, participated in most of the negotiations between the Malayan government and other parties to the Malaysia agreement. Like Lee's, Ghazali's account is full and, though no references are supplied, contemporary documentation patently supplements the author's recollections. Notwithstanding the considerable detail, however, the message is transparent: Malaysia was the liberation of Britain's last dependencies in Southeast Asia; it marked the triumph of democratic self-determination over colonialism. With a few exceptions (such as Malcolm MacDonald or Harold Macmillan "who helped to clear the cobwebs of colonialism"), British ministers and officials are portrayed as reactionaries, vainly attempting to stop the onward march of freedom. Observing the Sarawak river from a window in the istana (palace) at Kuching, Ghazali mused: "The river was tidal. Quite often it did not appear to know which way it was flowing. Even if it did flow it was very slow and with it were driftwoods and flotsam creating impediments to boats cruising by. It was almost a grotesque mimicry of the attitude of the colonial expatriates towards the Malaysia concept!" On one occasion he felt the need to remind the Tunku "that we were dealing with hard core die-hard colonialists who were living in the past". Since the Tunku "was a true democrat", Ghazali records his relief when Brunei decided against membership: "with undemocratic Brunei in, Malaysia could never claim to be based on parliamentary democracy".[4] According to this account, therefore, the British did not take the lead in the creation of Malaysia but, if anything, stood in its way. Although their memoirs differ in many respects, Ghazali and Lee depict the British as shrewd to the point of machiavellian and as arrogant though ultimately pragmatic. For both author-participants, of course, the British are not the heroes of the Malaysia story, nor are they their prime interest. Nevertheless, because the security of Southeast Asia was central to British strategic thinking and because nation-building was a preoccupation of the official mind of decolonization, the British contribution to the fashioning of Malaysia warrants further consideration.

While British opinion varied regarding the speed, indeed the wisdom, of decolonization, from the 1940s onwards successive governments publicly repeated a commitment to colonial self-government.[5] Until then colonial rulers had rarely sympathized with aspirations for national self-determination or had seen the need to prepare for the demission of empire. On the contrary, arguing in terms of cultural relativism and the sanctity of indigenous custom and practice, they had previously rejected the relevance of nationhood to societies outside the European tradition of nationalism and had dismissed Asian nationalists as self-serving oligarchs preying upon the untutored susceptibilities of the masses. By 1945, however, nationalism had acquired worldwide approbation. The Atlantic Charter and the shift in global power with the fall of Singapore were milestones in ending colonial empires and in the universal recognition of the right to national self-determination. Since the nation-state was by definition fundamental to the conduct of international relations and the basic unit of the currency of international organization, political leaders in Asia and Africa were encouraged in their struggle against European empires to formulate their objectives in terms of national self-determination.

World War II marked a significant change in colonial thinking too. Having previously rejected the relevance of nationalist claims, the British Government embarked on a new colonialism. It publicly acknowledged the principle of self-determination for subject peoples as the goal of colonial policy and adopted nation-building as the means to this end. To illustrate this shift in attitude, we might, for example, contrast the motto inscribed by Sir Herbert Baker above the doorway of the secretariat in New Delhi (inaugurated in 1931) with the progressive colonialism propagated by the BBC after the loss of Singapore in February 1942. The New Delhi motto stated: "Liberty will not descend to a people; a people must raise themselves to liberty; it is a blessing which must be earned before it can be enjoyed",[6] whereas in April 1942 BBC planners considered a series of broadcasts on the theme that "the British Commonwealth of

Nations has become part of a greater Commonwealth — the Commonwealth of Freedom". They envisaged the empire as an "incubator… hatching the eggs of independent nationhood. How the eggs got in the incubator it doesn't matter now so much, the important thing is 'are they being given the quickest possible development and what are we going to do about providing a decent poultry run in which so many independent chickens can scratch in the future?' "[7] With the pressure now on to effect an orderly escape from empire, nation-building became a key element in Britain's strategy of decolonization.

Nation-building acquired added importance with the advent of Cold War. Nation-states were erected as bunds against the surge of communism. "Our object must… be to identify our presence in South East Asia with the national aspirations of the area," Britain's commissioner-general advised the prime minister. "Our strongest card here against the expansion of communism is nationalism."[8] Thus, Britain prepared to withdraw from empire and relinquish power to new nation-states, not because of sentiment or altruism, but in order to shed costly overseas commitments, safeguard interests in former colonies, enhance influence with current allies and contain communism. Viewed in this light, decolonization might be interpreted as another stage of imperialism; it was an informal imperialism marked by a series of partnerships between former rulers and ruled on the one hand and between Britain and America on the other.[9] Partly evolutionary and partly instrumental, nation-building went hand-in-hand with decolonization. It was assumed that the building-blocks of economic development, social welfare and the "localization" of public services would be laid layer by layer. Upon these would be constructed institutions designed to foster both democratic self-government and social responsibility at local and later central levels. Constitutional engineering would be completed by the topping-out ceremony marking the transfer of power.

It might appear, therefore, that nationalist leaders were pushing at an open door provided, that is, they could demonstrate the viability of their nation-state and their authority to lead it. But what were the hallmarks of "genuine" nationalism? When was a political campaign a nationalist movement, and when was it rebellion, or insurrection, or an attempt to secede from a legitimate state? A common history, geography, racial origin, political destiny, language and culture were ingredients of national identity. Yet none on its own was the quintessential characteristic of all nations whose profiles varied. Indeed, rival groups within the same colony presented conflicting national projects and the struggle for home rule was accompanied by a contest between nationalists over who had the best claim to rule at home. In spite of, or perhaps because of, its ideological incoherence, nationalism became a highly tensile political tool. It was employed variously to lever power from alien governments, or to disparage rival claims to sovereignty, or to weld together disparate peoples, or to reinforce barriers between them. Whether inward-looking in its preoccupation with internal solidarity or outward-looking in its quest for independence, and whether obsessed with a mythic past or focused upon modernization, nationalism was fundamentally a boundary phenomenon reliant upon difference. It bound together those with shared values and aspirations and it set them apart from others. So far as the British were concerned, the test of legitimacy boiled down to self-interest; the British Government espoused the cause of those nationalists whose aspirations most closely coincided with their own. Thus it denied the claims of the Malayan Communist Party to represent the Malayan people and rejected the demands of the Partai Ra'ayat Brunei for Negara Kesatuan Kalimantan Utara (United State of Northern Borneo).

Whereas nationalism is dynamic, nationhood is static. While nationalism is a force instrumental in the creation of a nation; nationhood is the condition of being a nation. In common with nationalism, however, nationhood has spawned a variety of definitions and interpretations. In the context of de-colonization, what criteria were applied for assessing whether a dependency had reached nationhood? How did planners judged a colony's ability "to stand on its own feet"? How did they decide "when the time was right" for independence? Although they avoided explicit check-lists and precisely measurable standards, policymakers commonly tested the strength of nationhood against a number of benchmarks. The first of these was geographical size: it was deemed necessary to merge city-states and smaller territories (such as Singapore and Brunei) within larger entities. The second was social cohesion: racial and regional differences would have to be accommodated within elaborate, constitutional steel-frames, such as that drafted by the Reid Commission for Malaya and that recommended by Cobbold and Lansdowne for Malaysia.[10] Third, administrative experience would be monitored through the increasing localization of public services. Because it was clear that the governments of Sarawak and Sabah would remain dependent upon expatriate officers into the late 1960s, the Borneo territories failed this test for separate nationhood, while Brunei's dependence during the late 1950s and early 1960s on officers seconded from Malaya alarmed those who feared that British colonialism would be replaced by Malayan colonialism. A fourth criterion was political maturity. This was gauged according to the ability of country-wide parties to bridge communal and regional divides and secure popular support through elections. Although they had a preference for multi-racial movements, the British eventually reconciled themselves to the Malayan Alliance of mutually exclusive communal parties when it demonstrated its "nationalist" credentials (that is its pan-peninsula popularity) by the landslide electoral victory of 1955.

As regards security, fifthly, a nation-state was expected to safeguard its internal security but it was accepted that new states would defend themselves externally in concert with the former colonial power through treaties and military pacts. In the case of Malaya, Britain's involvement in internal security after 1957 was controversial. Its external defence was guaranteed by the Anglo-Malayan Defence Arrangement (subsequently extended to the whole of Malaysia) which was resented by Malay and non-Malay radicals, although, to the disappointment of Britain, independent Malaya refused to join the South East Asia Treaty Organization, thereby presenting a semblance of non-alignment. A sixth criterion for independence was economic viability. It was recognized that primary producers would remain vulnerable to world market forces and continue to need external funding for development; nonetheless, the British Government insisted that it should not to be saddled with financial responsibility after political power had been transferred to the leaders of new nation-states. Writing in connection with the West Indies, an official at the Commonwealth Relations Office stated: "It is clearly necessary that emergent Colonies should be economically viable before they can claim membership of the Commonwealth", although he added that "we do not want to go so far as to say that viability means they should be disqualified from receiving any form of assistance."[11] In the final stages of planning Malaysia, the British Government came under considerable pressure to cultivate goodwill in Kuala Lumpur by improving its financial settlement. In doing so, however, the prime minister pointed out "the limitations on our ability to help" because "the claims on Britain for overseas aid and the total of that aid are increasing very significantly".[12] A final benchmark of nationhood was legitimacy. It was essential for the departing colonial power to demonstrate to the international community — through transparent processes of consultation, democratic elections and the registration of new states as members of the United Nations — that the interests and wishes of the people had been satisfied and that the successor state was accepted by its nation. Public relations were of immense importance in this. Thus, reacting to local doubts and international criticisms, the British Government mounted a campaign to present through illustrated booklets and radio broadcasts "really convincing material" about the benefits which Malaysia would bring to its inhabitants as well as evidence of their consent to its creation.[13] Furthermore, in anticipation of a hostile report from the UN's examination of Borneo opinion in August–September 1963, a paper was produced elaborating the stages of the consultative process. In the event, it was not needed because the report of the UN mission was in general highly favourable to Malaysia. This international vindication of Malaysia, was the first publication produced by the new state's Department of Information and widely distributed on Malaysia Day.[14]

Notwithstanding these benchmarks, policymakers were on their guard against entrapment within rigid models of nation-building or commitment to specific timetables of decolonization. Multiple objectives whose sum fell short of a coherent scheme plus the inability to predict and control events meant that policy-making necessitated choice from amongst a range of competing options, none of which was wholly satisfactory. Sufficiently worldly-wise to realize that time might not be on their side, they adjusted to the unforeseen, compromised principles and risked premature concessions in order to retain at least some influence over developments. As the British high commissioner of Brunei put it, by 1963 "the risk of going too fast is less than going too slow".[15] World-weary from years of managing post-war decline, they accepted that they would not achieve all their goals and, in their bleaker moments, they forecast an outcome that left Britain worse off than before. Nevertheless, at first sight the creation of Malaysia does not appear to fall into this category. On the contrary, policymakers called the project a "Grand Design" and its outcome seemed to secure their interests and demonstrate their continuing power, justifying perhaps their critics' charge of "neo-colonialism".

Neo-colonialism and the Making of Malaysia

In its planning, implementation and consequences, Malaysia has been described and explained in terms of neo-colonialism. It has been claimed that Britain, firstly, devised the new state in order to promote its own economic and strategic interests; secondly, coerced and manipulated the Malayan Government and other "stooges" to merge disparate territories against the wishes of their inhabitants; and, thirdly, managed to ensure its continuing grip upon the area. The result was a state which lacked independence, sovereignty and national legitimacy. Its impact was to divide unnaturally the Malay world, to threaten the exercise of free relations between the countries of Southeast Asia and to undermine the well-being of its neighbours. Malaysia, it is said, provoked the hostility of Indonesia and the Philippines, and, instead of bringing stability to the region, fostered enmity between independent countries of Southeast Asia. As Indonesia's deputy foreign minister put it to the UN Security Council on 9 September 1964: "It was colonialism and imperialism which separated our peoples, artificially dividing our great family into differing units — thereby causing, if not opposition, almost complete estrangement."[16] Associated with the transparent polemic of Sukarno's rickety regime as well as with a crude form of Marxism, the neo-colonial thesis may now appear an easy target. Nevertheless, British attempts to subvert the republic, notably its undercover involvement in the Sumatran rebellion of 1957–58, have now been substantiated.[17] Moreover, the neo-colonial interpretation of the making of Malaysia has been sustained both in radical critiques and in the non-Marxist revision of British decolonization as another form of imperialism.[18] These make compelling reading and since any rebuttal would require evidential support from the archives, the following reassessment is based on a thorough examination of contemporary documentation of British policy-making.

Let us start with British intentions and plans. Policy-making was organic not mechanistic; at least, that was how it was regarded by the British. "Policy", wrote a Colonial Office official, "is like a tree which grows organically from year to year and adapts itself in the process to the changing circumstances which surround it".[19] It was driven by demands, nurtured by the bureaucratic process and buffeted by unexpected events. Notwithstanding rhetorical flourishes and public statements to the contrary, ambiguity and compromise frequently prevailed. Indeed, in their approach to Malaysia the British were not as single-minded and their policies were not as coherent as the charge of neo-colonialism suggests. Rather they responded to a variety of stimuli. Powerful among the tropisms encouraging growth was the local or indigenous initiative. In spite of the fact that the integration of all its dependencies in Southeast Asia had been Britain's long-term objective since the 1940s, ministers were inclined to wait upon events, at least until the 1960s. They were wary of "forcing the pace", attempted to "keep change within bounds" and reluctant to press ahead with any scheme unless it was favoured by Asian leaders and commanded popular support.[20] Assessing the prospects of closer association of the Borneo territories in 1957, the colonial secretary went so far as to recommend "some discreet moves in that direction", although he cautioned his colleagues that it would "take a long time to come about" and there was "no question of hurrying it".[21] When Tunku Abdul Rahman suggested Greater Malaysia in conversation with a British minister (a year before his celebrated speech launching the project), Harold Macmillan expressed doubts about its viability while his colonial secretary only went so far as to accept that it would provide "the least unsatisfactory future for them and for us which we can at present envisage for the long term".[22]

One would expect British policymakers to have been particularly sensitive to Britain's economic interests and to have promoted the Greater

Malaysia project for reasons of business. In fact, however, officials and ministers were either indifferent to, or dismissive of, the commercial advantages of Malaysia. This may surprise those who believe Malaysia to be the extension of the neo-colony of Malaya whose arrangements for independence had allegedly kept the country safe for British capitalism.[23] Yet their records show that Whitehall departments were not active in promoting British business in the area of Malaysia. Nor were they being lobbied by manufacturers seeking contracts, by traders concerned about possible tariff changes, or by investors apprehensive about the nationalization of foreign assets. Even Brunei's oil seems to have been immaterial. It is true that one of the principal reasons for the collapse of the negotiations over Brunei's entry into Malaysia was the dispute over the allocation of mineral revenues between federal and state governments. But, until the discovery of rich, offshore deposits was confirmed in June 1963, the prognosis of Brunei-Shell throughout the planning of Malaysia had been that mineral sources were in decline and that oil was a diminishing asset. This is not to say that Britain's economic interests were ignored. When they were reviewed, however, it was regularly concluded that British trade and investments were reducing in a region which was becoming less and less valuable to Britain as a supplier of primary products, as a market for manufactured goods and as a dollar-earner.[24]

In contrast to this indifference to the economic potential of Malaysia, the documents reveal an overwhelming anxiety that British defence commitments outweighed the economic returns from the region: "The conclusion is inescapable that our defence expenditure in the Far East is now out of all proportion to our economic stake there."[25] They also indicate that the government's priority was not to promote private enterprise but to reduce public expenditure — be it on the defence of Southeast Asia or for the economic development of the territories of the future Malaysia. Preoccupied with the costs and benefits of a world role, policymakers sought to retrench, not to parade a military presence. Their objective was not simply to spend less on existing commitments but to reduce the number and extent of those commitments. Consequently, they explored ways of replacing military methods of influence with non-military methods (such as diplomacy and development aid). They also investigated the possibility of transferring current defence obligations to the future Malaysia and of sharing their costs with Commonwealth allies.

Co-existing uneasily in the British mind with strategic considerations was the obligation to uphold the interests of Borneo peoples. Of the territories contemplating Malaysian membership, only North Borneo and Sarawak were genuine colonies. Britain's responsibility to provide for their welfare and respect their wishes in the event of a proposed change of sovereignty was genuine, profound and forcefully expressed by officials at the Colonial Office and by expatriate administrators in the field, not least the governors of North Borneo and Sarawak, Sir William Goode and Sir Alexander Waddell. Waddell became "extremely irritated" as the feeling grew that "the Tunku's object is Greater Malaya, not Greater Malaysia". To the impatience of ministers preoccupied with strategic matters rather than indigenous feelings, Goode persistently pointed out the dangers of a Malayan "take-over" of Borneo: "Any impression of being simply transferred as Colonies from Britain to Malaya will provoke a Merdeka Movement against K.L." that would be "potentially irresistible". Years later Goode recalled: "One Native Chief, a Dusun, said to me 'If the British are unwilling to stay longer, I'd rather have the Japanese than Malays to king over me'."[26]

There was much wrangling in Whitehall over priorities and ministers faced the conundrum of squaring different interests and fulfilling antithetical aspirations. Although the Malaysia project was referred to as the "Grand Design", its impact suffered from opposing objectives. For example, on the one hand, the imminent collapse of Lee Kuan Yew's government and the likely destabilization of Singapore underlined the need for immediate merger with Malaya; on the other hand, the misgivings of Borneo peoples about a "crash programme" or a "shot-gun marriage" with Malaya,[27] called for a gradual approach to territorial consolidation. The conflicting demands of regional security and the rights of indigenous peoples, therefore, together with tensions between global strategy and retrenchment placed the British in dilemmas which occasionally produced inter-departmental rancour and threatened to blight planning.

If British policy-making suffered from lack of co-ordination, so Britain's freedom for manoeuvre was constrained by local circumstances. Such an argument may be difficult to sustain in the light of instances of intervention that appear to demonstrate Britain's proclivity and capacity to manipulate local leaders and ride roughshod over the interests and wishes of the people. For example, the Cobbold report on Bornean opinion has been dismissed in some quarters as window-dressing for conduct that paid scant attention to that opinion.[28] In addition, military intervention in Brunei and police action in Singapore would appear to demonstrate a preparedness to resort to force. In December 1962 the rising of the Tentera Negara Kalimantan Utara (the military wing of Azahari's Party Ra'ayat Brunei) expressed popular opposition to the Greater Malaysia project and manifest support for an independent state of North Kalimantan (Negara Kesatuan Kalimantan Utara). The revolt was swiftly suppressed by the Gurkhas and other units. Soon afterwards its leaders were detained and pressure was brought to bear on the sultan to negotiate terms of Malaysian membership. Two months later, in anticipation of the ramifications of subversion throughout the region, operation "Cold Store" was mounted in Singapore and resulted in the detention of some 120 communist sympathizers and opponents of the ruling People's Action Party.[29] Meanwhile, members of the Clandestine Communist Organization in Sarawak and their sympathizers within the Sarawak United Peoples Party (which had consistently opposed Malaysia) were rounded up.[30] When, following the Manila Summit in early August 1963, Tunku Abdul Rahman complied with the wishes of Sukarno and Macapagal by agreeing to postpone the inauguration of Malaysia until the wishes of the Borneo peoples had been verified by a United Nations mission of enquiry, the energetic and tough-talking colonial secretary, Duncan Sandys, who felt that the Malayan prime minister had lost his nerve, went to Kuala Lumpur in order to prevent any further appeasement of the opponents of the Grand Design.[31] Another example that some might cite of Britain's desire to keep its hand on the tiller was the appointment, as its first high commissioner to Malaysia, of Lord Head who was a former cabinet minister and a forceful and authoritative figure to represent British interests.

Although these episodes suggest eager and largely successful deployment of strength and influence, yet the weight of evidence indicates the limitations of Britain's power as well as British forebodings at the time about the untoward effects of the use of force. Indeed, just as the Malayan Union debacle of 1945–46 had taught them not to compel compliance with their plans, so the twelve-year emergency had put them on their guard against being sucked into military confrontation. Nor, it should be pointed out, did they relish a scrap with Indonesia. Although Greg Poulgrain has been at pains to revise the view of Sukarno as the initiator of *Konfrontasi*,[32] Britain's involvement in the Sumatran rebellion of 1958 and preparations since 1960 to counter an Indonesian claim to the northern Borneo territories, on the lines of its bid for West Irian, did not equate with a propensity to foment military confrontation with Indonesia. On the contrary, it was in order to lower the international temperature that some senior British officials recommended further investigation of Maphilindo's potential for improving the prospects of peaceful co-existence between Malaysia and its neighbours.[33]

As it was, when crises blew up, Britain was often wrong-footed and caught with its back to the wall. For example, failure on the part of the intelligence service meant that the Brunei revolt turned out to be a close-run thing, while ministers were most reluctant to sanction mass arrests in Singapore on account of the worldwide criticism operation "Cold Store" would provoke. Far from being in the driving seat during the run-up to Malaysia, British ministers and officials frequently felt that they were being driven by Lee Kuan Yew, the Tunku and the Sultan of Brunei, and along routes which they did not wish to take. As in the case of the transfer of power to Malaya in 1955–57, so with the creation of Malaysia in 1961–63, the British found that they could not dictate terms. When the Sultan of Brunei decided at the last minute against joining, there was simply nothing the British Government could do about it. Neither veiled threats of coercion nor reasoned appeals to enlightened self-interest induced the sultan to change his mind. Similarly, although British administrators were appalled by Kuala Lumpur's colonial designs upon the Borneo territories, they were scarcely in a position to halt them and were hard-pressed even to moderate them. When Lee Kuan Yew unilaterally declared independence two weeks before Malaysia Day, the British circumspectly turned a blind eye to his "brinkmanship". It was, after all, because Britain's interest in Greater Malaysia derived, not from its power, but from its loss of power in the region that the British Government was in no position to apply coercion with any great effect when trying to promote its preferences.

Lacking compliant proxies, British representatives found their match in the leaders of the sovereign state of Malaya, the independent sultanate of Brunei and the quasi-independent Singapore. Each leader had his own agenda and vied with others. Each leader was subject to conflicting internal pressures and obliged to pursue multiple objectives. Nation-building spawned political parties and political parties reflected different national, sub-national and trans-national identities of the inhabitants of the Malaysian construct. Parties were also sustained by non-national links born of kinship, patronage and even personal greed. That political leaders wavered in their demands and shifted their allegiances was as much due to self-interested calculation as to any pressure exerted by Britain. For example, Tunku Abdul Rahman was under pressure from within his own party (United Malays National Organization, UMNO) as well as from the Pan Malayan Islamic Party and Malay radicals sympathetic to "*Melayu raya*" (the greater Malay world of the archipelago) not to compromise with the Singapore Chinese. Similarly, though for different reasons, the leaders of the Malayan Chinese Association, which was UMNO's partner in the Alliance government, were wary of merger which could lead to the loss of supporters to Lee Kuan Yew's People's Action Party. Not surprisingly, the Malayan prime minister blew hot and cold on Malaysia: sometimes he felt that, if it were to be done, it should be done quickly and in any case long before the run-up to the 1964 elections. Thus, he pressed the British for an early decision regarding the future of the Borneo territories and dismissed as neo-colonial British proposals for a transitional stage to safeguard the interests of Sarawak and Sabah. On other occasions, however, he played for time: he held Singapore at arm's length by setting conditions for its entry; he advocated a "Little Malaysia" without either Singapore or Brunei; he even threatened to withdraw from all plans for merger with any territory. When he was on the point of pulling out and the "Greater Malaysia" scheme was about to collapse, it was the blandishments of the British prime minister, not the strong-arms methods of his henchmen, that enticed the Tunku back to the conference table.[34] And at that conference table the Tunku's negotiating team drove very hard bargains, extracting from British ministers and officials a far more generous package of economic and military aid than the British had envisaged. Indeed, negotiations with the various "Malaysian" parties meant that the Grand Design, which had originally appealed to the British Government as the only realistic way of cutting both expenditure and commitments in the region, turned out to be far more expensive than had been expected.

The British relied, therefore, not on *force majeure* but on painstaking negotiations to reconcile the diverse objectives of the participating territories.[35] Months of discussions and consultations identified interests, assessed opinion, established principles, brokered compromises and eventually resulted in an uneasy agreement on the constitution of the prospective state. This constitution was neither a vindication of, nor a prescription for, nationhood. Rather, a framework was engineered to encourage what was hoped would be its natural development and to curb adventitious growth. As Cobbold put it in his conclusions to the commission's report, "It is a necessary condition that, from the outset, Malaysia should be regarded by all concerned as an association of partners, combining in the common interest to create a new nation but retaining their own individualities."[36] But, given the strength of those individualities, perhaps the most that could be expected of Malaysia was a federation of nations rather than a nation-state. By setting out at length and in detail provisions for federal and state institutions, citizenship, legislative powers, administrative arrangements, financial and public services, the protection of the special interests of the Borneo states and Singapore, and temporary arrangements covering a transitional period for the Borneo states and Singapore, the Malaysia agreement of July 1963 allocated powers and apportioned responsibilities, acknowledged majority interests and safeguarded minority rights, enshrined public service and reduced opportunities for corruption and arbitrary rule.[37] In short, the constitution of Malaysia was an elaborate set of contracts concluded after prolonged, multilateral negotiations. It was, in essence, an extension of the constitution of the already-independent Federation of Malaya which itself had been an artifice forged in a furnace of contradictions. It may subsequently have disappointed many, provoked active opposition in some quarters and been breached later by its very guardians, but the complex, interactive process of its making refutes the stark simplicity of the charge that the British Government devised Malaysia both single-mindedly and single-handedly. Whatever their intentions — and these, as we have seen, were several and ambivalent — the British were clearly not in a position to determine the shape of Malaysia.

Nor were the British able to guarantee Malaysia's future stability. As inauguration day drew near, the new state was placed in jeopardy by greater or lesser crises: unresolved disputes between Malaya and Singapore; a last-minute hitch in the relations between Malaya and Sarawak; an attempt by Kelantan to win an injunction against its establishment;[38] "Confrontation" with Indonesia; the Philippines' claim to Sabah; the United Nations enquiry into the wishes of the peoples of Borneo. Even if it survived these challenges, the benefits of Malaysia to the British looked uncertain. Two years earlier, Harold Macmillan had prophesied darkly that "it seemed likely that we should be faced with grave problems whether or not Greater Malaysia were achieved".[39] In fact, far from solving Britain's problems by reinforcing its grip upon the area while reducing the costs of influence, Malaysia turned out to be trouble for Britain, almost more trouble than it was worth. First of all, "Confrontation" was an unintended and unwelcome consequence. Instead of securing peace, it aggravated regional instability and, in so doing, damaged Anglo-American relations.[40] Moreover, the defence of Malaysia from external attack resulted in costs that would later force the British Government completely to review its position east of Suez and withdraw its military presence from Southeast Asia.[41] Secondly, the decision of the Sultan of Brunei to remain outside Malaysia saddled Britain with an expensive, embarrassing and open-ended commitment to the protection of an autocratic micro-state. Thirdly, Malaysia was prey to centrifugal forces: resentment of control from Kuala Lumpur festered in Sabah and Sarawak while the secession of Singapore in August 1965 appeared to expose the island to all the dangers that the British had wished to guard against, thus leaving their Grand Design in tatters. The outcome fell short of the objectives to fashion a single dominion from its former dependencies and to build a nation with the disparate territories and peoples of the area. Examination of Britain's role in the making of Malaysia reveals that the teeth of the imperial lion had long since decayed. For the shape and composition of the new state was determined as much by Britain's declining power and its incapacity to control developments as by a forceful strategy of planned decolonization.

Nation-Building and the Challenges of Independence

Just as the British had entertained doubts about Greater Malaysia, so Tunku Abdul Rahman's attitude to the project had been equivocal. While almost imperialistic in his advocacy of union with the Borneo territories, he always harboured misgivings about merger with Singapore. In early May 1961, as part of his diplomatic offensive to persuade the Malayan premier to espouse the scheme, Lee Kuan Yew urged its adoption with an appeal to nation-building:

National identification in such a large and powerful federation comprising a grand total of nearly10 million people with a total of 130,000 square miles as against the Federation's 50,000 and Singapore's 225 square miles would hold the hearts and loyalties of the people. Pride in a more powerful and viable state, which may be called the "Federation of Malaysia" or the "United States of Malaysia", would give a boost to nation-building to the mutual advantage of the three territories and would help to stabilise the future of the whole region.[42]

This argument made its mark and, within three weeks, the Tunku delivered his celebrated speech at the foreign correspondents' lunch in Singapore and, in so doing, effectively launched the planning process. When, a month later, the Tunku sent Macmillan a memorandum proposing the integration of the Borneo territories and Singapore with Malaya, he repeated Lee's point about the opportunities presented by Malaysia for nation-building:

> It is a matter for emphasis that such a federation, comprising a grand total of nearly ten million, in an area of 130,000 square miles, as against a Federation of 50,000 square miles, will have the effect of creating a greater importance in the hearts and minds of the people of these territories and a national pride which would go a long way in building up a feeling of loyalty to the country. The federation of Greater Malaysia or a Greater Malaya, whichever name may be decided upon, will be powerful and viable and will be able to give greater contribution in the support of the Commonwealth association.[43]

Both Lee and the Tunku envisaged Greater Malaysia as the structure for nation-building, as a framework to support the nation of the future. They did not seek to validate it by reference to history; nor did they pretend that it conformed with an existing, demonstrable nationhood. Ultimately nationhood would legitimate the state; at the moment of its inauguration, however, Malaysia was a state without a nation. Indeed, those identifying nationhood with ethnicity have gone so far as to argue that post-war realities had brought about an acceptance that Malaysia could never be a nation-state and that the only enlightened response "to the new reality" was to promote the "power sharing" concept and philosophy as had been done already in the Constitutions of 1948 (Federation of Malaya) and 1957 (independent Malaya) and was repeated in the Malaysian Constitution.[44] Because of strong trans-national kinship ties — or, alternatively, cross-state national ties — between the Malays of the archipelago, not even the threat posed by "Confrontation" with Indonesia (1963–66) would instil in the inhabitants of the new federation a common purpose, a shared experience, a sense of the menacing "other", or an over-arching national identity. Meanwhile, bonds between the federal components were tenuous.

In the absence of a mythic past, a common history, an ethnic homogeneity, a geographical coherence, how was the nation to be forged? Uncertainty over the name for the new state indicated lack of unanimity on its values, culture, and political identity. The Tunku's suggestion of "Greater Malaya" in June 1961 indicated his commitment to the Malayan formula of power-sharing and, thus, to Malay paramountcy. It alienated the Borneo territories, clashed with Lee's aspirations for a multi-racial meritocracy and presaged a contest for the ownership of the nation.[45] British and Bornean representatives repeatedly warned the Tunku of the perils of presenting Malaysia as a Malayan takeover while Lee Kuan Yew doggedly pinned down Kuala Lumpur on the detail of citizenship, taxation and trade arrangements. The contest came to a head in August 1965 with the exclusion of Singapore on account of Lee's attempt to move from state into federal politics and champion a "Malaysia for Malaysians".

The prospects for both Malaysia and Singapore were bleak at the moment of their separation. For the next four years Malaysia battled against further territorial fragmentation[46] and growing communalism which erupted in violence on 13 May 1969. Yet the "13 May incident" became the defining moment of the nation-state and is probably more significant in the collective memory than the achievement of independence in 1957, the conclusion of the emergency in 1960 or the foundation of Malaysia in 1963.[47] From this moment onwards Malaysia cut its lingering colonial links, consolidated the position of the *bumiputra* ("princes of the soil" of whom Malays were the majority) and planned for social and economic restructuring. Malaysia became a guided democracy, but, unlike Sukarno's, this was a guided democracy with sound economic foundations.

Exclusion from Malaysia was Lee Kuan Yew's "moment of anguish".[48] His reputation had rested on the achievement of independence through merger; for years he had maintained that Singapore would flourish only as part of a larger, multi-racial nation-state. Separation was more significant than a personal defeat for Lee, however; from the perspective of Singapore, it destroyed the foundations of the nation. The assumption that Singapore's survival depended upon merger with Malaya had underpinned the calculations of Lee, of the British Government and, to a lesser extent, of the Tunku during the planning of Malaysia. Now Singapore was divorced from its economic hinterland, exposed to renewed subversion and internationally vulnerable at a time when Britain was looking forward to winding down its military presence. Never having aspired to independence for Singapore, Lee was forced into a u-turn and had no option but to embark on nation-building in a separate state.

At this point, the narrative moves from what might be called "colonial records history" into a period where the British Government has more or less left the scene and for which its files are relevant only in so far as they deal with defence issues and the military base. Since access to the archives of all governments is in any case severely restricted for the most recent thirty years, the historian must turn to other sources for understanding the official mind of post-colonial nation-building: government publications, the press and political memoirs, notably those of Lee Kuan Yew whose name has been synonymous with Singapore for forty years.[49]

Since August 1965 nation-building in Singapore has differed from the process in many other post-colonial states: it has not depended on a mythological view of its origins and a hatred of foreigners. On the contrary, being a society of immigrants and unencumbered by a pre-colonial history, Singapore has neither raked over the past nor turned in on itself; rather it has pursued modern goals and has planned for a future in which the city-state will remain indispensable to the region. Nation-building here has also differed from the experience elsewhere in Southeast Asia largely because of features that distinguish the island from its neighbours, such as its size, location, commercial traditions and Chinese majority. As a result of separation from Malaysia, the state of Singapore resumed its precise, close-knit geographical definition. Unique amongst Southeast Asian countries in having an overwhelmingly Chinese majority, Singapore has greater ethnic homogeneity than all the others. Although Singapore is clearly at a disadvantage compared with its larger neighbours and likens its isolation in a Muslim world to the predicament of Israel, its compactness gave full scope to the dynamic leadership of Lee Kuan Yew and to the central planning and managerial control that have been crucial to the effectiveness of nation-building policies, notably in the areas of urban planning, housing, education, transport and other public services. Despite its size, the city-state has also benefited from a global reach since, being commercial rather than agrarian, it has taken maximum advantage of its geo-political position to develop as a trading, financial and communications centre. Again likening its predicament to that of Israel, Singapore has "had to leapfrog the rest of the region, and attract multi-national companies".[50]

By setting itself apart from the rest of Southeast Asia and projecting itself worldwide, the Republic of Singapore has acquired both a cosmopolitan role and a national — almost post-national — identity in much the same way as Venice and Genoa achieved pre-national identities in early modern Europe. In this leviathan, political liberty has been surrendered in return for security and public services. Yet, co-existing with the nanny state, is a strong culture of self-reliance, educational opportunity and economic liberalism. Locked together, state and the individual have cemented social solidarity, while planning and prosperity have engendered a national self-confidence. Side by side with self-confidence, however, stalks fear — fear of attack, fear of failure, fear of forgetting the rugged society's struggle to succeed. Fear, too, has reinforced national solidarity. For a pervading sense of vulnerability has led not only to an obsession with defence and internal security but also to an ethos of social conformity and individuals' dedication to the common good and collective will.

Not surprisingly, history has little appeal to this forward-looking society, but it has not been entirely dismissed as bunk. The story of the PAP riding the tiger of communism, is regularly retold. So, too, are successes and failures of the colonial period, notably the triumph of Raffles in 1819 and the surrender of Percival in 1942. Furthermore, as Singapore rose from the ashes of the Malaysia experiment, its leaders consciously forged the nation-state on the anvil of the colonial legacy. When Margaret Thatcher marvelled at Singapore's progress since 1965, Lee Kuan Yew is supposed to have responded: "We have applied the lessons which the British first taught us and then themselves promptly forgot."

NOTES

1   Avi Shlaim, *The Guardian* (London), 29 March 2003.
2   The literature on the impact of colonialism on national identities is immense,

particularly in the wake of the publication of Benedict Anderson's *Imagined Communities* in 1978.

3   See Lee Kuan Yew, *The Singapore Story* (Singapore, 1998).

4   Tan Sri Ghazali Shafie, *Ghazali Shafie's Memoir on the Formation of Malaysia* (Bangi, Malaysia, 1998), pp. 197–98, 242, 246 and 300.

5   For colonial policy and colonial self-government see D.J. Morgan, *The Official History of Colonial Development, 5: Guidance towards Self-government in British Colonies, 1941–1971* (London, 1980), and the multi-volume series, *British Documents on End of Empire* (London, 1992–).

6   Jane Ridley, "Edwin Lutyens, New Delhi, and the Architecture of Imperialism", *Journal of Imperial and Commonwealth History* 26, no. 2 (1998): 77, and *The Architect and his Wife. A Life of Edwin Lutyens* (London, 2002), p. 379.

7   Quoted in Siân Nicholas, " 'Brushing up your Empire': Dominion and Colonial Propaganda on the BBC's Home Services, 1939–45", *Journal of Imperial and Commonwealth History* 31, no. 2 (2003): 207–30.

8   Selkirk to Macmillan, 14 August 1961, PREM 11/3737, Public Record Office (now The National Archives), Kew.

9   For the development of this idea, see: John Gallagher, *Decline, Revival and Fall of the British Empire* (Cambridge, 1982); John Darwin, *Britain and Decolonisation* (London, 1988); Wm. Roger Louis and Ronald Robinson, "The Imperialism of Decolonization", *Journal of Imperial and Commonwealth History* 22, no. 3 (1994): 462–511; Wm. Roger Louis, "The Dissolution of the British Empire", in *The Oxford History of the British Empire, IV, the Twentieth Century*, edited by Judith M. Brown and Wm. Roger Louis (Oxford, 1999), pp. 329–56.

10   *Report of the Federation of Malaya Constitutional Commission* [Lord Reid], Col. 330, 1957; *Report of the Commission of Enquiry, North Borneo and Sarawak, 1962* [Lord Cobbold], Cmnd. 1794, 1962; *Malaysia. Report of the Inter-governmental Committee, 1962* [Lord Lansdowne], Cmnd. 1954. The Reid commission, composed of Commonwealth jurists, made recommendations for the constitution of independent Malaya. The Anglo-Malayan Cobbold commission assessed opinion in North Borneo and Sarawak regarding prospective membership of Malaysia. The Lansdowne committee, consisting of British, Malayan and Bornean representatives, drew up detailed proposals for the terms of membership of the Borneo territories.

11   H.A.F. Rumbold to A. Morley, 30 November 1955, DO 35/5076, Public Record Office.

12   Macmillan to Tunku Abdul Rahman, 12 July 1963, PREM 11/4349, Public Record Office.

13   See FO 953/2129, P5455/1 and also files 2128, 2130, 2131 and 2132, Public Record Office.

14 In response to a request (agreed at the Manila Summit, August 1963) from Macapagal, Sukarno and the Tunku, a UN mission conducted formal hearings for the "ascertainment" of the wishes of the Borneo peoples. Department of Information, Malaysia, *United Nations Malaysia Mission Report*, 16 September 1963.

15 Angus MacKintosh to Ian Wallace (Colonial Office), 14 October 1963, CO 1030/1457, no. 1, Public Record Office.

16 Ministry of External Affairs, Malaysia, *Malaysia's Case in the United Nations Security Council: Documents Reproduced from the Official Record of the Security Council Proceedings*, 1964, p. 8. The proceedings consisted of six meetings, 9–17 September 1964, as the result of which the council upheld Malaysia's complaint against Indonesian military incursions by 9 votes to 2 (the USSR and Czechoslovakia opposing).

17 See Matthew Jones, " 'Maximum disavowable aid': Britain, the United States and the Indonesian rebellion, 1957–58", *English Historical Review* 114, no. 459 (1999): 1179–1216.

18 For a restatement of the radical critique see Greg Poulgrain, *The Genesis of Konfrontasi: Malaysia, Brunei and Indonesia, 1945–1965* (Bathurst, NSW, and London, 1998); for non-Marxist literature on the "imperialism of decolonization" see note 9 above.

19 Trafford Smith, 17 November 1947, in R. Hyam, *British Documents on End of Empire: The Labour Government and the End of Empire 1945–1951* (London, 1992) III, document 235.

20 See, for example, David Goldsworthy, "Keeping Change within Bounds: Aspects of Colonial Policy during the Churchill and Eden Governments, 1951–57", *Journal of Imperial and Commonwealth History* 18 (1990): 81–108.

21 Memorandum by A. Lennox-Boyd for the Cabinet Colonial Policy Committee, 29 November 1957, CAB 134/1556, CPC(57)34, Public Record Office.

22 The Tunku raised the possibility of Greater Malaysia with Lord Perth (minister of state at the Colonial Office) on 10 June 1960. For Perth's record of their conversation and the reactions of Macmillan and other ministers, see CO 1030/1126 and PREM 11/3418. The quotation is from the colonial secretary's memorandum to the Cabinet Colonial Policy Committee, 15 July 1960, CAB 134/1559, CPC(60)17. The Tunku publicly announced the project in a speech to foreign correspondents in Singapore on 27 May 1961.

23 For example, Poulgrain has stated that one of Britain's guiding principles in the decolonization of Southeast Asia was "that the new political leaders who assumed the reins of power when the Colonial Office departed should be known to be amenable to continued British investment". *The Genesis of Konfrontasi*, p. 6. See also Malcolm Caldwell, "From 'emergency' to

'independence', 1948–57", in *Malaya: The Making of a Neo-colony*, edited by Mohamed Amin and Malcolm Caldwell (Nottingham, 1977).

24 For an examination of relations between business and government in Malaya/ Malaysia see Nicholas J. White, *Business, Government and the End of Empire: Malaya, 1942–1957* (Kuala Lumpur, 1997); "Gentlemanly Capitalism and Empire in the Twentieth Century: The "Forgotten" Case of Malaya, 1914–1965", in *Gentlemanly Capitalism and British Imperialism: The New Debate on Empire*, edited by R.E. Dumett (Harlow, 1999), pp. 175–95; and 'The Business and the Politics of Decolonization: The British Experience in the Twentieth Century', *Economic History Review* 53, no. 2 (2000): 544–64. See also A.J. Stockwell, "Malaysia: The Making of a Neo-colony?", *Journal of Imperial and Commonwealth History* 26, no. 2 (1998): 138–56.

25 Sir Arthur Snelling, "Defence in the Far East about 1970", 19 March 1963, CAB 134/2277, OC(O)(63)7.

26 Waddell to Sir Geofroy Tory (British high commissioner in KL), 27 July 1961, CO 1030/981, no. 412c; "Points for Sandys", notes by Goode, 16 July 1962, Goode Papers, Rhodes House, Oxford, Box 3, file 1, f3; Goode to Mubin Sheppard, 2 October 1984, Goode Papers, Box 5, file 5, f45.

27 For example, Lord Selkirk (UK commissioner-general in SE Asia) to Iain Macleod (secretary of state for the colonies), 24 August 1961, CO 1030/982, no. 498c; Selkirk to Ian Wallace (CO), 4 January 1963, CO 1030/1466, no. 26.

28 For example, "In retrospect the Cobbold Commission can be said to have functioned as an important 'cover' to legitimize the British decision to withdraw from Sarawak without having first granted self-government, as promised at the time of Cession [by Rajah Charles Vyner to the Crown in 1946] and as embodied in the nine Cardinal Principles [in the preamble to Sarawak's constitution of 1941]." Michael B. Leigh, *The Rising Moon. Political Change in Sarawak* (Sydney, 1974).

29 See Matthew Jones, *Conflict and Confrontation in South East Asia, 1961–1965. Britain, the United States and the Creation of Malaysia* (Cambridge, 2002): 109–21; and "Creating Malaysia: Singapore Security, the Borneo Territories and the Contours of British Policy, 1961–63", *Journal of Imperial and Commonwealth History* 2, no. 28 (2000): 85–109; T.N. Harper, "Lim Chin Siong and the 'Singapore Story' " in *Comet in Our Sky. Lim Chin Siong in History*, edited by Tan Jing Quee and Jomo K.S. (Kuala Lumpur, 2001), pp. 41–48.

30 Taking advantage of emergency powers after the Brunei revolt, "the Special Branch made widespread arrests of anyone suspected of any links, however tenuous, with Sarawak's Clandestine Communist Organisation including 50 members of SUPP. The effect was to deter SUPP moderates but to encourage

radicals and youth members to defect to the CCO", Ong Kee Hui (chairman, SUPP), *Footprints in Sarawak. Memoirs of Tan Sri Datuk (Dr) Ong Kee Hui, 1914–1963* (Kuching, 1998), p. 595. See also Sarawak Information Service, *The Danger Within. A History of the Clandestine Communist Organisation in Sarawak*, 1963.

31   The correspondence between Sandys and London during this tour is held both at the Public Record Office and in the Sandys Papers, Churchill College, Cambridge, 8/3, 8/14 and 8/32.

32   Poulgrain, *The Genesis of Konfrontasi*.

33   For example, the brief from Sir Burke Trend (secretary to the cabinet) for Macmillan (prime minister), 23 April 1963, on the Foreign Office memorandum, "Future defence of Malaysia", OP(63)6, PREM 11/4347.

34   Differences of principle between London and Kuala Lumpur delayed the first round of talks until November 1961. In June 1962 the Tunku threatened to withdraw Ghazali Shafie and Dato Wong Pow Nee from the Cobbold Commission. Next, on reading the Cobbold report he at first refused to proceed with further talks and, when he was persuaded to attend, only some major concessions prevented him from breaking off discussions.

35   The network of communication and consultation was complex. London received information from Lord Selkirk (UK commissioner-general, Southeast Asia, in Singapore), Sir Geofroy Tory (British high commissioner in KL), Sir William Goode (governor, North Borneo), and Sir Alexander Waddell (governor, Sarawak). The Tunku occasionally communicated directly with Macmillan; otherwise Kuala Lumpur preferred Tory as a channel, rather than the Malayan high commissioner in London, since messages via the former fed directly into the heart of British Government (Ghazali Shafie, *Memoir*, p. 92). Indeed, British officials championing the Borneo territories complained that Tory seemed to regard himself as a supernumerary of the Tunku's staff (Alastair Morrison, *Fair Land Sarawak. Some Recollections of an Expatriate Official* [Ithaca, 1993], p. 176). Attempts were made to co-ordinate views and policies in London by cabinet ministerial committees and inter-departmental committees of officials, such as the Cabinet Colonial Policy Committee, Cabinet Oversea Policy Committee, Cabinet Greater Malaysia Committee, Greater Malaysia (Official) Committee and Oversea (Official) Co-ordinating Committee. Problems of liaison persisted, even after July 1962 when Duncan Sandys became secretary of state for the Colonies as well as secretary of state for Commonwealth relations. In Southeast Asia, Selkirk co-ordinated territorial administrations through his office and also the British Defence Co-ordinating Committee and the Inter-territorial Conference (Borneo). The Malaysia Solidarity Consultative Committee, chaired by Donald Stephens (North Borneo/Sabah) consisted of local, regional leaders

and set out the guidelines for the Cobbold commission (of British and Malayan representatives) which in turn was followed by Lansdowne's inter-government committee that consisted of British, Malayan and Bornean delegates. Formal talks were held in London in November 1961, July 1962 and through May to July 1963, while British ministers visited the region from time to time during the planning period.

36 *Report of the Commission of Enquiry, North Borneo and Sarawak*, p. 78, para. 237. See also J.P. Ongkili, *The Borneo Response to Malaysia 1961–1963* (Singapore, 1967), p. 67.

37 The three-page Malaysia Agreement signed on 9 July 1963 was accompanied by a further 230 pages of eleven annexes. *Malaysia. Agreement concluded between the United Kingdom of Great Britain and Northern Ireland, the Federation of Malaya, North Borneo, Sarawak and Singapore,* Cmnd. 2094.

38 The state of Kelantan (governed by the Pan-Malayan Islamic Party) argued in the federal high court that Kelantan was a sovereign state and that only its sultan could make treaties on its behalf. It went on to claim that the Malaysia Act was "void and inoperative" and sought an injunction to restrain the Federation of Malaya and the British Government from implementing its provisions on Malaysia Day. *Straits Times*, 11 September 1963; CO 1030/1508; Richard Allen, *Malaysia: Prospect and Retrospect. The Impact and Aftermath of Colonial Rule* (London, 1968), pp. 174–75.

39 Cabinet Defence Committee minutes, 25 October 1961, CAB 131/25, D14(61)6.

40 The support of the United States, Australia and New Zealand was regarded as essential for the success of the Malaysia project, but the quadripartite talks in Washington in February 1963 revealed misgivings on the part of Britain's allies about its potentially destabilizing effects in the region and by August, it was clear that Macmillan and J.F. Kennedy differed in their approaches to Sukarno. FO 371/169695 and 169908, PREM 11/4349; see also Matthew Jones, *Conflict and Confrontation in South East Asia, 1961–1965. Britain, the United States and the Creation of Malaysia* (Cambridge, 2002), and John Subritzky, *Confronting Sukarno. British, American, Australian and New Zealand Diplomacy in the Malaysian-Indonesian Confrontation, 1961–65* (Basingstoke, 2000).

41 The release of British archives under the thirty-year rule has enabled historians to examine the redefinition of defence policy culminating in the decision to withdraw from east of Suez by 1971: David Easter, "Britain's defence policy in South East Asia and the Confrontation", Ph.D. thesis, London School of Economics, University of London, 1998; Phuong Pham, "The end to 'east of Suez'. The British Decision to Withdraw from Malaysia and Singapore, 1964 to

1968", D.Phil. thesis, University of Oxford, 2001; Saki Dockrill, *Britain's Retreat from East of Suez. The Choice between Europe and the World?* (Basingstoke, 2002).

42 Lee Kuan Yew, "Paper on the Future of the Federation of Malaya, Singapore and the Borneo Territories", n.d. [9 May 1961], CO 1030/973, no. E203.

43 "Integration of British North Borneo Territories and Singapore with the Federation of Malaya", enclosed in Tunku Abdul Rahman to Harold Macmillan, 26 June 1961, PREM 11/3418.

44 Tan Sri Ghazali Shafie, *Malay Nationalism and Globalisation* (Bangi, Malaysia, 2001), pp. 33–34.

45 See Cheah Boon Kheng, *Malaysia: The Making of a Nation* (Singapore, 2002), chapter 2: "The 'bargain' and contesting nationalisms".

46 KL had not kept the governments of Sabah and Sarawak informed of the impending departure of Singapore and this lack of consultation provoked some in Sabah to talk of secession. In 1966 Kuala Lumpur removed from office Sarawak's chief minister, Stephen Kalong Ningkan, on account of his advocacy of state rights and his resistance to the model of Malay dominance established in peninsular Malaysia.

47 See Cheah Boon Kheng, *Malaysia*, pp. 102–08; Gordon P. Means, *Malaysian Politics: The Second Generation* (Singapore, 1991), pp. 6–10; Karl von Vorys, *Democracy without Consensus: Communalism and Political Stability in Malaysia* (Princeton, New Jersey, 1975).

48 Lee Kuan Yew, *The Singapore Story*, p. 649; Albert Lau, *A Moment of Anguish. Singapore in Malaysia and the Politics of Disengagement* (Singapore, 1998).

49 See the massive second volume of Lee's memoirs, *From Third World to First: The Singapore Story, 1966–2000: Singapore and the Asian Economic Boom* (New York, 2000).

50 Lee Kuan Yew in interview with Peter Day, *BBC News*, 5 July 2000.

CHAPTER NINE

Nation-Building and the Singapore Story: Some Issues in the Study of Contemporary Singapore History

Albert Lau

"H ISTORY", AS Claude Levi-Strauss asserted, "is ... never history, but history-for".[1] Perhaps nowhere is the appropriation of this view that history must always be written from some viewpoint and, therefore, *for* some purpose in mind more evident than in its use for the agenda of nation-building. Few would deny that history and nation-building — defined by one commentator as "the creation by government of a cohesive political community characterized by an abiding sense of identity and common consciousness"[2] — are inextricably related, for history, so far as traditional arguments go, not only "offers lessons (be they true or false) to which leaders, nations and peoples respond" but is also "the shaper of national identity".[3] Indeed, as the editors of *Writing National Histories: Western Europe since 1800* point out, "Historical writing has been connected to the process of nation-building across Europe ever since the concept of the modern nation was first formulated in the American and French Revolutions of the late-eighteenth century."[4] In Singapore's experience of nation-building, however, the deliberative use of history in the fashioning of a national narrative — *The Singapore Story* — occurred belatedly, coming only after three decades of nation-building had lapsed. The use of history — and its perceived "politicization" — for the agenda of nation-building raises intrinsic conceptual and methodological concerns, as it did in the contemporary

Singapore experience, that invariably ignited ideological contestation regarding the integrity and purpose of history — and what is the proper way of portraying the past accurately.

History and Nation-Building

"The past" — "as it was" — is how history has been commonly defined. To be more precise, history is really about the "study" of the past, for the past "as it was" is irrecoverable and all we have are what historians, working with available records and archival materials, write about the past. Their retrieval, and representation, of the past has traditionally been validated by the methodology of "scientific" history based on the rigorous investigation of primary sources.[5] By retaining "objectivity", so the argument goes, historians could ascertain the "facts" and so report the "truth".[6] Of course, at the philosophical level, historians today recognize how this idealized "modernist" conception of historical "truth" is basically unrealistic: "facts", which are necessarily pre-selected by their incompleteness, do not exist naturally as facts but need to be so defined — or "interpreted" — by the historian; and any scintilla of "objectivity", which "implies the existence of vantage points absolutely without bias",[7] is simply unattainable in a subject where evaluation and interpretation are also intrinsic skills.

If history, as the critique of historical truth-claims has sought to show, is never neutral, then recalling the past for the highly politicized purpose of nation-building only opens it to further possible contestation. "History manifestly becomes a political battleground," argued Lysa Hong and Jimmy Yap: "Politicians who use history as a political weapon would claim that the version that they support is the most accurate and valid, if not the only acceptable way of understanding the past."[8] In the context of nation-building, the continued legimatory use of the past has, traditionally, been invoked for the purpose of fostering national consciousness and identity — and its corollary, instilling patriotism and citizenship.[9] "Most national history and most group history are of this kind," asserted William McNeill.[10] "Consciousness of a common past", he explained, "is a powerful supplement to other ways of defining who 'we' are. ...and formal written history became useful in defining 'us' versus 'them' ".[11] Indeed, for groups "struggling towards self-consciousness" and those whose "accustomed status seems threatened", the invoking of such "vivid, simplified portraits of their admirable virtues and undeserved sufferings"[12] has always been seen as an indispensable means of developing their continued instinct for national survival.[13] Such, for instance, was the consuming obsession of the Poles, as John Warren recounted from recent history:

> In an attempt to cripple the Poles' will to resist, German forces in the Second World War destroyed much of the historic centre of Warsaw. The destruction of that shared heritage was meant to convey the stark message that a people without a past are a worthless people. After the defeat of Germany, the Poles rebuilt Warsaw — exactly as it had been before the war.[14]

Propagating this so-called "mythistory"[15] as national history, however, presents dangers, as McNeill warns: "[T]he fact that a group of people accept a given version of the past does not make that version any truer for outsiders."[16] Instead, the capacity for inter-group conflict consequently intensifies: "a portrait of the past that denigrates others and praises the ideals and practice of a given group naively and without restraint, can distort a people's image of outsiders so that foreign relations begin to consist of nothing but nasty surprises."[17] Notwithstanding such concerns, it seems apparent that the "use of the national past to legitimize (or delegitimize) particular governments and regimes remains as widespread as ever".[18] No government or nation could afford to reject the past for the sake of insuring its present and future: "A nation or any other human group that knows how to behave in crisis situations because it has inherited a heroic historiographical tradition that tells how ancestors resisted their enemies successfully is more likely to act together effectively than a group lacking such a tradition".[19] That governments and politicians continue to appeal to history or, in some cases, "mythistory" in the fashioning of their national narratives should not be too surprising, for they had recognized instinctively what their detractors had failed to acknowledge fully: as narrative history has always been written for some purpose, it is in a sense inevitably political,[20] and therefore becomes "a potent ideological mechanism in the work of nation-building".[21]

The Use of History in Singapore's Nation-Building

And yet, in Singapore's experience of nation-building, there was an initial reluctance to reclaim and use the past.[22] Gripped by the preoccupation with the immediate tasks of national political and economic survival after its sudden and tumultuous separation from Malaysia in 1965, its leaders sought to direct Singaporeans to "examine the present, think of the future, and forget the past".[23] As one Singapore minister, S. Dhanabalan, acknowledged, "We were all too preoccupied with surviving the present to worry about recording it for the future."[24] Consequently, history, which "has no immediate practical use", was dropped from the primary school curriculum from 1972 in favour of more "useful studies" geared to Singapore's industrial needs.[25] The past was perceived as a hindrance to the nation-building efforts. "Powerful shadows from the past, and the ghosts of things dead, obscure and bedevil the road to a brighter and more united future," observed Devan Nair, "Rival and jealous gods of the past bar entry at all the gates which open out into the uplands of the Future."[26] The future rather than to their past was where Singaporeans were exhorted to look. Singapore's short history, it was argued, offered no proud Golden Age or a glorious heroic historiographical tradition that could be usefully called upon to galvanize its peoples for national mobilization goals or to transcend the mentalities of their separate ethnic and cultural consciousness. What the island's history revealed instead was not only the record of Singapore's sustained physical and political vulnerability but also the concomitant story of its domination by the successive colonial powers of the day. The search for such a usable past in a plural, immigrant, society, it was further feared, could also lead unwittingly to the strengthening of ethnic and cultural identities with disastrous consequences. As Rajaratnam commented:

> As pasts go, I confess, this is not much of a past in a world when countries can boast of histories dating back thousands of years. ...

Singapore's genealogical table, alas, ends as abruptly as it begins. However we could have contrived a more lengthy and eye-boggling lineage by tracing our ancestry back to the lands from which our forefathers emigrated — China, India, Sri Lanka, the Middle East and Indonesia. The price we would have to pay for this more impressive genealogical table would be to turn Singapore into a bloody battle-ground for endless racial and communal conflicts and interventionist politics by the more powerful and bigger nations from which Singaporeans had emigrated. The present government ... [therefore] has been careful about the kind of awareness of the past it should inculcate in a multi-cultural society.[27]

From the early 1980s, however, the dismissal of its past gave way to growing concern about the political wisdom of forgetting Singapore's national history. In an apparent volte-face, Singapore officials started to warn against the "indecent haste to obliterate our historical heritage"[28] and the drive to "create a sparkling new Singapore with no trace of the past".[29] That history was "an essential part of our national development"[30] and had its "proper use"[31] was at last officially — if belatedly — acknowledged. It was not the love of nostalgia or "some obscure research reasons"[32] that brought about this apparent reappraisal but the unleashing of new political and societal forces that, in the official mind, could potentially threaten Singapore's long-term security, viability and ethos of survival. Singapore had survived its early difficult years, and after a decade and a half of steady growth and prosperity, the future had appeared less fearsome. What worried Singapore's leaders was not only how modernization and urban renewal, while necessary in land-scarce Singapore, had transformed its physical landscape beyond recognition, but also how the rapid pace of development was impacting its society to such an extent that "our young and future generations will not know how Singapore was like before".[33] "Because what is worth preserving from the past are not all that plentiful," Rajaratnam warned, "we should try to save what is worthwhile from the past from the vandalism of the speculator and the developer, from a government and a bureaucracy which believes that anything that cannot be translated into cold cash is not worth investing in."[34] Struck by the Polish authorities' single-minded determination to rebuild Warsaw "exactly as it was before the war", Rajaratnam surmised that they were not only trying to replicate the physical buildings but also to recapture the "intangibles" — "its character, its atmosphere, and its texture" — precisely because they knew that to have built a modern Warsaw would have meant "if not obliterating then at least weakening to a significant degree, the Polish people's awareness of their long and memorable past". Because the Poles had "a different kind of national accounting" when it came to rebuilding Warsaw, they could "today stand up stubbornly and defiantly to assert their identity and desire for freedom in the face of a more powerful, superior and demanding adversary".[35] That the Polish experience underscored an important use of the past for nation-building was not lost on Rajaratnam — nor was its implied relevance to Singapore's own sovereign existence as a strategically placed but vulnerable nation-state:

> The history of Poland, because of its strategic or, more accurately, unlucky location, has been one of repeated invasions by marauding armies which sought the subjugation and elimination of the Poles as an independent people. Had the Poles not had a strong sense of the past, they would have disappeared as a people as have so many in the course of mankind's chequered and violent history.[36]

Even more alarming than the destruction of Singapore's physical heritage were the effects of these rapid changes on the formative experiences of the post-1965 generation, to whom "the turbulence of the colonial and Malaysian era, and the difficulties of the first years of independence, are only sagas of epic proportions, heard at second hand, not vivid personal experiences". Growing up in an orderly and successful present, they were "less used to hardship than to affluence, less aware of the fragility of our prosperity, and have higher expectations of what life ought to offer".[37] Such a change in the population, as Lee Hsien Loong pointed out, "must affect the political process" and the challenge for the government was to "keep alive a sense of our heritage".[38] An understanding of Singapore's history, officials felt, could offer "lessons" so that "history need not repeat itself":[39] "We must know the story of how Singapore came to be what it is, so that we never forget what an unnatural fact our very existence is, and why the price of this continuing is constant vigilance."[40] In particular, young Singaporeans needed to understand that order, stability and racial harmony should not be taken for granted ("We ignore our tribal faultlines at our peril," observed George Yeo[41]); that "there are no such things as permanent prosperity and permanent success";[42] and that "our future as a nation is not predestined but will depend on our commitment and preparedness to work for our common good."[43] Otherwise, as Rajaratnam warned, "From my study of history, I conclude that decline and collapse appear to be the unavoidable fate of successful nations."[44]

Without such "historical moorings", officials feared that Singaporeans could, at best, evolve into a "rootless and transient society",[45] without a sense of identity, and endangering Singapore's future prospect as a nation, as Lee Hsien Loong warned: "The long-term survival of a country, especially a small one, depends in large measure on a strong sense of identity."[46] Without the latter, Singaporeans would lose the "security of belonging" that could help them "weather difficult times" together.[47] "[A] people with poor memories", observed George Yeo, "can be a fatal weakness in crises".[48]

> When we study the lives of our forefathers and the way they responded to challenges, we abstract lessons for ourselves. In this way, we build upon the accumulated knowledge and wisdom of our ancestors ... We must never lose this sense of our past because it is a great source of spiritual strength in a crisis. Societies with shallow cultures are easily destroyed.[49]

Without this awareness among its young, its leaders feared that Singapore could not be expected to master its future. This sense of the past, as S. Jayakumar asserted, was therefore "essential to understanding the present process of nation building".[50]

The soul searching about Singapore's history gave rise, from the mid-1990s, to a more interventionist phase which saw the introduction and integration of National Education (NE) into the school curriculum from 1997. Explaining its background, Education Minister Teo Chee Hean reiterated:

> NE was included in our school curriculum because it was found that many Singaporeans, especially those of school-going age and younger Singaporeans knew little of our recent past and the people closely associated with our recent history. They did not know how Singapore became an independent nation. Many of our young people did not know when Singapore gained independence, and that Singapore was once part of Malaysia. Neither were our young able to explain Singapore's separation from Malaysia in 1965. Another disturbing indicator was reflected in a survey conducted by *Lianhe Zaobao* in 1996 that found a large majority of the 659 respondents from secondary schools expressing little interest in nation building.[51]

At the official launch of the programme on 19 May, Deputy Prime Minister Lee Hsien Loong outlined its aim to help young Singaporeans "develop national cohesion, the instinct for survival and confidence in our future", or what he called the "DNA to be passed from one generation to the next". It was necessary, he said, to foster a sense of identity to "strengthen their emotional attachment to the nation, and their sense of rootedness", ensure that they understood Singapore's "unique challenges, constraints and vulnerabilities, which make us different from other countries", and instil in them "the core values of our way of life, and the will to prevail, that ensure our continued success and well being". In implementing the programme, history was given a major role: "[O]ur young must know the Singapore Story — how Singapore succeeded against the odds to become a nation," he said, "... Knowing this history is part of the becoming a Singaporean. It is the backdrop which makes sense of our present."[52]

The launch of NE, followed in 1998 by the staging of a grand multimedia exhibition, *The Singapore Story: Overcoming the Odds* in July, which attracted over half a million people, and the launch in September of the first volume of Senior Minister Lee Kuan Yew's memoirs, *The Singapore Story: Memoirs of Lee Kuan Yew*, helped to keep Singapore history very much in the spotlight. In his opening address at the exhibition, Prime Minister Goh Chok Tong reiterated the importance of history to help Singaporeans understand the "vulnerabilities and constraints" that "will always be there" and how the "painful episodes" of the race riots in 1964 and 1969 would always be an "integral part" of the Singapore Story that all Singaporeans should know. "Each succeeding generation of Singaporeans," he said, "must learn about the nation's history, and understand how it is relevant to their future. Then, 100 years from now, we will have more chapters to recount, more stories to tell".[53] In writing his memoirs, Senior Minister Lee too had in mind to impart a sense of the past to future generations. He had not intended to write his memoirs, he said, but was persuaded to do after he was "troubled by the over-confidence of a generation that has only known stability, growth and prosperity",[54] an observation he had made in a speech in 1996:

> ...The present generation below 35 has grown up used to high economic growth year after year, and take their security and success for granted. And because they believe all is well, they are less willing to make sacrifices for the benefit of the other in society. They are more concerned about their individual and family's welfare and success, not their community or society's well being.
>
> But this is very dangerous, because things can go terribly wrong very quickly. These people are not aware of Singapore's vulnerabilities. All they read and see is No. 1 or No. 2 competitive country, No. 1 seaport, No. 1 airport, No. 1 airline and so on. Sometimes they complain that we are driving people too hard and making life too stressful, so why not settle for No. 2 or 3, or 4! But it does matter, for if we are not near the top in competitiveness, there is no reason why we should have a seaport, or an airport, or an airline — or indeed why there should be a separate independent Singapore. It is as simple as that.[55]

Though not official history, Lee's memoirs provided, as British premier Tony Blair noted, "unique insights into the history of modern Singapore".[56] Written by "a man who, almost single-handedly, built a great nation from a small island",[57] it is personal — but still authoritative — history. "As current history, *The Singapore Story* is without equal," wrote former Australian Prime Minister, Malcolm Fraser.[58] But because Lee had wanted to "give young Singaporeans an objective account of why and how Singapore sought merger with Malaya but in two years was asked to leave Malaysia",[59] his book also stirred controversy from across the Causeway, driving Malaysian leaders and opinion-makers to question his perspective and account of personalities and events that led to the difficult period in both nation's history. All these NE-related developments helped to secure the position of history as a pillar in Singapore's nation-building agenda. "Like the prodigal son, history is returning to Singapore," noted Asad Latif of the *Straits Times*, "National Education has offered it a place to stay. ... a revolution has occurred. This is the critical fact of Singapore's recent history."[60]

Engaging the Recent Past: Issues and Controversies

History's return and its "proper" use by the state invariably open it to possible contestation. To the ruling party's political opponents, like former Barisan Sosialis leader, Lee Siew Choh, the latest attempt by the People's Action Party (PAP) government at "[r]ewriting, reversing history" was dismissed as a scheme to "cover up past misdeeds which they do not want posterity to know about."[61] Not unexpectedly, among other observers, the heavy political hand of the government in fashioning the national narrative also contributed in no small measure to the perception that it was official "propaganda", designed with some secret political agenda in mind. NE's "obsession" with "a set of lessons to be learnt from certain historical events", for instance, so worried one letter-writer to the *Straits Times*, who saw this as an attempt to "preclude historical controversy" and "engender a form of selective amnesia" as facts could be interpreted "in such a way that the lessons learnt are those which are conducive to the preservation of the political status quo". He cautioned that NE should not degenerate into "a mind-numbling, flag-waving form of jingoism which would strain the credulity of the student as he matures intellectually" and warned that there was a real danger in politicizing history: "Political involvement in National Education may lead the cynic to dismiss the whole campaign as little more than political propaganda."[62] Another writer opined that allowing the youth to "find out the facts from as many sources as are available and be given the option for making up their own minds" was preferable to "any process of indoctrination".[63] Others read the politicization of history as an ideologically-inspired rear-guard attempt by the ruling PAP government to create a "crisis mentality" as part of its ongoing attempt to "sustain hegemony over the state" — the possible result of indents made by the opposition to its parliamentary monopoly from 1981.[64] As Loh Kah Seng argued:

> While it [the Singapore Story] does allow a range of possible perspectives, all of these nonetheless focus on the basic concept of 'vulnerability'. The persistent admonition that the nation is racially explosive discourages the public from dismissing dubious ideas as PAP propaganda since to do so would be, in effect, to threaten one's own economic future. The Singapore Story thus pre-determines how Singaporeans perceive and interpret the reality they experience, and to the extent that they regard the regime's ideas uncritically as 'common-sense' truisms, they partake in the government's ongoing hegemony.[65]

While the PAP's overarching political dominance has made the close identification of party and national interests almost impossible to separate, and there is a sense of how this coincidence could be advantageous in insuring through the national narrative its "hegemony", it does not appear that party survival alone, in this case, was, as some have argued, its overriding objective in the construction of national history. Certainly, such an overt, interventionist, scheme carried risks of being misconstrued and rejected as PAP "propaganda", as it obviously had, and could rebound against the party instead. That the weak political opposition was not its match and that the ruling party already had, in its political arsenal, an impressive track record to boast and other, surer, instruments of power to sustain its political legitimacy and dominance would argue against too ready an acceptance of a reductionist interpretation of its use of national history.

That its use of history could be misconstrued as propaganda, the PAP had already anticipated. While acknowledging that NE, like similar programmes in Japan and the United States, was a "process of indoctrination", Lee Hsien Loong, however defended its necessity on national grounds at his opening address during its launch: "If countries like Japan and US, with long histories and deep roots, have found it essential to pass on national instincts systematically from generation to generation, all the more Singapore, a young country barely one generation old, must make a concerted effort to imbue the right values and instincts in the psyche of our young."[66] As for its version of national history, Lee, while not denying that it was not propaganda, asserted that it was also neither mythistory but a narrative "based on historical facts" and was therefore "objective history, seen from a Singaporean standpoint". "We are not talking about an idealized legendary account or a founding myth, but of an accurate understanding of what happened in the past, and what this history means for us today." Neither was it "definitive" history. Not all the records were available, he said, but as archives yielded their secrets, progressively, "a more complete picture will emerge".[67]

The more vociferous contestation of its version of national history came not from within but from without — its close neighbour, Malaysia. "Singapore's very existence," observed Anthony Reid, "represents something of a challenge to Malaysia's self-image."[68] Sharing a common history, it was perhaps inevitable that the clash of interpretations over key events that defined the *raison d'etre* for their existence as separate, independent, nation-states would occur, especially when, in recounting its national history, Singapore was disinclined to "gloss over them". "Amnesia is not an option," declared Lee Hsien Loong in his NE address, "We cannot pretend that incidents involving race and religion never happened. They are part of our history."[69] What Singapore's leaders were now willing to openly tackle were the "delicate issues" of the two race riots in Singapore in 1964, which they charged, "had been instigated deliberately to intimidate Singapore's Chinese population" and the "fundamental" nature of the issues which led to its separation from Malaysia.[70] In his memoirs, the Senior Minister elaborated on and provided his perspective on these two defining issues. The race riots, he said, were instigated by the incendiary statements and "flagrant falsehoods" of key United Malays National Organization (UMNO) leaders, of whom the UMNO Secretary-General, Syed Jaafar Albar, was the main protagonist, with the knowledge of, and backed by, the Malaysian Deputy Premier, Tun Abdul Razak for the purpose of re-establishing UMNO's political influence among the Singapore Malays, thus reclaiming the ground it had lost to the PAP in the 1963 election, and to further use the Singapore Malays as pawns to consolidate Malay support for UMNO in Malaya.[71] On separation, the fundamental problem was over whether the new Federation should be a truly multi-racial society, a "Malaysian-Malaysia" which the PAP championed through the Malaysian Solidarity Convention that it led, or one dominated by Malay hegemony. Reflecting on the "real reasons" for separation, Lee wrote: "They must have concluded that if they allowed us to exercise our constitutional rights, they were bound to lose in the long run. The Malaysian Solidarity Convention would have rallied the non-Malays and, most dangerous of all, eventually made inroads into the Malay ground on the peninsula ... This was the nub of the matter."[72] In a comment certain to rile Malaysian leaders, Lee opined that the "PAP leaders were not like the politicians in Malaya. Singapore ministers were not pleasure-loving, nor did they seek to enrich themselves."[73] He revealed how Tun Razak, for example, had once offered Dr. Goh Keng Swee, then Singapore's deputy premier, some 5,000 acres of prime rubber land as a bribe, which Goh turned down.[74]

Lee's account drew a rash of angry cries from Malaysian leaders who retorted that the book "merely reflects one man's highly partisan interpretation of history", was selective in its use of sources and deeply biased in its arguments, and was nothing more than a "tool for self-aggrandizement".[75] The Malaysian Premier, Dr. Mahathir Mohamad accused Singapore of being "insensitive" by dredging up "such old issues, it's no use".[76] "[W]e try hard not to raise difficult issues," he said, "while they do the opposite."[77] Deeply "hurt" by Lee's insinuations about his father, Education Minister Najib Tun Razak said that the Senior Minister should not have written about the dead who could not defend themselves.[78] Then Defence Minister Syed Hamid Albar, the son of the late former UMNO-Secretary, charged Lee with "manipulating the facts to make them appear as if that was what had actually happened … he is trying to recall history based on his own perspective and his own interpretations".[79] Providing the Malaysian perspectives on the defining events, Syed Hamid said that, contrary to Lee's charges that his father had provoked the race riots, there was already "a strong, valid discontent among the Malay population on the way Lee Kuan Yew had treated them".[80] On why Singapore was expelled, he said that it was "because of its communal politics promised under the cover of multi-racialism" and accused Lee of putting PAP candidates in the 1964 Federation elections "to instigate the Chinese population in Malaysia to support the PAP when the understanding was that the PAP should limit its political activities to Singapore".[81] Mahathir observed that "When Singapore was part of Malaysia, Singapore leaders wanted to see the Chinese in Malaysia controlling politics; so when we warned them to stop it, they became angry at us, and it was for that reason that the late Tunku Abdul Rahman opined that it was best they stay out of Malaysia."[82]

Denying that he had written a distorted account in his memoirs "to justify what I have done or to prove I was right", Lee Kuan Yew said, "That would have been a waste of time. I was not always right. It was good fortune that on some critical issues, things turned out well, otherwise I would have come to grief and the Singapore story would have had a different ending."[83] Dismissing the Malaysian charge that he was being "insensitive", Lee said that it was only their way of saying, "why are you saying things which I don't like to hear".[84] But he had an obligation to tell Singaporeans "why I did these things, what took place and why they should take note of my experience. If my experience is irrelevant, throw the book away. I believe it is not irrelevant".[85] As Lee expected his book "to be scrutinized and criticized", he had a team of researchers who "took pains to check and re-check my facts":[86]

When I started I did know how much work it needed. It was not simply sitting down to say 'Once upon a time' and then spin a story off the top of my head. A whole team of researchers went through 30 years of my correspondence, notes of meetings, Cabinet papers and other documents in the archives, to gather and marshal the data for me to work on. I did not write an official history of Singapore. It is my account of what I did, why I did it, and about the people who worked with me or against me.[87]

While his book remained his version of events, it was an account based on sources that may be verified independently:

What I have written, I have checked against the records, especially when recounting the race riots of 1964. My account is supported by documents submitted to the commission of inquiry which was held in Singapore by the Malaysian judiciary to investigate the causes of the riots. The documents are still in the archives ... My narrative is also substantiated by reports of British, Australian, New Zealand and American diplomats in Kuala Lumpur made at that time.[88]

On Tun Razak's offer of a bribe, Lee revealed that Dr. Goh had "told me of this offer at the time it was made" and had also noted this in his oral history account recorded in 1982. In the same account, Goh had also recorded that Tun Razak had assured him that he was in control of Syed Jaafar Albar. Asked by Lee on 31 October 1997 whether he would stand by what he had said in his oral history account, Goh replied on 4 November 1997 that "he stood by every word in his oral history". Lee said that both of them decided it was better to publish "these facts while we are still alive to substantiate them than to speak from our graves". "To write or dictate oral history to be published after my death, would not be right," he added, "If I am not prepared to speak while I am alive, I do not deserve to be heard from my grave."[89] His statements were not directed at the families of those he had named who had been "hurt" but "I had to write the truth because it was crucial to an understanding of what happened."[90] Lee reiterated that, as he could write his memoirs "but once", he "set out to be accurate, to make a contribution to the historical records of Singapore ... I do not propagate falsehoods, not in a serious document like this. This is not a political tract".[91] The consequences for him would have been grave: "If there are false or untrue statements, I will stand contradicted and my credibility demolished."[92] Indeed, as Prime Minister Goh Chok Tong commented, the Senior Minister's remarks carried force: "As he put it quite poignantly, he is an old man, is there any reason for him to put in untruths because if the untruths are proven, then his whole life's reputation is gone. His integrity is gone." But Lee's account, as Goh emphasized, "is not the official history of Singapore". He hoped that, "as new materials are made available elsewhere, historians will look at the materials and they will then use the materials to either substantiate SM's account of what took place, especially in the years when Singapore joined Malaysia and before that, or as well as to prove SM wrong if they could have new materials to do so."[93]

To professional historians, however, the very notion of engaging the recent past, especially one that has witnessed such vigorous political contestation, underscores some of the more practical issues of writing contemporary history. Comparisons with "current affairs", "enlightened journalism" or "speculative history" are apt to arise, as would doubts about the stunted perspectives, the inadequate documentation, and subjective bias that normally characterize the writing of contemporary history.[94] Good history writing, it is argued, requires an objectivity that is tempered by the vantage point of time and the use and analysis of available archival documentation — all that contemporary history, apparently, is not.

The contemporary historian's lack of historical perspective, therefore, offers a serious objection. "Thinking in time" is what a historian has been normally trained to do, and consequently the greater the distance between the historian and his subject, so it is argued, the better history he is able to write. This ability to view events in the perspective of time, however, is hampered when the historian writes about the recent past. The problem of a limited perspective is of particular relevance to Singapore. As the island attained its own sovereign statehood only in 1965, much of its post-independence history would therefore be, by definition, contemporary history, and any attempt to document the account of its story of nation-building would be immediately confronted at the onset by this constraint of a stunted perspective. Would such an enterprise therefore be doomed from the start? Perhaps it should be apparent that historical distance from the subject does not in itself always guarantee the writing of good history. Taking Professor Geoffrey Elton's definition of historical perspective as "truly understanding an age from the inside",[95] and not, as commonly understood, as an interpretation of events in the light of hindsight, that objective may be better realized by a contemporary historian working "from within" the period he is studying. He would be better positioned to capture the "atmosphere" of the age to an extent which no future historian, however perceptive, may ever succeed in recapturing. "The 'superstition of historical distance'," as Gordon Wright puts it, "can blind us to the fact that the contemporary historian may produce a more faithful account than his later successor, who will possess a fuller documentary record plus the blessings of long perspective but who will suffer from the astigmatism caused by the distortions of time."[96] Indeed, as Devan Nair recounted from his own personal involvement in the nation-building process in Singapore, a participant's first-hand perspective could afford valuable insights that would otherwise be unavailable to a historian studying an age from the outside: "This would be history at first hand, written by those who lived, fought and won through daunting events and experiences, which are not likely to be repeated for the younger generation of Singaporeans." Regrettably, however, "those who make history seldom find time to write it themselves," he lamented, but "it would be a tragedy if future generations of Singaporeans had to depend on second-hand versions."[97] That a participant in a historical event will have a unique perspective that is often not fully understood by historians writing about the subject was also noted by Lee Kuan Yew:

History does not happen in clear cut units like courses for credits in an American university. It is after forces let loose in tumultuous events have run their course that the historian comes along to mark out neat periods and narrates them in clear-cut chapters.[98]

The objection that writing contemporary history offers only a limited perspective is further compounded, according to some scholars, by a more pervasive problem when it is applied to recent Singapore history: the apparent dominance of a singular perspective — the PAP's "template" of history, which has a tendency to "crowd out alternative voices in the narration of Singapore's history". Lysa Hong observed, for instance, that Rajaratnam's account of party history — the "PAP's First Ten Years" which appeared in the *PAP Tenth Anniversary Celebration Souvenir 1964* — has become "a classic ... for casting the template for the history of Singapore", particularly of the struggle of the non-communists against the communists within the PAP. "More than 30 years after it was written," she wrote, "the understanding of the period has not moved one iota from Rajaratnam's rendition of it". Written by the "victors"[99] — leaders "at centre stage of a government that has been in almost absolute power since 1965", and men who could also "claim privileged knowledge" — the accounts become "an exercise in legitimizing 'us' and not others. The others (political foes) are reduced to negative labels on the extreme fringes".[100] Having "shared the struggle for a time, and yet had departed from its true path"[101] and lost the political game, they "also lost their voice as agents of history because of the institutional and political constraints on them".[102] T.N. Harper noted, for instance, that in the "dominant national narrative", the role of former PAP leader, Lim Chin Siong, who was detained in February 1963 for his pro-communist activities, has become "an adjunct to the master narrative of Lee Kuan Yew and others" in the "authorized version" of the struggle — "He has not vanished from it entirely; but is seen always at a distance and most often through the eyes of his adversaries".[103] Given the dominance of the PAP "template", alternative views "has to come from slippages in the dominant discourse itself".[104]

Notwithstanding the perception that such a dominant "template" exists, it should be obvious that the existence of a version of the past, however compelling, does not in itself constrain any scholar who so wishes from producing other counter versions consistent with the historical evidence. The crux of the matter, it could be argued, is not so much a question of the dominance of a perceived "template", but something more fundamental:

the quality of the evidence. The existence of the PAP "template", for instance, had not stopped former Barisan Sosialis leader, Dr. Lee Siew Choh, from contesting it, as he did in his series of lengthy letters to the *Straits Times* to argue his case that the PAP referendum for the merger with Malaya in 1961 was "a most dishonest referendum"[105] and was "undemocratic, unfair and unjust"[106] because it did not put a simple "yes" or "no" question, and the important questions were framed by the ruling PAP alone, without consultation. But, as Mohamad Maidin, the Parliamentary Secretary for Education, pointed out, "Historical controversy ... must be consistent with the facts. Facts will not and cannot be ignored, however inconvenient." Replying to Lee's charges, and referring the former to the "facts", including the parliamentary debates on the subject, Maidin pointed out that Dr. Lee "forgets his history": "The Barisan lost the argument and lost the Referendum. The PAP carried the majority of the people and 35 years later, in defiance of the facts, Dr. Lee is trying [to] rewrite the record and reverse that verdict of history."[107] The PAP had acted openly, responsibly and constitutionally on the referendum, he said, "Its actions are all on the public record." Reiterating the government's view, he asserted:

> The Singapore story is based on facts and documents, and the consensus of historians who have studied them. Since the facts and documents are all on record, any dispute can be resolved impartially and objectively. It is objective history, seen from a Singaporean point of view.
>
> The facts of the Singapore story will always be subject to reinterpretation in the light of new information or fresh analysis, like all other historical facts.[108]

Maidin's reference to the "facts" of history puts into context another objection to the writing of contemporary history: the problem of available archival evidence. What if the "facts" are not accessible or only "selected" facts have been made available? Would this not distort the narrative? How could historians presume to write authoritatively about recent history when they have no access to the classified official documents which would not yield their secrets for at least another thirty to fifty years — or forever — under official legislation? In writing his memoirs, the Senior Minister, for instance, said that he had started work only in 1995, the year documents in the British archives were made available under the "thirty-years rule" on the declassification of documents. Similarly, archival records were also made available around this time in Australia and the United States.[109] It was the availability of such records that enabled his research team to accumulate "[m]ore than 20 filing bins of documents ... over the last three years", disclosed Andrew Tan, who headed Lee's research team.[110] The importance of having archival sources is borne out in my own experience in writing *A Moment of Anguish: Singapore in Malaysia and the Politics of Disengagement*,[111] which was an attempt to understand a defining episode in Singapore's contemporary history — the twenty-three months that Singapore was part of Malaysia and the circumstances that contributed to its eventual separation and independent statehood. It was indeed fortuitous that, at the time when I embarked on my study in 1996, the various archives in the United Kingdom, Australia and the United States, and, more significantly, the Singapore archives, were opened, and I was able to consult, for instance, Special Branch and police reports, kept at the archives of the Internal Security Department, Ministry of Home Affairs, and also certain files from the Prime Minister's Office which were made available at the National Archives of Singapore. A major drawback for the historian writing about contemporary events in Singapore has always been the unavailability of primary sources, particularly of confidential categories of indigenous records, which remained largely classified apparently because of their "sensitive" nature. The alternative use of foreign archives to document indigenous history, however, has not escaped criticism among historians concerned about the writing of more "autonomous" history using indigenous sources. But unless these latter records exist or are made available, it is likely that, for certain categories of historical studies, the reliance on foreign archives will continue to be indispensable for the writing of contemporary Singapore history. In the circumstances of my own study, which coincided with the renewal of interest in history and National Education in Singapore, the opening of the foreign and local archives enabled the circumstances of the controversial and pivotal race riots in Singapore in July and September 1964 to be documented with greater precision from primary records, including Special Branch accounts, for the first time. Because of the threat of the race riots to law and order, the latter sources were especially useful in providing a perspective as seen from the viewpoint of the security services, whose role it was to investigate the causes and nature of the riots. The archival records also permitted the documentation of what was little-known before: the secret negotiations for the abortive "disengagement" some six months before the actual separation and the behind-the-scenes manoeuvrings, particularly the role of key personalities who contributed to the climatic parting in 1965. In short, it was the availability of archival documentation that permitted a more comprehensive and in-depth study of the subject that was not possible in earlier works.

That a historian requires his sources to write good history is a methodological truism. But, as the contemporary historian is wont to argue, it is perhaps less ingenuous to say that, without access to classified documents, no satisfactory historical analysis can be made of recent events. Not all classified records are likely to be made available to historians even after the lapse of a period of time. A measure of incompleteness is therefore inevitable. Records which are of "current" significance to government departments, or which are of a security or politically sensitive nature, may never be made available to scholars. On his part, the writer of contemporary history has certain other compensating advantages in that he has not only a richer wealth and variety of other sources available — for instance, the larger output of secondary writing, memoirs, diaries, journals, newspapers, film and sound recordings, videos, oral interviews — but also better means of authenticating their reliability, all of which make the contemporary historian's task, to some degree, even more exacting. What seems clear, however, as the *Straits Times* leader argued, is that while disclosure of these facts must be in accordance with accepted norms, there is scope for a great deal more to be divulged, especially from indigenous archives. On the ups and downs of the Singapore-Malaysia equation, it commented that "The definitive history of that period has yet to be written. Such knowledge would be in the public interest; it should therefore be in the public domain." The editorial added that it was counter-productive for all this information to gather dust while people speculated about important sequences on the basis of scrappy media reports, faulty memory and the possibly biased recollections of some of the players. The wrong conclusions were all too likely.[112]

The contemporary historian's attempt to reconstruct the recent past raises a final objection: the question of subjectivity. Inevitably, the greater involvement of the historian in writing about contemporary issues, it is argued, must necessarily colour his judgement. In a contested field like writing national history, the potential is also correspondingly heightened, as seen in the reaction to the publication of Lee's memoirs. Syed Hamid Albar, for instance, suggested that "Our historians should also write a book on the split, lest the only book be penned by someone so prejudiced against the Malaysian leaders and people."[113] Indeed, Malaysian commentators and academics had not been slow to defend their nation's honour. Rustam Sani, for instance, rejected the Singapore interpretation as "propagandistic", "one-sided", and "dogmatic" and said that the construction of the Singapore narrative was an attempt by the Singapore Government to "play the Malaysia bogey card, like Germany under the rule of Hitler" so as to create "its own holocaust" to "remind Singaporeans of the need for upholding national unity and defending the existence of the Government. The alternative was re-absorption into the Malaysian entity".[114] Another, a Malaysian academic, Farish A. Noor, accused the "older generation of Singapore's leaders" of wishing to "pass on the bad blood of the past to the young, with the hope that this latent animosity would continue to grow and fester in the future" and called on Singapore to "stop playing games with history".[115] But the problem of bias is by no means confined only to the writing of contemporary history. Complete objectivity in the writing of history in general is an ideal to be approximated. As Malaysian historian Cheah Boon Kheng, writing about the "sensitive topic" of Sino-Malay racial clashes in Malaya in the post-surrender interregnum from 1945–1946 noted, "I am mindful of the need to treat the topic objectively and not to pass moral judgements or to take sides ... I too am aware that I have my own sympathies and aversions and hope I have been able to control my feelings in an academic study."[116] As a Singaporean writing about the subject of the separation, it is natural to assume that I will have a Singaporean perspective on the subject. But as a historian my aim must be to offer a perspective of those events based on the available evidence. That the subject of the separation is contested history makes this all the more necessary, as I noted in the preface of *A Moment of Anguish*: "In embarking on this task, as in writing about contemporary history, I am aware that the field is open to controversy, not least, in this instance, because of the possibly still sensitive nature of the subject."[117] In view of the different historical viewpoints presented by Kuala Lumpur and Singapore, the availability of foreign archives on the subject proved particularly valuable in my own study for another reason: they provided "a third-party" perspective on the various issues and controversies that engulfed relations between the two countries. The key British, Australian, New Zealand and American observers who reported on events for their respective home governments were seasoned diplomats and shrewd analysts who had access to top government leaders in Kuala Lumpur and Singapore and often had good insights into their thinking. Their confidential dispatches made keen commentaries about the political tactics and maneuverings of the various local political forces, as well as the perceived motivations which directed them. Depending on whether they reported from the vantage point of either Kuala Lumpur or Singapore, shades of differences in emphasis would invariably surface. But taken together, their views provided a useful foil to the perspectives offered by the local participants.[118] Singapore's charge that the race riots in 1964 were politically inspired, for example, would seem to be borne out by such "third party" assessments. The historian's task therefore must be to weigh the evidence objectively and then ensure that the reportage of his findings is consistent with the 'facts' and not merely the product of his personal bias and unsubstantiated assertions. Indeed, while bias, including nationalist bias, is inevitable, the business of a historian, as Nicholas Tarling put it, "is to be as objective as possible. The fact that you cannot be completely objective does not mean that you should not try": "History is not an arena where narratives contend, no narrative being better than the others. We have been trying to make sure that some 'narratives' are better than others. Documents, peer review, common sense and experience make historians as objective as possible."[119] "The foundation of true scholarship", as my former colleague, Wong Lin Ken, wrote, "rests on integrity" and the historian "redeems his craft and upholds his reputation if he remains intellectually honest".[120]

In the final analysis, there seems to be little distinction between the contemporary historian's experience and that confronting historians writing about earlier eras. In both contexts, the historian is faced with similar problems of incomplete documentation, perspective and objectivity. Not only would there be the need to constantly and critically examine, analyze and assess the available evidence, the historian would also be required to judiciously synthesize and interpret his findings, and revise them if necessary, in the light of new evidence and perspective. As John Tosh put it, "It can be argued that scholars today [writing on the recent past] are too close to the events of this period to achieve sufficient detachment, and that they are further handicapped by their limited access to confidential records. But although the job cannot be done as well as historians would like, it is important they do it to the best of their ability."[121]

For Singapore, the "proper" use of contemporary history in its nation-building programme reflects an ongoing dilemma in its effort to construct a national identity. Imbued with neither ethnic homogeneity nor cultural distinctiveness, its leaders had sought through economic opportunities and incentives and social programmes to weld its peoples by giving them a stake in the imagined "nation".[122] But as Prime Minister Goh observed in August 2002, the use of the latter instrument created yet another predicament:

The more we educate Singaporeans and the more economic opportunities we create for them, the more internationally mobile they will become. The more they gain from subsidized HDB [Housing Development Board] housing, the more money they have to buy cheaper houses in Australia. Will Singaporeans be rooted to Singapore? Will enough Singaporeans stay here, to ensure our country's long-term survival?[123]

The issue, as the prime minister put it starkly, was whether the majority of Singaporeans called Singapore "home". The matter of "rootedness" is apparently of much concern to the country's political leadership. Earlier, in 1999, the prime minister had already warned: "Whether we like it or not, more Singaporeans will take wing, given the pace of globalization and their own personal mobility. As Singaporeans become even more cosmopolitan, the issue of concern to us is whether they will become less rooted to Singapore. We now have to even compete for the hearts of Singaporeans against attractions elsewhere."[124] There was a need for "cultural reserves" in the face of globalization trends that may fragment "our sense of being Singaporeans", as George Yeo explained:[125]

[A]n increasing number of Singaporeans have now moved out to other lands in search of fame and fortune. They are lost to Singapore if they lose their sense of being Singaporean. But if they organize themselves, retain their Singaporean identity and maintain links with institutions, families and friends in Singapore, such a Singapore diaspora can greatly enhance our national strength and our international competitiveness. ... Our nationhood deprives us of easy access to our traditional hinterlands. But it gives us a unique opportunity to internationalize ourselves in a way which preserves us as a self-consciously Singaporean community, locally and overseas. ... If we fail, those who come will feel no bond to the nation and those who leave will, over a generation, melt into a worldwide Chinese or Indian diaspora. If we succeed, we will transcend the geographical limitation of our size and remove the ʾclaustrophobia that now cramps our spirit.[126]

In the face of uncertain times and unique challenges, the reclamation of the past made political and economic sense. As Teo Chee Hean saw it, "This shared history, especially key defining moments, provides the social glue to bind the people together and enhances the sense of identity, community and comradeship."[127] For a nation, like an individual, needs a good memory. It was David Mcculough who said, "A nation that forgets its past can function no better than an individual with amnesia." For Singapore, amnesia, it seems, is not an option.

NOTES

1   Claude Levi-Strauss, *The Savage Mind* (London: Weidenfeld & Nicolson, 1966), p. 257; cited in Beverley Southgate, *Why Bother with History? Ancient, Modern, and Postmodern Motivations* (London: Routledge, 1996), p. 81.

2   Michael Leifer, *Dilemmas of Statehood in Southeast Asia* (Singapore: Asia Pacific Press, 1972), p. 1.

3   John Warren, *The Past and its Presenters: An Introduction to Issues in Historiography* (London: Hodder & Stoughton, 1998), p. 160.

4   Stefan Berger, Mark Donovan and Kevin Passmore, "Apologias for the nation-state in Western Europe since 1800", in *Writing National Histories: Western Europe since 1800*, edited by Stefan Berger, Mark Donovan and Kevin Passmore (London: Routledge, 1999), p. 3.

5   Richard J Evans, *In Defence of History* (London: Granta Books, 1997), p. 3.

6   Beverley Southgate, *History: What and Why? Ancient, Modern and Postmodern Perspectives* (London: Routledge, 1996), p. x.

7   Ludmilla Jordanova, *History in Practice* (London: Arnold, 2000), p. 94.

8   Lysa Hong and Jimmy Yap, "The Past in Singapore's Present", *Commentary* 11, no. 1 (1993): 31.

9   Warren, p. 170.

10 William H McNeill, *Mythistory and Other Essays* (Chicago: University of Chicago Press, 1986), p. 13.

11 Ibid., p. 11.

12 Ibid, p. 13.

13 Warren, p. 167.

14 Ibid., p. 162.

15 McNeill defined "mythistory" as a "mingling of truth and falsehood, blending history with ideology, results": "Myth and history are close kin inasmuch as both explain how things got to be the way they are by telling some sort of story. But our common parlance reckons myth to be false while history is, or, aspires to be, true. Accordingly, a historian who rejects someone else's conclusions calls them mythical, while claiming that his own views are true. But what seems true to one historian will seem false to another, so one historian's truth becomes another's myth, even at the moment of utterance." See McNeill, pp. 3, 12.

16 Ibid., p. 13.

17 Ibid, p. 14.

18 Kevin Passmore, Stefan Berger and Mark Donovan, "Historians and the Nation-state", in *Writing National Histories: Western Europe since 1800*, p. 281.

19 McNeill, pp. 13–14.

20 Southgate, *Why Bother with History*, p. 81.

21 Dayang Istiaisyah bte Hussin, "Textual Construction of a Nation: The Use of Merger and Separation", *Asian Journal of Social Sciences* 29, no. 3 (2001): 406–7.

22 See also Albert Lau, "The National Past and the Writing of the History of Singapore", in *Imagining Singapore*, edited by Ban Kah Choon, Anne Pakir and Tong Chee Kiong (Singapore: Times Academic Press, 1992).

23 Ong Pang Boon, "It is Necessary to Preserve Our History", *Speeches: A bimonthly selection of Ministerial Speeches* 5, no. 3 (1981): 48. (Henceforth, *Speeches*)

24 S. Dhanabalan, "Windows into Singapore's Past", *Speeches* 8, no. 3 (1984): 33.

25 Ong, "It is Necessary to Preserve Our History", p. 48.

26 Devan Nair, "Nation Building and the Jealous Gods of the Past", in C.V. Devan Nair, *Not by Wages Alone: Selected Speeches and Writings of C.V. Devan Nair 1959–1981* (Singapore: NTUC, 1982), p. 315.

27 S. Rajaratnam, "The Uses and Abuses of the Past'", *Speeches* 8, no. 2 (1984): 5.

28 Ong, "It is Necessary to Preserve Our History", p. 47.

29 Dhanabalan, "Windows into Singapore's Past", p. 33.

30 George Yeo, "Importance of Heritage and Identity", in *Speeches* 13, no. 1 (1989): 47.

31 Rajaratnam, "The Uses and Abuses of the Past", p. 6.

32 S. Jayakumar, "Awareness of Our History Must be Promoted", *Speeches* 7, no. 2 (1983): 61.

33 Ibid.

34 Rajaratnam, "The Uses and Abuses of the Past", p. 9.

35 Ibid., pp. 2 and 9.

36 Ibid., p. 2.

37 Lee Hsien Loong, "Singapore — Nation at the Crossroads", *Speeches* 10, no. 4 (1986): 50.

38 Ibid., pp. 52–53.

39 *Singapore Parliamentary Debates*, 5 March 1985, col. 199.

40 Lee, "Singapore — Nation at the Crossroads", pp. 52–53.

41 George Yeo, "Civic Society", *Speeches* 17, no. 6 (1993): 54.

42 S. Rajaratnam, "Life-and-Death Struggle with Communists in 1950–60's", *Speeches* 8, no. 3 (1984): 13.

43 Tay, Eng Soon "The 1950's — Singapore's Tumultuous Years", *Speeches* 8, no. 3 (1984): 50–51.

44 Rajaratnam, "Life-and-Death Struggle with Communists in 1950–60's", p. 13.

45 Ong, "It is Necessary to Preserve Our History", pp. 48–49.

46 Lee Hsien Loong, "The National Identity — A Direction and Identity for Singapore", *Speeches* 13, no. 1 (1989): 29.

47 Ong , "It is Necessary to Preserve Our History", p. 48.

48 George Yeo, "Transmitting Historical Memories", *Speeches* 22, no. 2 (1998): 54.
49 ———. "The New Asian and His Heritage", in *Speeches* 17, no. 4 (1993): 58.
50 Jayakumar, "Awareness of Our History Must be Promoted", p. 61.
51 Teo Chee Hean, "Know the Singapore Story", *Speeches* 24, no. 3 (2000): 78.
52 *Straits Times*, 20 May 1997.
53 Goh Chok Tong, "The Singapore Story", *Speeches* 22, no. 4 (1998): 1–2.
54 Lee Kuan Yew, *The Singapore Story: Memoirs of Lee Kuan Yew* (Singapore: Times Edition, 1998), p. 8.
55 Lee Kuan Yew, "Picking Up the Gauntlet: Will Singapore Survive Lee Kuan Yew?", *Speeches* 20, no. 3 (1996): 30.
56 See comments by Tony Blair, "About the author and his memoirs" in Lee, *The Singapore Story*.
57 See comments by Kiichi Miyazawa, "About the author and his memoirs", in ibid.
58 See comments by Malcolm Fraser, "About the author and his memoirs", in ibid.
59 *Straits Times*, 16 September 1998.
60 Asad Latif, "What Future for the Past?", *Sunday Times*, 13 July 1997.
61 Lee Siew Choh, "The Truth about 1962 Merger Referendum", *Straits Times*, 16 June 1997.
62 Donald Low How Tian, "Syllabus Should Have Room for Historical Controversy, Creativity", *Straits Times*, 24 May 1997.
63 Gopal Baratham, "Who will Recount the Objective Truth?", *Straits Times*, 22 May 1997.
64 In the Anson by-election, J.B. Jeyaretnam defeated the PAP candidate and ended its thirteen-year parliamentary monopoly.
65 Loh Kah Seng, "Within the Singapore Story: The Use and Narrative of History in Singapore", in *Crossroads: An Interdisciplinary Journal of Southeast Asia Studies* 12, no. 2 (1998): 2 and 17.
66 *Straits Times*, 20 May 1997.
67 Ibid.
68 "Can the Truth be Resolved — Once and for All?" *Sunday Times*, 1 November 1998.
69 *Straits Times*, 20 May 1977.
70 Ibid.
71 See the account in Lee, *The Singapore Story*, pp. 551–69.
72 Ibid., p. 656.
73 Ibid.
74 Ibid., pp. 656–57.
75 "UMNO Youth Defends Founding Fathers of Malaysia", *Straits Times*, 19 September 1998.

76 *Straits Times*, 15 September 1999.
77 *Straits Times*, 17 September 1998.
78 "Tun Razak's son 'hurt' by memoirs", *Straits Times*, 17 September 1998.
79 "SM Lee 'Trying to Fan Racial Dissatisfaction' ", *Straits Times*, 17 September 1998.
80 *Sunday Times*, 1 November 1998.
81 Ibid.
82 Ibid.
83 *Straits Times*, 17 September 1998.
84 Ibid., 16 September 1998.
85 Ibid.
86 Ibid., 21 September 1998.
87 Ibid., 17 September 1998.
88 Ibid., 16 September 1998.
89 Ibid., 21 September 1998.
90 Ibid., 19 September 1998.
91 Ibid., 16 September 1998.
92 Ibid.
93 *Sunday Times*, 27 September 1998.
94 See Albert Lau, "Some Conceptual Issues in the Study of Contemporary South East Asian History", *Journal of the History Society* (1987–88): 16–20.
95 Geoffrey Elton, *The Practice of History* (London: Fontana), p. 30.
96 Gordon Wright, "Contemporary History in the Contemporary Age", in *The Future of History: Essays in the Vanderbilt University Centennial Symposium*, edited by Charles F. Delzell (Nashville: Vanderbilt University Press, 1977), p. 225.
97 Devan Nair, "The PAP's Central Task", *Not by Wages Alone*, pp. 332–33.
98 Lee Kuan Yew, "History is not Made the Way it is Written", *Speeches* 3, no. 8 (1980): 4.
99 Gopal Baratham, "Who will Recount the Objective Truth?", *Straits Times*, 22 May 1997.
100 Hong Lysa, "Making the history of Singapore: S Rajaratnam and CV Devan Nair", in *Lee's Lieutenants: Singapore's Old Guard*, edited by Lam Peng Er and Kevin Y L Tan (St Leonards: Allen & Unwin, 1999), p. 99.
101 T.N. Harper, "Lim Chin Siong and the 'Singapore Story' ", in *Comet in the Sky: Lim Chin Siong in History*, edited by Tan Jin Quee and Jomo K.S. (Kuala Lumpur: INSAN, 2001), p. 4.
102 Hong Lysa, "Making the History of Singapore", p. 99.
103 Harper, p. 3.
104 Hong, "Making the History of Singapore", p. 101.

105 Lee Siew Choh, "Voters were Misled and not Given Any Real Choice", *Straits Times*, 3 June 1997.
106 Lee Siew Choh, "The Truth about 1962 Merger Referendum".
107 Mohamad Maidin Packer Mohd, "Lee Siew Choh Trying to Rewrite Record, Reverse History", *Straits Times*, 7 June 1997.
108 Mohamad Maidin Packer Mohd, "S'pore Story Based on Facts and Documents", *Straits Times*, 28 May 1997.
109 *Straits Times*, 16 September 1998.
110 Ibid., 12 September 1998.
111 Albert Lau, *A Moment of Anguish: Singapore in Malaysia and the Politics of Disengagement* (Singapore: Times Academic Press, 1998).
112 Editorial "Time to Write the Definite History", *Business Times*, 28 May 1997.
113 *Sunday Times*, 15 November 1998.
114 Rustam A. Sani, "Why S'pore, KL Ties will Stay Volatile", *Straits Times*, 18 July 1998.
115 Farish A. Noor, "Singapore Playing Games With History", <http://jaring.my/just/Singapore2.htm>.
116 Cheah Boon Kheng, *Red Star Over Malaya: Resistance and Social Conflict During and After the Japanese Occupation, 1945–1946* (Singapore: Singapore University Press, 1983), p. xv.
117 Lau, *A Moment of Anguish*, p. v.
118 Ibid., p. vi.
119 *Straits Times*, 16 August 2000.
120 See Wong Lin Ken's review of Southeast Asian History and Historiography: Essays presented to D.G.E. Hall, in *Journal of Southeast Asian Studies* 8, no. 2 (1977): 236.
121 John Tosh, *The Pursuit of History: Aims, Methods and New Directions in the Study of Modern History*. Revised Third Edition (London: Longman, 2002), p. 49.
122 Jon S.T. Quah, "Globalization and Singapore's Search for Nationhood", in *Nationalism and Globalization: East and West*, edited by Leo Suryadinata (Singapore: ISEAS, 2000), p. 77.
123 Goh Chok Tong, *Prime Minister's National Day Rally Speech 2002* (Singapore: Ministry of Information, Communications and the Arts, 2002), pp. 53–54.
124 Goh Chok Tong, "Strengthening the Singapore Heartbeat", *Speeches* 23, no. 5 (1999): 12.
125 CJW-L Wee, "The Need for National Education in Singapore", *Business Times*, 31 May 1998.
126 George Yeo, "Importance of Heritage and Identity", in *Speeches* 13, no. 1 (1989).
127 Teo Chee Hean, "Know the Singapore Story", *Speeches* 24, no. 3 (2000): 79–80.

CHAPTER TEN

Nation and Heritage

Wang Gungwu

THE SUBJECT of nation and heritage here has been couched in very broad terms, although the focus will be on Southeast Asia.[1] It is obvious that the region has to be placed in the context of the Asian experience as a whole. What would also be essential is to look at the global picture and note the rapid spread of the idea of nation-states during the twentieth century. In that wider context, the various political cultures within the region and their roles for nation-building in the past century need to be examined. The underlying issue is the political heritage that has guided this nation-building task. The two aspects of the heritage especially relevant are, first, the models from the West, including the colonial transition, and secondly, the earlier examples of national development in Asia itself.

Forty years ago, political leaders in East and South Asia faced the choice of nation-building either through capitalism and liberal democracy, or through socialism in its many manifestations, from the moderate social democratic forms in Nehru's India and U Nu's Burma, and variations of these in Indonesia, to the revolutionary international communism of the Soviet Union variety in China, North Korea and Vietnam. The modernizing leaders of Asia also had to build their new nations under the shadow of the Cold War. Given the anti-colonial backgrounds that they had all experienced, and the need to argue for self-determination through the exercise of democratic rights, there was no alternative but to do so in the framework of a world of nation-states as represented in the United Nations Organization.

These leaders were aware that the concept of nation-states was alien to Asia. The forms had been evolved in Europe but, even in Europe, there was a great deal of variety.[2] The new Asian states after 1945 did not, of course, have to copy any one of them. But they did seem to have taken them as guides, if not as exact models. Their leaders were keen not to make the mistakes of the West. For example, between the 1950s and 1970s, none of them wanted their countries to be like those of Eastern and Central Europe, which had come under the control of the Soviet Union,[3] nor like the disorderly and chaotic examples of Italy and Greece and the fascistic dictatorships of Spain and Portugal. They were more likely to look to the successful examples of nation-states like Britain, United States, France, Netherlands, Switzerland and the Scandinavian states.[4]

Now, some fifty years later, where are the new Asian nations going? Nation-building has not been easy. Has this been because the task is universally difficult, or especially so in Southeast Asia because the nation-state is an alien institution? Are there elements in earlier histories and the cultural heritage that make the peoples less ready for nation-building? Has there been a tendency to follow Western models too closely, a failure to consider local ways to do the job? Or has rapid globalization been an obstacle to the evolution of distinctive Southeast Asian patterns? Have the travails of the nation-building efforts, the achievements and failures, contributed to our understanding of the phenomenon in general, as has been suggested by the studies of Benedict Anderson?[5]

Various kinds of national identities have existed among peoples in Asia before modern times, but the potential "nations" did not have a uniform name to call themselves. In Southeast Asia, we can identify historical identities among the Vietnamese, the Khmers, the Thais of Siam, the Burmans, the Javanese, and the Malays of the peninsula, all of whom were potentially capable of defining themselves as nations if necessary.[6] There had been no need for them to do so before their encounters with European institutions, and the urge to identify as nations, especially as nation-states, did not surface in most cases until the twentieth century.

An important condition before modern times was the formation and development of states. There had been feudal, monarchical, or imperial states, many with elaborate administrations. But the precondition for Southeast Asian nationhood was the establishment of a new kind of state structure appropriate to a nation-state. Recent books on ethnic politics in the region remind us of the complexities which various states faced in trying to build nations among the different peoples who happened to live within the state's new political borders.[7] Obvious examples are countries with large numbers of immigrants (Chinese, Indians and other South Asians, Arabs, Europeans, and other Southeast Asian peoples who had migrated in search of a better livelihood) who arrived within the past couple of centuries.[8] But there are also many others which involve indigenous peoples with strong territorial rights.[9] The various hill-tribes of Burma, Thailand and Vietnam are minorities that accept to a greater or lesser degree their place in the new national identities of the respective countries. The Malays in southern Thailand and the Moros in the southern Philippines, the Ibans, Kadazans and others of Eastern Malaysia, and the various *suku* (indigenous peoples) with their historic lands in various parts of the Indonesian archipelago, are well-known. This mix of "nations without states" in each of the countries of Southeast Asia all testify to the efforts needed to provide a clear national identity for such multi-cultural, multi-lingual, even multi-nationality conditions.

The nation-building history project referred to in the opening essay (Chapter 1 of this volume)[10] will produce books on the nation-building experiences of the original five members of ASEAN when it was first formed in 1969. These will describe the series of policies over the past forty to fifty years that directly or indirectly sought to build new nations out of the complex situations the national leaders have found within the borders of their countries. The challenge is to apply the methods of history to a major contemporary phenomenon. Among the most important issues it will deal with is to examine the origins of certain policies, how decisions were made and implemented, and what the results were after the policies were introduced. It seeks to find out whether the policies were totally or only partially successful, how they affected other features of nation-building. For example, did the early policies narrow down the options for

254 • *Wang Gungwu*

the next stage of nation-building? Or did they open up new possibilities for the country to develop politically or economically? What were the cumulative effects of the specific nation-building policies on education, culture, the social classes, the national self-image, and ultimately on the sense of national identity?

These questions remind us of at least two aspects of the region's political heritage. For most colonies, the idea that some kind of nation-state was the source of the wealth and power was a revelation. The Western empires that were based on nation-states had come to dominate all of Asia. The new generation of local leaders was led to hope that they too might create nation-states for their own countries one day. Those in Southeast Asia received encouragement from the example of Japan and later from that of China, India and elsewhere. It is appropriate to begin with the models from the West, including the colonial transition.

The example of the modern Philippines provides a good starting-point. It is different from the other parts of the region because most of it was under direct European rule longer than any other country in Southeast Asia.[11] Its local-born educated élites felt the impact of the European state earlier than others. As part of the Spanish empire, they would have been aware of the anti-colonial movements which led to the independence of several new states in South and Central America. Some of the young Filipinos who were provided with higher education were sent to Spain to continue their studies. They saw various versions of the European nation-state which had become the model for the new states that won their independence from Spain. The most outstanding of them was Jose Rizal who had a sophisticated understanding of European ideals. Although he was more of a reformist and not, strictly speaking, the kind of national leader we find in the twentieth century, he introduced the European ideas that became the hallmark of early Filipino nationalism.

Furthermore, when the United States went to war with Spain and defeated the Spanish in the Philippines, the Americans presented themselves as an earlier example of colonials rebelling successfully against the metropolitan power. Ironically, this former colony succeeded the Spanish as a new imperial power and proceeded to rule over the Philippines as their own colony.[12] But it did confirm that an independent nation-state was the route to take for modern progress. In many ways, this unique intervention by an ex-colonial nation played a part in shaping the idea of the nation-state for the region. From the beginning, the United States tried to distinguish itself from the other imperial powers by insisting that its role was tutelary. Its stay would be temporary and its job was to prepare the Philippines to take its rightful place in the family of nations. It took the high moral ground in sharp contrast to the imperialist expansion by the Japanese that had made Taiwan its colony only five years earlier and sought to remain there permanently.[13]

The three other European empires in Asia did not share the American position. They all expected to stay indefinitely, quite convinced that the native peoples were not ready for nationhood, although they had begun to face growing anti-colonial sentiments in the 1920s and 1930s. They certainly took note of the fact that the new Asian empire of Japan was in the making and that one of their senior members, Spain, had been ousted by another potential imperial power. They would not take seriously the American claim to be less imperial than themselves. Although Britain, France and the Netherlands had different approaches towards their respective colonies, none of them contemplated helping their subjects to build their own nations. Only when young nationalists began to demand the same political rights that the British, French and Dutch peoples enjoyed did colonial officials trouble to challenge these nationalists to prove themselves worthy of independence.

The Dutch were the most confident, having held territory longest in the region and being convinced of their ability to resist the changes asked for by local leaders.[14] They saw no need to encourage their subjects to think of themselves as becoming citizens of a nation-state sometime in the future. In any case, they saw that there were two levels of response among the nationalists, who were not only against Dutch colonialism, but also against Chinese dominance in business. The earliest expressions of nationalism came from Indonesian businessmen, particularly in Java. They included leaders of aristocratic backgrounds, who complained about the collusion between the Chinese and Dutch colonial officials. This may seem familiar today, but the resentments exploited by Dutch officials who hoped to appease such sentiments by changing their policies towards the Chinese minority were of a different order.

But the nationalists could not be distracted so easily from their main purpose. They had an understanding of nation that was drawn from European history itself. For example, many had studied the history of the Dutch and appreciated the way the Dutch founded their nation as an anti-colonial enterprise against the Spaniards. The revolt of the Spanish Netherlands was the first example in modern history of a successful anti-colonial war.[15] It lasted almost a hundred years, with the Dutch finally winning independence in time to begin its own trading empire in Asia in the seventeenth century. This provided the framework for the initial expression of Indonesian nationalism. The speeches of leaders like Sukarno and Hatta referred to the heroic examples of Dutch patriots to underline their right to fight for freedom as colonial subjects of the Dutch themselves. The Dutch remained unsympathetic and thought the Indonesian independence enterprise was wholly premature. In their eyes, the geography of the Netherlands East Indies as well as its ethnic mix did not have the conditions for any viable nation-state to be built there. That such an independent nation did eventually emerge after World War II is, in fact, one of the wonders of modern Southeast Asian history.[16]

Unlike the Dutch, the British and French had much larger and more extensive empires. For the British, Southeast Asia was the area in between their empire in India and their vast trading interests in China. As long as India was not independent, it was unthinkable for any other of their territories to ask for it. And, indeed, most unfortunately for Burma, it came to be administered as part of the Indian part of the empire, as were parts of the Malay peninsula during the first half of the nineteenth century.[17] But for the opening of China in the 1840s, the Malay states would also have been much more closely tied to imperial interests in India. In any case, the invention of indirect rule reduced the urge to seek independence among the élite groups who were given roles in the newly emerging modern administration. Thus the question of providing a British model for a future nation-state to be formed out of what was called Malaya was simply not relevant before the Pacific War.

Similarly with the French in their Indochina territories. As relative latecomers, they had moved quickly to develop these lands for their economic interests as well as making them especially useful for their expansion plans in China. Unlike the British, however, they had stronger educational ideals and were quick to impress on the Vietnamese the superiority of French civilization. Although Vietnam was divided into three at the time, it was an ancient pre-modern state and, in key ways, already an embryo nation.[18] Nevertheless, the Vietnamese nationalist response to the French did not depend on French tutelage. With China in the background, they were constantly affected by the shape and intensity of an evolving Chinese nationalism.

The main point to make here is that, with the exception of the Philippines and a few young Indonesian nationalist leaders, none of the colonies learnt directly from the European model of a nation-state. I shall argue later that, prior to the end of World War II, the models which inspired the future Southeast Asian leaders largely came from Asia itself. Nevertheless, Europe was ultimately the most important for every group of leaders. The reason for this was that the West won that war in Asia. They were responsible for the management of the decolonization process and the recognition of new nations by the United Nations Organization, the most notable example being the acceptance of Indonesia.[19] They were the powers the nationalist leaders had to struggle against in order to define their nationhood. And, not least, it was from Western political and legal literature that the politicians learnt to argue their case and prepare themselves for the nation-building tasks they would have to perform.[20]

That literature is very important for the political heritage. The study of modern nation-building had first been studied in depth by historians of Western Europe. The historians illuminated the general features of the subject and explained the variable nature of the phenomenon, including the use of history itself as a basis for the creation of nation-states. For example, the historians of the American and French Revolutions really made the subject of nation-building significant.[21] Their work led to sophisticated historical analyses of earlier nations like Britain, Spain, Portugal and the Netherlands.[22] These in turn inspired other writers, artists and scholars to stimulate the kinds of nationalism that led to the dramatic unification of the German and Italian peoples.[23] Later, historians joined with linguists, philosophers and other intellectuals to help shape the nations of Central and Eastern Europe.[24] It was only later that sociologists and political scientists began to work out the theoretical frameworks to explain the phenomenon.

It is not clear if each of the new Southeast Asian leaders themselves read these works of history and theory. What we do know is that the ideas in them had found their way into the press, political pamphlets and other popular writings. For example, following the end of World War II, the ideas derived from the work by historians of European nationalism and the foundations of the nations in Europe, together with the histories written of the successful nation-states of Europe, were widely known. Nationalist leaders everywhere became familiar with both the justifications and the mechanisms of nation-states. Some of their younger and better-educated supporters would have kept up with the emerging theoretical literature, also by Western social scientists, who analysed contemporary examples in systematic ways and offered more sophisticated constructs.[25]

For the former colonial territories of Southeast Asia, an early study of how nationalism might determine the region's future was the Institute of Pacific Relations report in 1942 by Rupert Emerson, Lennox Mills and Virginia Thompson.[26] Another influential work was that by McMahon Ball[27] which linked nationalism with communism and explored the juxtaposition of new nations with "the internationalist conspiracy" of communist parties. Rupert Emerson had studied both British Malaya and Netherlands East Indies.[28] He was more sensitive than the others to the problems of nation-building within colonial boundaries where the dominant majority had many minority peoples to contend with.

Local scholars began to make their impact from the 1960s. But the dominance by political scientists, sociologists and anthropologists continued, except in the Philippines, where Filipino historians competed for attention with the Americans.[29] For Indonesia, the writings of George Kahin, Sartono Kartodirdjo, Benedict Anderson, and Taufik Abdullah received international attention.[30] For Malaya (including Singapore), the list is longer, and the writings on early nationhood by Stephen Milne, K.J. Ratnam, Syed Husin Ali, Chan Heng Chee, William Roff, Khoo Kay Kim, Cheah Boon Kheng and Gordon Means are pioneering efforts.[31] The dominance of social scientists has been more significant for Burma and Indochina. Burma, for example, interested several political scientists like Lucian Pye, Joseph Silverstein and Robert Taylor, but its government did not encourage its own scholars to do similar studies. Indochina was long dominated by the protagonists of both sides of the Vietnam War and scholars are only beginning to get out from under its shadow.[32]

In most of these studies, the emphasis tended to be on the immediate heritage of a modern state. The historical and cultural roots of ethnic nations have received less attention. This is understandable because the basic research on these roots has been patchy and uneven. Until more systematic work has been done to analyse their role in the way the nation-states have progressed during the last five decades, their contributions, whether positive or negative, cannot be properly assessed. Interestingly, there is far more detailed knowledge available about the national emergence of a country like Japan and also about the complex elements that have gone into the formation of multi-cultural, even multi-national "nations" like China and India. Let me now turn my attention to the experiences elsewhere in Asia.

*   *   *

Southeast Asian political leaders started by looking at other experiences in Asia. For the first half of the twentieth century, East Asia was especially important for the way nationalism evolved in Asia. The word "experience" reminds us that Southeast Asian attention to nationalism goes back at least a hundred years. The way Japan had responded to Western advances in Asia impressed many of the first generation nationalists. Japan had surprised the world by defeating the Qing empire in 1895. For the young nationalists of Vietnam, Indonesia and Burma, Japan became an inspiration after the Russo-Japanese War. Of course, the leaders all recognized that this nationalism came as a response to the West and that it was the European nation-state that should serve as their model.[33]

The exceptional background of the Philippines produced the first violent demonstration of a conscious anti-colonial nationalism in the region. Their leaders like Bonifacio and Aguinaldo did not have the opportunity to know Europe directly but, by the end of the nineteenth century, they had understood how the Western challenge had been the inspiration for an emerging Japan. They were also aware, through Hong Kong, of the Chinese élites who were using Western models to criticize the ineptness of their own government. These included Sun Yat-sen and his followers who were moving towards taking revolutionary action to achieve a modern state. Also, several people of Chinese descent participated in the Philippine nationalist movement. So even in this exceptional case, awareness of East Asia was present very early.[34]

Another special case is that of Thailand. Although it did not experience colonial conquest and had its own interpretation of the Western challenge, the Thai monarchy was impressed with Japanese nationalism. King Chulalongkorn was acutely aware of the threat to his kingdom's independence. As the only other ruler in Asia not actually having foreign officials running his government, he identified with a sovereign ruler like the Meiji emperor. Although his country's position was precarious, he had sufficient independence to work out his response to powerful imperial countries like Britain and France and try to learn from the modernizing Japanese nation. The idea that Thailand should become a nation-state was shaped by younger members of the Chakri royal family who had studied in Europe, notably in France, Britain and Switzerland. Equally important was the fact that the first generation of bureaucrats was trained in Europe in diplomacy and international relations in order to help Thailand preserve its sovereignty. The Thais had studied European experiences directly as a sovereign state. The issues that concerned them were thus highlighted in different ways, and nation-building in Thailand was obviously different from the kind which grew out of anti-colonialism in the rest of Southeast Asia.[35]

Even among the others, there were differences in what they saw elsewhere in Asia. Let me first contrast the response of two countries, Vietnam and Burma. In Vietnam, the French brought all of the country under French control only after the Meiji revolution had already begun. The Vietnamese response to the French was directly influenced by the Sino-French war of 1884 which was fought partly along the borders of Vietnam and China. Thus, from the very beginning, the Vietnamese leaders looked also at China.[36] They observed that China's approach to the West was ineffective, whereas Japan's was exceptionally successful. Also, by the end of the century, the Chinese themselves had been defeated by the Japanese. When the Russians were also defeated by the Japanese, reports in the world press had an even greater impact. But, for reasons of history and geography, Vietnam continued to be deeply influenced by the experiences of China. Even when they were comparing Japan and China, it was to China that their nationalists turned for lessons on how to deal with the West. Among those who influenced the early nationalists in Vietnam was Liang Qichao, a reformist nationalist, followed later by the revolutionary approach of Sun Yat-sen.[37] Only when Ho Chi-minh emerged as leader did they look beyond China to the Communist International, a different model altogether. Even then, the communists in China also turned to Comintern, and close links were retained for decades between the two communist parties.[38]

The Burmese nationalists, on the other hand, were struck by the fact that the Japanese were able to beat the Russians at war. The fact that it was British newspapers in Rangoon that brought them the news added another dimension to their nationalism. Unlike the rest of Southeast Asia, Burma was governed as part of British India and had looked to the Indian National Congress and to British left-wing socialists for ideas about anti-colonial nationalism. Thus, as in India, some of the earliest anti-colonial literature available was based on the Irish experience of fighting the British. Later, the experience of the Boers in South Africa, including Gandhi's nationalist awakening, was especially relevant. In this way, the Indian National Congress developed sophisticated ideas about anti-colonial nationalism which influenced the early Burmese. They were learning from the Indians while at the same time drawing upon the Japanese for a contrasting experience.[39]

Southeast Asia consists of countries with such different histories that it should not surprise us that some of them looked in quite different directions. It is worth noting that the Japanese experience was important early, and that the Chinese experience was not influential until later on. That China should have had an impact was due partly to the fact that there were so many people of Chinese descent in Southeast Asia and partly because of the fierce opposition that the Chinese organized against Japanese nationalism.[40] The two rival nationalisms impinged greatly on the minds of Southeast Asian nationalists throughout the 1920s and 1930s. That rivalry reached its emotional peak when a full-scale war between China and Japan broke out in 1937. This was then followed by the Japanese invasion of the Western colonies in Southeast Asia and, for three-and-a half years, their occupation of most of the region itself. Over time, they directly influenced the way the region developed their own responses to the modern idea of a nation-state.[41]

In short, early nationalism in the region had two sources of inspiration. It was marked by anti-colonialism mixed with fear of Western power, but it was also suffused with admiration of Western wealth and power and the Japanese formula for dealing with the West. These were the main features during the early period when the first nationalist leaders began to speak their minds on the subject. Ultimately, however, it was the colonial experience and the different reactions against it that determined the way nationalism developed in each country. That experience led to the feeling that nothing would matter until the colonial powers were made to leave. To this extent, there was ambiguity about the comparative relevance of European and other Asian experiences. The Japanese claimed that they had invaded Southeast Asia to free the people from colonial rule, to drive the West out of Asia. Many Southeast Asian leaders showed that they would accept that claim only if it helped them achieve independence for their respective countries. Indeed, if the war had not gone badly for the Japanese so quickly and there had been more time for the Japanese to win over more of the nationalist leaders, the relationship between that leadership and the Japanese would have been much more intimate and historically significant. It has to be acknowledged that some of the Japanese in the occupied territories did a good job in wooing and training local nationalists. They were particularly successful in Indonesia and, for a while, also in Burma.[42] They even made converts among the Indian soldiers in the British army in Malaya and helped to form the Indian National Army to support the Japanese campaigns to liberate India from the British.

The nationalist message that the Japanese brought to Southeast Asia had much more impact than has so far been acknowledged. The neglect of their contribution was largely because the Japanese lost the war and the colonial powers returned. The result was that there has been a negative image of the Japanese throughout the region. The most obvious example can be found in what the British did on getting back to Malaya. They presented a very positive picture of their colonial rule in comparison with the Japanese Occupation, and successfully diminished, if not totally eradicated, the nationalist message the Japanese had offered. Nationalism tended thereafter to be seen as potentially fanatical and aggressive.[43]

This is related to another image, that of Chinese nationalism, notably that found among the large numbers of Chinese in British Malaya. The Sino-Japanese war greatly speeded up and intensified the growth of Chinese nationalism among the overseas Chinese in Southeast Asia. Overseas Chinese nationalism had become a heritage and duty since the days when Sun Yat-sen aroused support from ordinary overseas Chinese for his nationalist movement. It began as a narrow, parochial form of nationalism expressed largely as an anti-Manchu movement in China.[44] That had obvious appeal to Chinese who originated from Guangdong and Fujian, the people most resentful of the Manchu conquest. It is not surprising that the sense of a Chinese national identity grew strong from the south. Unlike northern China, where the mandarinate were prepared to work with a Manchu Son of Heaven and where the people had come to accept the Manchu as having become Chinese in many ways, anti-Manchu sentiments in the south remained strong for over 200 years down to the beginnings of the twentieth century.[45]

The powerful triad or secret society movements that had flourished in provinces like Fujian and Guangdong carried the seeds of an anti-Manchu nationalism to other Chinese. Thus when Sun Yat-sen turned to these triads for support of his first political party, the Xingzhong Hui, this anti-Manchu feeling greatly helped him to reach out to all those who were living overseas. This was the easy part. It was only later that the nationalists realized that succeeding the Qing empire required a more inclusive way of looking at nationalism.[46] This is a problem that has persisted to the present day, touching on issues of a common civilizational heritage and of imperial borders that marked the lands where China has legitimate national sovereignty. But the events leading to the Sino-Japanese War of 1937–45 brought a more focused view of the new Chinese nation, one that created an increasingly fierce nationalism.[47] When this became manifest in Southeast Asia, it began to have a negative impact on the indigenous leaders in Southeast Asia and eventually complicated the question of nationalism for them. On the one hand, they admired China and Japan for facing up to the West in their different ways. On the other hand, they were anti-colonial and grew uncomfortable with the fact that these powers had brought so many Chinese to their countries, migrants who were openly committed to fight for a Chinese nation. Some of these Chinese were also increasingly active in a wide range of patriotic affairs and organized successful national salvation movements among all overseas Chinese in the region. This simply highlighted to indigenous nationalist leaders that this business of anti-colonialism was more complicated than just driving out the West. There grew the fear of what would happen if the Chinese form of nationalism were to take root in their countries. Added to that was the ambivalent attitude towards Japan by the end of World War II. What had begun with admiration had ended up with a mixture of fear and resentment against Japanese occupation. Thus, there is a multi-layered picture of nationalism to place beside the anti-colonial nationalism of Southeast Asians.

By the early 1950s, when anti-colonialism had achieved its objective and the colonial powers were beginning to leave, the image of nationalism was no longer as heroic and positive as before. By the time they achieved their objectives, the new leaders had learnt to be sceptical about the nationalism of Japan. Its association with militarism and aggression had become linked through war-time propaganda with the Nazi nationalism of Germany and the fascism of Italy. The nationalist leaders found themselves in a paradoxical position. As they started on their early nation-building tasks, they found themselves seeking to stress the constructive aspects of nationalism. Even to this day, the leaders speak at times in highly nationalist terms on matters like unity and sovereignty, but speak in anti-nationalist terms on issues of multinational trade and regional cooperation. The latter has been further stimulated by recent developments in economic globalization and the transnational study of the social sciences that have been introduced to a new generation of bureaucratic and technocratic leaders in these countries.

When the nationalist leaders achieved statehood if not nationhood, the task of nation-building had to begin. The nation-building history project deals with what has been going on for the last fifty years in Southeast Asia. The project members are all historians. It was agreed that the project would not start with theories, models, or ideas of what nations should or should not be like, but would look at what these national leaders actually did when they got into power. When they had their countries to run, and if they stuck to their own rhetoric and believed what they were saying, what did they do to build their nations? For the task of nation-building, political unity and economic development were clear priorities. For example, that could mean expanding business networks quickly to ensure economic growth, and investing in education for longer-term social cohesion. But what did the Southeast Asian leaders actually do when they came to power?

The project would concentrate on what the leaders actually did from day one of independence, what happened when they made their first decisions. It was common experience that, with a blueprint of what a nation should be like, one that sets down ideals explaining why the colonial power had to go, and what greatly needs to be done, the people expect you to implement these promises. And when the new regime starts to implement them, what happens? As all politicians who have campaigned successfully have found when they actually get into power, there are many constraints on what they can and cannot do, and many factors that they did not have to take into account when they were making speeches before. Hence there is a focus on the actual business of nation building.

Here is where the experiences elsewhere may be especially relevant. Each of the major nation-building countries like Japan, China and India could be seen as drawing deeply from their own political cultures.[48] Their experiences deserve to be studied for the light they may throw on Southeast

Asia. For better or worse, the long continuous histories have been tapped in East and South Asia to consolidate the modern state. To many scholars, such a heritage provides cultural ballast that gives the new peoples the best chance to achieve nationhood. To others, the burdens of the past might actually prevent or delay the formation of a new nationality that embraces the ideals of a democratic citizenry. The studies of the new nations of Southeast Asia so far have not stressed the region's various political heritages. Although it is not necessary to underline all the ingredients and characteristics of such heritages, it is hoped that by tracing the specific actions of political leaders while they have been nation-building, it can be shown how their respective political heritage has guided their actions and made a difference to how their nations have developed.

There is, of course, also the external environment. The Cold War in Asia was obviously a factor in shaping the nation-building process. Almost immediately after these countries gained their independence, a sort of globalization came into the region in a very strong way, in the form of the Cold War.[49] We normally think of globalization as something that is very recent but the term can be extended back. In many ways, whether in terms of "world systems" as perceived by Wallerstein or Gunder Frank, globalization was there when the Europeans circumscribed the globe and their ships arrived in Asia.[50] Whether it was Magellen in the Philippines or the Portuguese arriving in Malacca and Macau, it was the beginning of strong links between the economies of Asia and the West. Even the earlier Silk Route that brought East Asian goods to the West and Western goods across Asia may be considered part of the phenomenon. By the time of the industrial revolution in the nineteenth century, the globalized economy was controlled by a few European countries. Today, it has reached into every part of the world and the struggle between the dominant United States economy and a number of international institutions that depend on it promises to shift the foundations of global power. How will the new nation-states of the world survive that tussle?

During the nineteenth century, the globalization was of a much more specialized and narrow variety. But it diversified and expanded in range and depth before the end of World War II, a perfect example of a globalized war that involved everybody. But even before the war, the world had experienced its most intense period of globalization. This was when the Great Depression hit everybody.[51] It started in New York on Wall Street, but spread to the rest of the world. No country was free from it. The Southeast Asian trade figures from 1930 to 1940 show how much the region suffered with the rest. China's figures were complicated by many other factors and harder to assess, but even Japan was affected very drastically. But, in Southeast Asia, in areas that had nothing directly to do with Wall Street, it was amazing how their economies and their markets collapsed in the face of the depression.[52]

After the war, fairly early on, with the nation-states just beginning in Southeast Asia, they were immediately faced with the Cold War at their doorstep. This story began in 1949, when Hong Kong became the border in the global war between capitalism and communism. It was described by some as the West Berlin of Southeast Asia. The rhetoric of the time was to look at Hong Kong as part of the Southeast Asia that formed the capitalist side of the Cold War and, in this way, project the new nation-states into the forefront of the war against communism. Thus the Vietnamese were not allowed to get their independence earlier because they were on the wrong side of the Cold War. Other countries tried very hard to avoid choosing between the two sides. Burma and Indonesia wanted to stay neutral, an almost impossible position during the Cold War.[53] Suddenly Southeast Asia was fragmented into three parts: with two major neutralist countries, with Vietnam divided between communists and anti-communists, and with the others very uncertain what to do. Had the British overtures to the People's Republic of China in 1950, prior to the Korean War, been successful, who knows how Malaya and Singapore would have related to China. The local leaders at the time probably thought it was fortunate that the British overtures were rejected by the PRC, and an Anglo-American line was drawn to link British Malaya to Thailand and the Philippines.[54]

Clearly, taking sides in the struggle between the superpowers had an impact on the way nation-building policies were made. In Southeast Asia, the Vietnam War was certainly a determining force for many national leaders, whichever side they were. Choices were made which had long-term consequences on policies. The perceived need for a regional security system experienced many ups and downs, from the externally-sponsored Southeast Asia Treaty Organization (SEATO) to many transitional associations and informal arrangements, then to the Association of Southeast Asian Nations (ASEAN) which proved to be the most successful of them all.[55] That this has now been enlarged to include all ten states in the region, and that ASEAN is playing a bigger role in global forums, raises interesting questions on the continuing tasks of nation-building within the region. Do all these external events impinge directly on how nation-building decisions are made? Have they already had a distinctive, if not a unique, effect on the nation-building process of each of its members?

Thus, almost from the beginning, nation-building has been shaped by a regional concern of a strategic nature, one that had not so much to do with Southeast Asia as with the global conflict between the two superpowers and their allies.[56] The Cold War caused regional circumstances to change so rapidly and so unexpectedly after independence that none of those nationalist leaders were really able to implement what they had said they were going to do. We are probably too close to the Cold War to stand back to see exactly what the Cold War did to mould, shape, or start nation-building projects in Southeast Asia. We still need to understand how the Cold War actually changed the picture and channelled nationalist efforts or nation-building efforts in directions that had not been predicted before and did not fit any particular model of experiences elsewhere.

The experience of other parts of Asia has never been the dominant one for Southeast Asia. The anti-colonial experience, however, has been. It could be that the political heritage of the West should concern us more here. That influence has come in two very different ways. One is where the nationalist leaders have taken Western nation-state models as the highest form of what they wanted to achieve after their colonial leaders left. In a strange way, almost all of them first wanted to re-create what made colonial powers powerful in the first place. While the Indonesians looked at the Dutch experience, the classic models were the nation-states of Britain and France. They built their nations organically on historical experiences and that led them to shape their nations in quite different ways. Indeed, most nationalist leaders, whether consciously or not, began by assuming that these two nations should be the models. After all, they became the two most powerful nations in the world for 200 years. That power could not have been an accident.

Secondly, nations that developed late in Europe, as Germany and Italy did, did not have the centuries of organic growth that Britain and France had.[57] Their nationalism was distorted by the fact that their leaders wanted to nation-build in a hurry. They used state power to force the pace of nation-building in a way that Britain and France never had to do. In the end, because of their imperialistic ambitions, countries like Germany and Italy became negative examples. In any case, they had little to do with Southeast Asia and so were easily ignored. Although, in the end, Britain and France had to retreat back to their own home countries, they remained very impressive models in the minds of the nationalists.

It is clear the Philippines was an exception because its revolution was aborted by the Americans and they had a secondary colonial experience. Also, the Americans were a different kind of colonial power. They refused to be old-style empire builders and provided a mixed message to the Filipinos, partly encouraging their nationalism and partly controlling it. It was a kind of guided nationalism that encouraged its leaders to be relatively benign and friendly towards the colonial power. That was the secret of American success. That exception also led it to become a useful example to serve as a norm for how well some of the new nation-states of Southeast Asia were treated by former colonial powers during the Cold War.

The fact is, all the other colonial powers left the region while the Americans became more and more involved in a new capacity as a superpower. Even after the Vietnam War, they remained in the region because of their commitments in Taiwan, the Philippines and Thailand. The American advances into the region have to be taken into account in any study of nation-building in Southeast Asia. American influence has, on the whole, been a moderating influence in the region, and has spread to the others through American education, American ideals, and American popular culture in all its forms. These have so far had a countervailing effect against more radical forms of nationalism, but how that would eventually develop is still uncertain. These populist notions require close attention, because they reach out to ordinary people in new ways. How that would influence future ideas about being a nation, being patriotic, even being nationalistic is not yet clear.

The most important single element is the American elaboration through their social science scholarship today, of a multi-culturalism that the American nation stands for.[58] However that is defined, multi-culturalism is very controversial and in Canada, Australia, or New Zealand it takes different forms.[59] It defines new states drawn from immigrant peoples from the old world of nation-states and empires. There is a new set of starting points, a different way of outlining nationalist goals, and implicit in this is the idea that a nation can be created from people coming from different origins, different linguistic, cultural and ethnic backgrounds. The United States has been successfully created in this way. East Asians remain sceptical about this model, but Southeast Asians do not find it so difficult to understand. Some of them are historically multi-cultural and multi-ethnic to a similar extent.

Two influential models are now present. The first generation had looked to Britain and France as the ideal nation-states, but the influence and dominance of the United States in the economies of this part of the world have raised some really difficult questions for the new nationalist élites. These questions are not necessarily about the democratic institutions and human rights arguments which would threaten the privileges of the élites. But much more insidious and ultimately challenging to nationalism is this multi-cultural ideal which is being projected not only by the United States, but by countries like Australia and Canada, and has been a subject of growing interest in Europe as well.[60] There is an increasing view that in societies that are multi-ethnic and multi-cultural to begin with, any artificial efforts to bring about national unity through coercion and by discriminatory laws will be doomed to failure. If this view becomes accepted, it would be the most important single contribution that the Americans could make to the new generation of Southeast Asians.

Finally, if I may take Malaysia as an example, the difference between someone like former Prime Minister Mahathir and someone like former

Deputy Prime Minister Anwar Ibrahim is instructive. Mahathir stands for the generation whose nationalist ideals are based on their understanding of the British nation-state and the anti-colonialists who wanted to emulate the model. Anwar is a product of a modern Islamic universalism, with its own perspective of nationalism and the nation-state, but also belonging to a new generation of nationalists who have been exposed to trans-national, multi-national, multi-ethnic, and multi-cultural ideals.[61] This generation has modified some of the rhetoric and ideals for the nation, although they are yet to find a clear sense of direction as to where they are eventually going. It may be that these ideals will be thwarted and defeated for a while, but it is too early to say that their time will not come.

NOTES

1   This is a revised version of the Annual Lecture for the year 2000 published in *Journal of the Malaysian Branch of the Royal Asiatic Society*, vol. 73, pt. 2, 2000, pp. 5–30.

2   H. M. Chadwick, *The Nationalities of Europe and the Growth of National Ideologies* (Cambridge: The University Press, 1945); Charles Tilly, ed., *The Formation of National States in Western Europe* (Princeton: Princeton University Press, 1975); Ernest Gellner, *Nations and Nationalism* (Oxford: Basil Blackwell, 1983); Montserrat Guibernau, *Nationalisms: The Nation-State and Nationalism in the Twentieth Century* (Cambridge: Polity Press, 1996).

3   Miron Rezun, *Nationalism and the Break-up of an Empire: Russia and Its Periphery* (Westport, Connecticut: Praeger, 1992).

4   Hugh Seton-Watson, *Nations and States: An Enquiry into the Origins of Nations and the Politics of Nationalism* (London: Methuen, 1977); Hans Kohn, *Nationalism: Its Meaning and History* (Princeton: D. Van Nostrand, 1967).

5   Benedict Anderson, *Imagined Communities: Reflections on the Origin and Spread of Nationalism* (London: Verso Editions and New Left Books, 1983).

6   D.L. Steinberg et al., *In Search of Southeast Asia: A Modern History*, revised edition (Honolulu: University of Hawaii Press, 1987); O.W. Wolters, *History, Culture, and Region in Southeast Asian Perspectives* (Singapore: Institute of Southeast Asian Studies, 1982).

7   Benedict Anderson, *The Spectre of Comparisons: Nationalism, Southeast Asia and the World* (New York: Verso, 1998); David Brown, *The State and Ethnic Politics in Southeast Asia* (London: Routledge, 1994).

8   Wang Gungwu, "Migration and Its Enemies", in *Conceptualizing Global History*,

edited by Bruce Mazlish and Ralph Buultjens (Boulder, Colorado: Westview Press, 1993), pp. 131–51.

9   Grant Evans, ed., *Asia's Cultural Mosaic: An Anthropological Introduction* (New York: Prentice-Hall, and Singapore: Simon and Schuster, 1993); Peter Kunstadter, ed., *South-east Asian Tribes, Minorities, and Nations*, 2 vols. (Princeton: Princeton University Press, 1967); F.M. Le Bar, G.C. Hickey, and J.K. Musgrave, *Ethnic Groups of Mainland Southeast Asia* (New Haven: HRAF Press, 1964); Gehan Wijeyewardene, ed., *Ethnic Groups across National Boundaries in Mainland Southeast Asia* (Singapore: Institute of Southeast Asian Studies, 1990).

10 This is a project sponsored by the Institute of Southeast Asian Studies, Singapore. The authors involved are Taufik Abdullah, Charnvit Kasetseri, Reynaldo Ileto, Cheah Boon Kheng and Edwin Lee.

11 Teodoro A. Agoncillo, *Filipino Nationalism, 1872–1970* (Quezon City: R.P. Garcia, 1974); Anderson, *The Spectre of Comparisons*; O.D. Corpuz, *The Roots of the Filipino Nation*, 2 vols. (Quezon City: Aklahi Foundation, 1989).

12 Reynaldo C. Ileto, *Filipinos and their Revolution: Event, Discourse, and Historiography* (Quezon City: Ateneo de Manila University Press, 1998).

13 Ramon H. Myers and Mark R. Peattie, eds., *The Japanese Colonial Empire, 1895–1945* (Princeton: Princeton University Press, 1984).

14 Bernhard Dahm (trans. Mary F. Somers Heidhues), *Sukarno and the Struggle for Indonesian Independence* (Ithaca: Cornell University Press, 1969); Herbert Feith and Lance Castles, eds., *Indonesian Political Thinking, 1945–1965* (Ithaca: Cornell University Press, 1970); Yong Mun Cheong, *H.J. van Mook and Indonesian Independence: A Study of His Role in Dutch-Indonesian Relations, 1945–1948* (The Hague: Martinus Nijhoff, 1982).

15 Pieter Geyl, *The Revolt of the Netherlands, 1555–1609* (London: Ernest Benn, 1932).

16 Mohammad Hatta, *Portrait of a Patriot: Selected Writings* (The Hague: Mouton, 1972); R.W. Liddle, *Ethnicity, Party, and National Integration: An Indonesian Case Study* (New Haven: Yale University Press, 1970); Sukarno, *An Autobiography* (as told to Cindy Adams) (Hong Kong: Gunung Agung, 1966).

17 Hugh Tinker, *The Union of Burma* (London: Oxford University Press, 1967); F.N. Trager, *Burma: From Kingdom to Republic* (New York: Praeger, 1966); C.M. Turnbull, *The Straits Settlements, 1826–67: Indian Presidency to Crown Colony* (London: Athlone Press, 1972).

18 Joseph Buttinger, *The Smaller Dragon: A Political History of Vietnam* (New York: Praeger, 1958); Hans Antlov and Stein Tonnesson, eds., *Imperial Policy and Southeast Asian Nationalism, 1930–1957* (London: Curzon Press, 1995).

19 Alastair M. Taylor, *Indonesian Independence and the United Nations* (London: Stevens, 1960).

20 G. McT. Kahin, ed. *Government and Politics in Southeast Asia* (Ithaca: Cornell University Press, 1959).

21 Hans Kohn, *Nationalism: Its Meaning and History*.

22 John Armstrong, *Nations before Nationalism* (Chapel Hill: University of North Carolina Press, 1982); Raymond Carr, *Spain, 1808–1939* (Oxford: Clarendon Press, 1966); Tilly, *The Formation of National States in Western Europe*.

23 Hans Kohn, *Prelude to Nation-States: The French and German Experience*; Richard Bessel, ed., *Fascist Italy and Nazi Germany: Comparisons and Contrasts* (Cambridge: Cambridge University Press, 1996).

24 Hugh Seton-Watson, *Eastern Europe between the Wars* (Cambridge: The University Press, 1945); R.H. Seton-Watson, *A History of the Czechs and Slovaks* (London: Hutchinson, 1943).

25 Feith and Castles, ed., *Indonesian Political Thinking, 1945–1965*; William L. Holland, ed., *Asian Nationalism and the West* (New York: Macmillan, 1953); Urmilla Phadnis, *Ethnicity and Nation-Building in South Asia* (Delhi: Sage, 1990).

26 Rupert Emerson, Lennox Mills and Virginia Thompson, *Government and Nationalism in Southeast Asia* (New York: Institute of Pacific Relations, 1942).

27 W. McMahon Ball, *Nationalism and Communism in Southeast Asia* (Carlton: Melbourne University Press, 1952).

28 Rupert Emerson, *Malaysia: A Study in Direct and Indirect Rule* (New York: Macmillan, 1937); and *From Empire to Nation* (Cambridge: Harvard University Press, 1960).

29 Agoncillo, *Filipino Nationalism*; Teodoro A. Agoncillo, *The Revolt of the Masses: The Story of Bonifacio and the Katipunan* (Quezon City: University of the Philippines Press, 1956); Corpuz, *The Roots of the Filipino Nation*; Reynaldo C. Ileto, *Pasyon and Revolution; Popular Movements in the Philippines, 1840–1910* (Quezon City: Ateneo de Manila University Press, 1979).

30 George McT. Kahin, *Nationalism and Revolution in Indonesia* (Ithaca: Cornell University Press, 1952); Taufik Abdullah, ed., *The Heartbeat of the Indonesian Revolution* (Jakarta: P.T. Gramedia Pustaka Utama, 1997); Taufik Abdullah, ed., *Sejarah Lokal di Indonesia: Kumpulan Tulisan* (Yogyakarta: Gadjah Mada University Press, 1985); Benedict Anderson, *Java in a Time of Revolution: Occupation and Resistance, 1944–1946* (Ithaca: Cornell University Press, 1972); Sartono Kartodirdjo, *Modern Indonesia: Tradition and Transformation, a Socio-Historical Perspective* (Yogyakarta: Gadja Mada University Press, 1984).

31 K.J. Ratnam, *Communalism and the Political Process in Malaya* (Kuala Lumpur: University of Malaya Press, 1965); William Roff, *The Origins of Malay Nationalism* (Kuala Lumpur: University of Malaya Press, 1967); Chan Heng Chee, *Nation-Building in Southeast Asia: The Singapore Case* (Singapore: Institute of Southeast Asian Studies, 1971); Khoo Kay Kim, "The Beginnings of Political Extremism,

1915–1935", Ph.D. thesis, Department of History, University of Malaya, 1973; Cheah Boon Kheng, *The Masked Comrades: A Study of the Communist United Front in Malaya, 1945–1948* (Singapore: Times Books, 1979); S. Husin Ali, ed., *Ethnicity, Class and Development: Malaysia* (Kuala Lumpur: Persatuan Sains Sosial Malaysia, 1984); Gordon P. Means, *Malaysian Politics* (London: University of London Press, 1970); R.S. Milne and K.J. Ratnam, *Malaysia: New States in a New Nation* (London: Frank Cass, 1974).

32 Lucian W. Pye, *Politics, Personality and Nation Building: Burma's Search for Identity* (New Haven: Yale University Press, 1962); Josef Silverstein, ed., *Burmese Politics: The Dilemma of National Unity* (New Brunswick: Rutgers University Press, 1980); Robert H. Taylor, *The State in Burma* (London: Hurst, 1987).

33 E. Herbert Norman, *Japan's Emergence as a Modern State: Political and Economic Problems of the Meiji Period* (New York: Institute of Pacific Relations, 1940); Delmer M. Brown, *Nationalism in Japan: An Introductory Historical Analysis* (Berkeley: University of California Press, 1955).

34 Agoncillo, *The Revolt of the Masses*; Teresita Ang See, *Chinese in the Philippines: Problems and Perspectives* (Manila: Kaisa Para sa Kaunlaran, 1997); Josefa Saniel, *Japan and the Philippines, 1868–1898* (Quezon City: University of the Philippines Press, 1962).

35 Charles F. Keyes, *Thailand: Buddhist Kingdom as Modern Nation-State* (Boulder: Westview Press, 1989); Thongchai Winichakul, *Siam Mapped: A History of the Geo-Body of a Nation* (Honolulu: University of Hawaii Press, 1994); Vichitvong Na Pombhejara, ed., *Readings in Thailand's Political Economy* (Bangkok: Bangkok Printing Enterprise, 1978); David K. Wyatt, *Politics of Reform in Thailand: Education in the Reign of King Chulalongkorn* (New Haven: Yale University Press, 1969).

36 Henry McAleavy, *Black Flags in Vietnam: The Story of a Chinese Intervention* (London: Allen and Unwin, 1968); David Marr, *Vietnamese Anticolonialism, 1885–1925* (Berkeley: University of California Press, 1971).

37 David Marr, *Vietnamese Tradition on Trial, 1920–1945* (Berkeley: University of California Press, 1981); Hue Tam Ho Tai, *Radicalism and the Origins of the Vietnamese Revolution* (Cambridge, MA.: Harvard University Press, 1992); Willaim J. Duiker, *Ho Chi Minh* (Crows Nest, NSW: Allen & Unwin, 2000).

38 Huynh Kim Khanh, *Vietnamese Communism, 1925–1945* (Ithaca: Cornell University Press, 1982); Nguyen Khac Vien, *Tradition and Revolution in Vietnam* (Berkeley: University of California Press, 1974). For a recent study that connects some of the extensive Vietnamese links with other parts of Southeast Asia, Christopher E. Goscha, *Thailand and the Southeast Asian Networks of the Vietnamese Revolution, 1885–1954* (London: Curzon, 1999).

39 Josef Silverstein, *Southeast Asia in World War II: Four Essays* (New Haven: Southeast Asian Studies, Yale University Press, 1966); Steinberg et al., *In Search of Southeast Asia*; Tinker, *The Union of Burma*; Trager, *Burma: From Kingdom to Republic*.

40 Stephen Leong Mun Yoon, "Sources, Agencies, and Manifestations of Overseas Chinese Nationalism in Malaya, 1937–1941", Ph.D. thesis, University of California Los Angeles, 1976; Ann Arbor, Michigan: University Microfilms, 1978; Yoji Akashi, *The Nanyang Chinese National Salvation Movement, 1937–1941* (Lawrence: Centre for East Asian Studies, University of Kansas, 1970); Peter Duus; Ramon Myers and Mark R. Peattie, eds., *The Japanese Wartime Empire, 1931–1945* (Princeton: Princeton University Press, 1996).

41 Silverstein, ed., *Burmese Politics*.

42 Anderson, *Java in a Time of Revolution*; Harry J. Benda, *The Crescent and the Rising Sun: Indonesia Islam under the Japanese Occupation, 1942–1945* (The Hague: W. van Hoeve, 1958); Harry J. Benda, ed., *Japanese Military Administration in Indonesia: Selected Documents* (New Haven: Yale University Southeast Asian Studies, 1965).

43 Ahmad Boestaman, *Dr Burhanuddin: Putera Setia Melayu Raya* (Kuala Lumpur: Pustaka Kejora, 1972); Ariffin Omar, *Bangsa Melayu: Malay Concepts of Democracy and Community, 1945–1950* (Kuala Lumpur: Oxford University Press, 1993); Cheah Boon Kheng, *The Masked Comrades*; R.K. Vasil, *Politics in a Plural Society*, (Kuala Lumpur: Oxford University Press, 1971); Yeo Kim Wah, *Political Development in Singapore, 1945–1955* (Singapore: Singapore University Press, 1973).

44 Wang Gungwu, *China and the Chinese Overseas* (Singapore: Times Academic Press, 1991).

45 Wang Gungwu, "Questions of Identity during the Qing Dynasty", Paper presented to the 3rd International Sinology Conference, Taipei, 2000.

46 Wang Gungwu, *The Revival of Chinese Nationalism* (Leiden: International Institute for Asian Studies, 1996) (Collected in the volume as chapter 8).

47 Akashi, *The Nanyang Chinese National Salvation Movement*; Leong, "Sources, Agencies, and Manifestations of Overseas Chinese Nationalism in Malaya"; C.F. Yong, *Tan Kah-Kee: The Making of an Overseas Chinese Legend* (Singapore: Oxford University Press, 1987); C.F. Yong and R. B. McKenna, *The Kuomintang Movement in British Malaya, 1912–1949* (Singapore: Singapore University Press, 1990).

48 Partha Chatterjee, *The Nation and Its Fragments: Colonial and Postcolonial Histories* (Princeton: Princeton University Press); Masao Maruyama, *Nationalism in Postwar*

Japan (Tokyo: Institute of Pacific Relations, 1950); Jonathan Unger, ed., *Chinese Nationalism* (New York: M.E. Sharpe, 1996).

49 Michael Antolik, *ASEAN and the Diplomacy of Accommodation* (Armonk, New York: M.E. Sharpe, 1990); Dewi Fortuna Anwar, *Indonesia in ASEAN: Foreign Policy and Regionalism* (Singapore: Institute of Southeast Asian Studies, 1994); Russell H. Fifield, *The Diplomacy of Southeast Asia, 1954–1958* (New York: Harper, 1958).

50 Janet Abu-Lughod, *Before European Hegemony: The World System, AD 1250–1350* (New York: Oxford University Press, 1989); Andre Gunder Frank, *ReOrient: Global Economy in the Asian Age* (Berkeley: University of California Press, 1998); Immanuel Wallerstein, *The Modern World-system*, 3 vols. (New York: Academic Press, 1974, 1980, 1989).

51 John K. Galbraith, *The Great Crash, 1929* (Boston: Houghton Mifflin, 1955); John Arthur Garraty, *The Great Depression* (San Diego: Harcourt Brace Jovanovich, 1986).

52 Ian Brown, "Rural Distress in Southeast Asia during the World Depression of the Early 1930s: A Preliminary Reexamination", *Journal of Asian Studies* 45, no. 5 (1986): 995–1026; Ronald Dore and Radha Sinha, eds., *Japan and World Depression: Then and Now, Essays in Memory of E.F. Penrose*, New York: St Martin's Press, 1987; J.T.M. van Laanen, *The World Depression (1929–1935) and the Indigenous Economy in Netherlands India* (Townsville, Queensland: James Cook University of North Queensland, 1982).

53 Laurence W. Martin, ed., *Neutralism and Nonalignment: The New States in World Affairs* (New York: Praeger, 1962).

54 Stanley S. Bedlington, *Malaysia and Singapore: The Building of New States* (Ithaca: Cornell University Press, 1978); Richard Clutterbuck, *Conflict and Violence in Singapore and Malaysia, 1945–1983* (Singapore: Graham Brash, 1984); Khoo Kay Kim and Adnan Hj Nawang, eds., *Darurat, 1948–1960* (Kuala Lumpur: Muzium Angkatan Tentera, 1984); Lee Kuan Yew, *The Singapore Story: Memoirs of Lee Kuan Yew* (Singapore: Times Editions, 1998); Nicholas Tarling, *Nations and States in Southeast Asia* (Cambridge: Cambridge University Press, 1988).

55 R. Nagi, *ASEAN: 20 Years, A Comprehensive Documentation* (New Delhi: Lancers Books, 1989); Wang Gungwu, "Nation Formation and Regionalism in Southeast Asia", in *South Asia Pacific Crisis: National Development and the World Community*, edited by Margaret Grant (New York: Dodd, Mead and Company, 1964), pp. 125–35, 258–72.

56 Wang, "Nation Formation and Regionalism in Southeast Asia".

57 Bessel, ed., *Fascist Italy and Nazi Germany*; Eugene Kamenka, ed., *Nationalism, the Nature and Evolution of an Idea* (London: Edward Arnold, 1976).

58 J. Buenker and L. Rafner, eds., *Multiculturalism in the United States: A Comparative Guide to Acculturation and Ethnicity* (New York: Greenwood Press, 1992); Nathan Glazer and D.P. Moynihan, *Beyond the Melting Pot* (Cambridge: MIT Press, 1963).

59 A.J. Fry and Ch. Forceville, eds., *Canadian Mosaic: Essays on Multiculturalism* (Amsterdam: Free University Press, 1998); David Goodman, D.J. O'Hearn and Chris Wallace-Crabbe, eds., *Multicultural Australia: The Challenges of Change* (Newham, Victoria: Scribe, 1991).

60 Richard Caplan and John Feffer, *Europe's New Nationalism: States and Minorities in Conflict* (New York: Oxford University Press, 1996); Russell F. Farnen, ed., *Nationalism, Ethnicity, and Identity: Cross National and Comparative Perspectives* (New Brunswick: Transaction Publishers, 1994); Gerard Noiriel, *The French Melting Pot: Immigration, Citizenship, and National Identity* (Minneapolis: University of Minnesota Press, 1996); Tariq Modood and Pnina Werbner, eds., *The Politics of Multiculturalism in the New Europe: Racism, Identity, and Community* (New York: Zed Books, 1977).

61 Mahathir Mohamad, *The Malay Dilemma* (Kuala Lumpur: Federal Publications, 1970); Anwar Ibrahim, *The Asian Renaissance* (Singapore: Times Books International, 1996); Erwin Rosenthal, *Islam and the Modern National State* (Cambridge: Cambridge University Press, 1965); Bassam Tibi, *Arab Nationalism: A Critical Enquiry* (trans, and ed. Marion Farouk-Slugett and Peter Slugett) (London: Macmillan, 1981).

Index